How to
Make
Money in
Stock
Index
Futures

How to Make Money in Stock Index Futures

Courtney D. Smith
Vice President and Director of
the Commercial Support Group
Paine Webber, Inc.

McGraw-Hill Book Company

New York   St. Louis   San Francisco
Auckland   Bogotá   Hamburg
Johannesburg   London   Madrid
Mexico   Montreal   New Delhi
Panama   Paris   São Paulo
Singapore   Sydney   Tokyo
Toronto

Library of Congress Cataloging in Publication Data

Smith, Courtney.
   How to make money in stock index futures.

   Includes index.
   1. Stock index futures—Handbooks, manuals, etc.
I. Title.
HG6043.S65   1985   332.63′222   84-17150
ISBN 0-07-059107-5

1234567890   DOC/DOC   898765

0-07-059107-5

The editors for this book were William A. Sabin and Kate Scheinman, the designer was Dennis Sharkey, and the production supervisor was Sally L. Fliess. It was set in Melior by University Graphics.
Printed and bound by R. R. Donnelley & Sons.

Contents

Preface

Stock index futures have exploded across the investment scene and are rapidly changing many investment methods. This has been in response to fundamental changes in the stock arena: the world of stock
investment has become increasingly complex and
stock prices are more volatile.

Many investors bought stocks only to witness the
market go up and their stocks go down. Large pension
and mutual funds have consistently underperformed
the broad market averages. This has adversely
affected the retirement plans of many investors while
presenting a short-term loss of capital for many others.

It is little wonder that many investors are looking
for alternatives to traditional investments. Exchange-
traded options came into being in the 1970s and were
the first wave of alternative investments presenting
both investment and hedging possibilities. Stock
index futures and options are the next wave.

This introductory book has been written to help private investors and professionals alike take advantage
of the new opportunities for profit and risk management that stock index futures present. These opportunities will move from the fringes of the investment
community to the forefront.

Private professional investors will no longer be at
the mercy of the market but will instead be able to
control the amount of risk they desire in their investments. Mutual fund managers will eventually be
graded on their ability to make money rather than on
their ability to outperform the broad averages. This
will have far-reaching consequences for investors.

This book was written with the assumption that the
reader is familiar with investing in stocks but knows
little about commodity futures. Thus, the first several
chapters give the basics of the futures market. People
with little exposure to futures should be relatively
comfortable with them by the end of Chapter 4. Readers should then be able to implement the strategies
and ideas that comprise the rest of the book.

To Courtney Jr.

How to
Make
Money in
Stock
Index
Futures

Introduction

Stock index futures are the most exciting investment products since exchange-traded options. Investors and hedgers now have several substitutes for investing in stocks when they expect a major change in the direction of the market. Think the market is going to rally? Buy a stock index futures contract! Think your portfolio of stocks is about to dip in value temporarily? Sell a futures contract!

Stock index futures represent a new level in flexibility in investing. They increase the number of paths open to investors just as options did. Stock investors can now buy the market just as easily as they buy an individual stock.

For years investors had to buy mutual funds or carry very large portfolios if they wanted to trade the market. Yet mutual funds have consistently underperformed the market by several percentage points a year. Stock index futures have changed all that.

In the past, many investors, believing the market was going to go up, bought stocks. They watched as the market did go up, while their portfolios dropped in value. These investors may have the ability to call the market direction but not the ability to pick individual stocks. Stock index futures provide a viable investment vehicle for this kind of investor.

Stock index futures have a place in most moderate-sized investor portfolios. They are new tools in the fight for investment profits.

Purpose of This Book

The purpose of this book is to provide a useful guide to the understanding, trading, and hedging of stock index futures. It outlines the basics of the futures market, order placement, trading techniques, futures evaluation, hedging considerations, and trading plans.

It is not a get-rich-quick type of book, but rather is written for serious students of investing.

Assuming that the reader is not familiar with futures but is familiar with the stock market, this book discusses those aspects of the futures market that are necessary to begin trading. Novice traders may also wish to inspect some of the books listed in the last section of this book.

Futures Contracts

Fortune 500 companies are major users of futures contracts to protect themselves against adverse price movements. Over 50 percent of the open futures contracts are carried by companies hedging themselves against price risk. The futures marketplace is an arena of prudent business as well as one of speculation.

Popularity

The futures markets are very popular for investments. Trading volume is large and growing rapidly. For example, futures volume on all exchanges grew 24 percent from 1982 to 1983. Much of the volume growth came as a result of innovative products such as stock index futures.

Volume has become so large over the last decade that the dollar value of all futures contracts traded in the United States in 1983 was worth more than the value of stocks traded on the two largest stock exchanges.

The volume of contracts has also become very large. Stock index futures are the most successful new contracts in futures trading history. Value Line volume grew from 528,743 contracts in 1982 to 724,979 in 1983, New York Stock Exchange (NYSE) volume went from 1,432,913 to 3,513,733, and the Standard & Poor's (S & P) 500 exploded from 2,935,532 to 8,101,697! Stock index futures have climbed in only two years to become one of the most popular commodity futures traded.

What Is a Futures Contract?

A futures contract is a legally binding contract to make or take delivery of a commodity within a set time period. The quantity, grade, and time period are set in the contract. People who buy futures contracts are "long" futures and are required to take delivery of the commodity if they hold the contract to expiration. People who sell a futures contract are "short" futures and are required to make delivery of the commodity if they hold the contract to expiration. This is the case with traditional commodities. The situation with stock index futures is simpler. We'll explain the difference in a later chapter.

It is possible to buy or sell a futures contract without owning or intending to own the commodity. A futures contract can be liquidated and the legal obligation to make or take delivery eliminated by taking a futures market position opposite to the original position. For example, suppose you bought a futures contract on the NYSE Index. You have an obligation to take delivery of the contract on the expiration date. However, you can liquidate the contract by selling another contract of the NYSE Index. The reverse is also true. A new short cancels an existing long and a new long cancels an existing short.

Traders who are long are expecting higher prices, while traders who are short are expecting lower prices. This is the same as in the cash stock market.

Spreads

A futures spread is similar to an options spread. A long position is initiated in one contract and a short position is initiated in another contract. Spreads can be between contract months of a futures contract, for example, long March S & P 100/short June S & P 100. Alternately, they can be between the various indexes, for example, long December Value Line/short December S & P 500.

We'll go into many of these concepts later in the book. In addition, we will show how to evaluate futures contracts and spreads.

Organization of This Book

There are eight chapters and a list of recommended sources in this book.

Chapter 1, the introduction, lays some groundwork. Chapter 2 discusses some of the basics of the futures market and the major players in the market. A brief history of the futures market is included to provide historical perspective. Chapter 3 outlines the mechanics of commodity trading. You will learn which orders to place, the differences between stock margins and commodity futures margins, the definitions of volume, open interest, and commissions, and other details needed to trade stock index futures.

Chapter 4 outlines the attributes of the major stock index futures contracts. This section will be useful as a reference and for preliminary analysis of the future price direction of the futures contract. Chapter 5 gives the basics of analyzing the price action of the futures contract from a technical point of view. The chapter will discuss the major techniques of predicting the future price direction of the futures market. We do not discuss the methods of analyzing the underlying cash stock indexes. There are many fine books already devoted to that topic.

Chapter 6 is the most important chapter in the book for the advanced trader and hedger. It details the valuation of the futures contract in relationship to the cash index. This is vitally important for all traders, hedgers, and spreaders. Chapter 7 lists a number of specific strategies for hedging and investing in stock index futures.

Chapter 8 outlines a basic trading plan for stock index futures investors. A discussion of money management and its importance and a simple money management technique are presented. At the end of the book there is a section presenting useful sources of information. These sources range from books to software to chart services.

The Futures Market and Its Participants

The commodity futures exchanges form the centerpiece of the commodity futures industry. All of the money spinning around the commodity world has the exchanges as its vortex. The development and history of commodity exchanges provide a useful perspective for the novice commodity trader.

There are two main types of markets: spot, or physical, markets, where actual goods are sold, and futures markets, where trading is in contracts for future delivery. The histories of the two types of exchanges are linked. Physical exchanges were the first exchanges, and many of these evolved into futures or forward(s) markets.

Division of labor and specialization of processes create the necessity for exchange. If individuals were to create all of their desires, wants, and necessities by themselves, there would be no exchanges of labor or goods between people. Exchanges spring up to facilitate the transfer of goods and services between individuals. Robinson Crusoe did not need an exchange until Friday came along. Exchanges now exist in abundance. The corner grocery store and the used car lot are examples of exchanges.

Markets have existed longer than economists. History records the existence of markets from ancient times. The first markets were local and serviced a small geographical location because of the high cost of transportation. Goods and services required for local use were produced locally. The first exchanges were for items whose value was so great that the cost of transportation was not a barrier. Precious metals and spices are the archetypal commodities that were traded around the world and across political bounda-

5

ries and cultures. Precious metals and spices are a concentrated form of wealth. They have a high value combined with a low weight. This made them ideal as the first commodities traded widely. As the cost of transportation declined through the increased use of waterways and, eventually, roads, items of lesser value entered the marketplaces of the world.

The ancient Greeks and Romans had well-established trading centers. The agora of Athens was initially founded as only a marketplace but later developed into a political arena. In fact, the word "agora" means market. The Roman forum developed from a marketplace into a political center in much the same way the Greek agora developed. The Romans developed large distribution centers for goods acquired throughout the Roman empire, and markets sprang up around these distribution centers.

The medieval trade fairs descended from the Greek agora and Roman forum. These fairs brought merchants together at particular times of the year to exchange raw materials and finished goods. In time these fairs became permanent fixtures, and merchants opened offices at each of the marketplaces. The first exchanges offered a wide variety of goods—whatever anyone carried to the fair was sold—but many of the exchanges eventually specialized in particular products or groups.

Originally, the markets traded in physical goods alone. Raw material markets eventually separated their products by various grades to facilitate pricing and selling. Rudimentary arbitration agencies were developed to adjudicate disputes. These two refinements were necessary to make the development of futures markets possible. Merchants were then able to order goods of a known quality for a set delivery time in the future without having to see the actual goods.

Europe was not the only area having exchanges. Commodity exchanges were formed in the United States and Japan in the 1700s. These exchanges were physicals exchanges. Each tended to specialize in a narrow range of commodities, such as cotton and furs. Forward contracting started in Japan in 1730 on the Osaka Rice Exchange. Forward contracting is similar to futures contracts. A forward contract is a contract where one party agrees to deliver a set quantity of a commodity at a predetermined time. For example, a cotton mill could contract with a cotton farmer to deliver 1000 bales of cotton to the mill on December 13. Rice, the most widely used food in Japan, was the most popular commodity traded in Japan, but edible oils, cotton, and precious metals were also traded.

New York City was the early leader in marketplaces in the United

States. Several exchanges were set up in the 1700s to trade in fibers, produce, and other items. The New York Mercantile Exchange that exists today was originally called the New York Produce Exchange and dates from this time period. The 1800s saw the establishment of major exchanges in other parts of the country. Chicago, New Orleans, Savannah, Minneapolis, and Kansas City developed large commodity exchanges, many of which exist to this day.

The futures markets evolved out of the dominant cash markets to fill a need that was not being met by the existing exchanges. The futures market added the concept of time to the trading of commodities. It therefore fulfills a very different need than that which the cash market fulfills by allowing the trading of commodities in the future.

The futures market evolved out of business people's need to transfer their risk of carrying inventory to speculators who were willing to accept the risk, hoping to profit by a gain in the value of the commodity. Businesses earn profits usually by processing or distributing a product. They usually do not have the resources or capital to withstand a possible drastic fall in the value of their inventory. Businesses seek ways to reduce the possibility of a fall in the value of their inventory. A drop in the value affects their cash flow and balance sheets negatively.

A futures contract is a contract to take or make delivery of a particular grade of a commodity at a particular time in the future. An individual who is to take delivery is said to be long the commodity while the person who is to deliver the commodity is said to be short the commodity.

The usual way that merchants use the futures market is to hedge the value of the cash commodity. In other words, merchants will transfer the risk of price change on the cash commodity to other people. This means they own the specific product. Merchants will profit if the price of the goods in inventory moves higher and will lose money if the value declines. Merchants who do not use commodity futures are speculating that the value of their goods will appreciate in price. Most businesses are not interested in speculating on the value of their inventory. They are far more eager to profit by processing or distributing their goods. They remove the speculative element of their business by transferring the risk of inventory appreciation or depreciation to others.

Merchants are usually long the cash commodity because they typically own it. A short position in the futures market is used to offset the long cash position. Remember, the short futures contract requires merchants to make delivery of their goods at a set time in the future.

The net effect of the hedge is to make the merchants flat in the market. In other words, the long cash position is offset by the short futures position. These merchants no longer have a stake in the price of the inventory because they will no longer profit or lose on a change in the price of the commodity.

For example, let us assume that a merchant owns 5000 bushels of corn. The merchant wants to profit by selling them to a cornflake manufacturer. It is September, and the delivery of the corn to the manufacturer won't be made until December. The merchant worries that a decline in the price of corn will eliminate the profit margin and even cause him to lose money. He is willing to forego the possibility of gaining by a price appreciation if the risk of loss is eliminated or sharply reduced. The merchant is speculating on the price of corn until the corn is delivered to the manufacturer in December. The profits and losses of the business are dependent on the price of corn. He can reduce or possibly eliminate the risk by using the futures market.

The merchant goes to a commodity broker and sells one contract of December corn. Another term for selling is "shorting." Shorting a contract requires the merchant to deliver 5000 bushels of corn to someone in December. The merchant can settle the contract in one of two ways: he can deliver the corn or buy a futures contract. In buying a futures contract, the merchant offsets the original position and is no longer in the market. He has no obligation to deliver the 5000 bushels of corn.

The effect of the original sale of the corn contract is to make the merchant essentially immune to price fluctuation. The merchant is now long in the cash market and short in the futures market. He will be indifferent to price fluctuation. The merchant owns the corn but has entered into a contract requiring the delivery of corn to someone else in December. Remember, the contract can be removed simply by buying another futures contract.

Let us look at the effect of the two possible scenarios of higher or lower corn prices on the corn merchant.

Higher prices

September 1

Cash corn: $2.00
December corn futures: $2.20
Action: Sell one December corn futures.

December 1

Cash corn: $3.00
December corn futures: $3.00

Actions: Cover December corn futures position by buying one December corn contract. Sell cash corn.

Result: Gain on cash corn position of $1.00. Loss on futures position of $.80. Net price for cash corn after both transactions is $2.20 ($3.00 cash price minus $.80 loss on futures transaction). Note that the net price received for the corn is the same as the selling price of the December corn futures contract.

Lower prices

September 1

Cash corn: $2.00
December corn futures: $2.20
Action: Sell one December corn futures.

December 1

Cash corn: $1.00
December corn futures: $1.00
Actions: Cover December corn futures position by buying one December corn contract. Sell cash corn.

Result: Loss on cash corn position of $1.00. Gain on futures position of $1.20. Net price for cash corn after both transactions is $2.20 ($1.00 cash price plus $1.20 profit on the futures transaction). Note that the net price received for the corn is the same as the selling price of the December corn futures contract.

Note the price of the futures contract and the price of the cash corn converged on the last day. This convergence generally occurs in all futures contracts. Stock index futures prices converge with the underlying stock index on the last trading day. For example, the price of the December New York Stock Exchange Index futures contract will be identical to the price of the New York Stock Exchange Index of cash stocks on the last day of trading of the futures contract.

The usefulness of futures contracts is clearly seen when the net selling prices of the two price scenarios are compared. In both cases the final net price to the merchant is $2.20. The merchant becomes relatively indifferent to subsequent price movements after hedging with commodity futures. As will be seen later, the owner of stocks or options is able to use the stock index futures contracts in the same way the corn merchant used the corn futures to transfer risk of price loss.

The most common type of hedge is the one just described, the short hedge. This is a hedge where the hedger owns a commodity, for example, stocks, and wishes to protect against a dropping of the value of the inventory. The opposite hedge is called a long hedge. A long hedge occurs when a hedger is short the cash commodity and long the futures contract. One is short the cash when one is committed to delivery of a commodity at a set time in the future. For example, if a corn exporter agrees to deliver 5000 bushels to a client in December, this hedger could buy a futures contract to protect against a rise in price. Remember, the long hedger is concerned that prices increase between the time of sale and the time of delivery. An increase in price would be against the interest of the hedger as a higher price would cost the hedger more than was expected when the sale was made. The long hedge locks in the price of the commodity at the time of sale and eliminates negative price surprises.

The opposite of the short hedge is the long hedge. This is done by a merchant who has already sold the commodity. Exporters who have sold their inventory are short the commodity and need to protect themselves from price increases. Processors who know what their processing will be because of sales commitments are also considered short the cash market. Long hedges will protect these processors from the reduction of their profit margin through price increases.

A second major purpose of futures contracts is price discovery. Futures markets are used as a way of discovering the price for a particular product. The futures markets act as a central point for all market participants, such as processors, growers, investors, and distributors, to meet in one location and trade the commodity. Before exchanges existed, market participants had to talk to many other people before they could estimate a fair price at which to buy or sell. A lack of exchanges increases the cost of buying and selling because of the vastly greater time necessary to transact business. For example, before the beginning of currency futures, foreign exchange traders would make numerous phone calls just to keep abreast of the price. Now, traders can watch video screens to keep on top of market action and use the phone calls to trade and monitor market news. The existence of exchanges also increases the liquidity of the market and makes for a more realistic price. "Increasing liquidity" means increasing the volume trading in one location. The more people trading a market, the more reasonable the price. Before exchanges, farmers would bring their corn to merchants to sell. The merchants often bid absurdly low prices for the corn because there was no one else in the room to compete. Farmers would have to go up and down the street looking for bids from merchants before deciding to whom they should sell.

The price discovery mechanism of futures markets is not as important for stock index futures as it is for other commodities. The major difference is that with stock index futures you are dealing with the prices of a multitude of items whereas with other futures there is basically one item, although there may be multiple grades of that single item. In addition, there is no single market for other cash commodities. Stock index futures rely on the cash stock market, mainly the New York Stock Exchange, to provide the price discovery mechanism for the cash index. Nonetheless, even the futures market provides the price discovery for the value of the stock index in the future. For example, the S & P 100 discovers the price of the index of the cash stocks comprising the index. The market for the futures contract keeps one eye on the value of the cash index and one eye on expected value of the cash index when the futures contract expires.

The exchanges provide the arena for the activities outlined above. They provide the physical environment for the trading and the bookkeeping (clearing of contracts) between the players. In addition, the exchanges provide rules and arbitration for the exchange members. Information about the traded commodities is also often collected and disseminated to the members. They also ensure that participants meet financial requirements.

The futures exchanges also initiate the process of the creation of new futures contracts to be traded on the exchanges. This process usually begins with various committees of the exchanges and eventually ends up with the Commodity Futures Trading Commission for approval.

In general, there are several criteria of viability of a new futures contract. The commodity must be standardized. Many commodities come in multiple grades. For example, treasury bonds have many different coupon rates. The exchanges have been instrumental in setting standards for the grading of various commodities. In the case of stock index futures, the product does not need to be graded because it comes in only one flavor. The Value Line Index is a standardized product without grades. Stock index futures thus satisfy the criterion of standardization.

There must also be good support from hedgers and commercial users. Futures markets have a reputation for being arenas of wild speculation. This is far from the truth. Virtually no commodity futures contract has persisted that did not have the support of the actual users of the commodity. Without the participation of the users who wish to reduce their price risk, the chances of success of a contract are extremely slim. The Commodity Futures Trading Commission publishes a monthly list of the contracts of commodity futures, the type of traders holding them, and whether they were long or short.

This report, called the *Commitment of Traders Report*, shows clearly that viable contracts need the use and support of the commercial interests. Exhibit 2-1 shows the chart for S & P 500 futures from a copy of the *Commitments of Traders Reports*. Notice the high number of hedgers holding contracts in relation to speculators. S & P 500 is not unusual in the preponderance of hedgers using the markets.

The use of commodity futures often follows seasonal patterns. In the case of wheat, the heaviest use of futures occurs after the harvest when there is the greatest quantity of wheat available to sell. It is too early to tell what seasonality there may be in commercial use of stock index futures, but there are indications that seasonality exists in stock prices. For example, there is a tendency for stock prices to dip just prior to the tax reporting date, April 15. Investors apparently sell stocks to pay their tax bills and the extra selling often depresses prices.

Commodity exchanges exist in many cities of the world, from Kuala Lumpur to London to Kansas City. There are currently four exchanges in the United States that trade stock index futures: the Kansas City Board of Trade, the New York Futures Exchange (a subsidiary of the New York Stock Exchange), the Index and Option Market (a division

EXHIBIT 2-1 A chart for S & P 500 futures showing the international monetary market commitments of traders in all futures combined and indicated futures, March 31, 1983 (Commodity Futures Trading Commission).

FUTURES	TOTAL	REPORTABLE POSITIONS								NONREPORTABLE POSITIONS	
		NON-COMMERCIAL				COMMERCIAL		TOTAL			
	OPEN INTEREST	LONG OR SHORT ONLY		LONG AND SHORT (SPREADING)							
		LONG	SHORT	LONG	SHORT	LONG	SHORT	LONG	SHORT	LONG	SHORT
		(S&P 500 INDEX X $500.00)									
ALL	17,732	3,952	6,329	196	196	6,192	2,737	10,340	9,262	7,392	8,470
OLD	17,729	3,952	6,329	196	196	6,192	2,737	10,340	9,262	7,389	8,457
OTHER	3	0	0	0	0	0	0	0	0	3	3
		CHANGES IN COMMITMENTS FROM FEBRUARY 28, 1983									
ALL	-5,109	-3,949	-1,152	-1,736	-1,736	+1,790	-627	-3,895	-3,515	-1,214	-1,594
		PERCENT OF OPEN INTEREST REPRESENTED BY EACH CATEGORY OF TRADERS									
ALL	100.0%	22.3	35.7	1.1	1.1	34.9	15.4	58.3	52.2	41.7	47.8
OLD	100.0%	22.3	35.7	1.1	1.1	34.9	15.4	58.3	52.2	41.7	47.8
OTHER	100.0%	*	*	*	*	*	*	*	*	100.0	100.0
	NUMBER OF TRADERS	NUMBER OF TRADERS IN EACH CATEGORY									
ALL	132	41	61	6	6	20	14	66	79		
OLD	132	41	61	6	6	20	14	66	79		
OTHER	0	0	0	0	0	0	0	0	0		

CONCENTRATION RATIOS
PERCENT OF OPEN INTEREST HELD BY THE INDICATED NUMBER OF LARGEST TRADERS

	BY GROSS POSITION				BY NET POSITION			
	4 OR LESS TRADERS		8 OR LESS TRADERS		4 OR LESS TRADERS		8 OR LESS TRADERS	
	LONG	SHORT	LONG	SHORT	LONG	SHORT	LONG	SHORT
ALL	25.7	15.5	34.1	24.8	24.2	14.9	32.6	23.4
OLD	25.7	15.5	34.1	24.8	24.2	14.9	32.6	23.4
OTHER	*	*	*	*	*	*	*	*

* LESS THAN .05 PERCENT.

of the Chicago Mercantile Exchange), and as this book goes to press (August 1984), trading was initiated on the Major Market Index on the Chicago Board of Trade. There are also stock index futures traded in the United Kingdom, Canada, and Australia. The initial success of the stock index futures will probably lead to additional locations and index futures around the world.

Commodity exchanges are organized into memberships. The typical exchange requires that a membership be held in the name of an individual, though a corporation may provide the money for the purchase and the individual may assign his or her privileges to the corporation. Large brokerage firms may not "own" any seats on the Chicago Board of Trade but may control seats through the use of employees as members. The main privilege of members is the ability to trade on the exchange floor. Only members are allowed to trade on the floor. Members are also allowed to participate in the administration of the exchange through management positions and committees.

There are requirements that must be met to become a member of a commodity exchange. The prospective member must have sufficient capital to buy a seat. Seats are bought and sold in an auction, much as it is in futures trading. The bids and offers are posted at the exchange. Prices can range from as little as $6000 to as much as $350,000, depending on the exchange, the trading privileges, and the current trading situation. The 1982 high and low seat prices at exchanges trading stock index futures were:

	High	Low
New York Futures Exchange	$38,000	$6,000
Index and Options Market at the		
Chicago Mercantile Exchange	285,000	242,500
Kansas City Board of Trade	69,000	48,000

Many memberships are controlled by companies. Companies nominate one of their employees as a prospective member. The company provides a financial guarantee and gives the nominee a loan to buy the seat. The new member usually assigns the rights of the seat to the company, and the company has the employee agree to give back the seat if he or she leaves its employ.

Individuals may also trade on the floor by leasing a seat from a seat owner. The exchanges have occasionally issued trading permits. These permits typically have a limited life of 1 to 3 years, and the user is charged a monthly or quarterly fee. Trading permits allow permittees to trade a single commodity or a limited group of commodities. Commodity exchanges have sometimes allowed the permits to be swapped for memberships upon payment of additional fees. Trading permits allow exchanges to expand their membership lists to attract traders to new and unproven futures contracts. Trading permits will be one of the means through which exchanges will compete to become the most popular for stock index futures.

A major advantage of being a member is access to the trading floor. Trading in stock index futures can then be done directly rather than through a broker. Members can trade their own accounts or execute orders for others. Some traders find the instant communication with the floor to be valuable. Members pay significantly lower commission costs. Exchange members pay exchange fees usually amounting to less than $2.00 per trade instead of commission charges. Active traders may find this the most important benefit.

Management of the exchange is accomplished through a board of directors, various officers, and many committees. The board of directors is the most important body, as it sets policy and makes final decisions in most cases. The board may act as a judge in major disciplinary cases of the exchange. The board is typically composed of elected members and representatives of the public and major users. The administration of the exchange is accomplished by the president. The president is a salaried employee of the exchange and has the same functions as a chief executive officer of a corporation. Members make their biggest impact on the management of the exchange through the exchange committees. Committees exist to provide guidance to the president and the board of directors and to deal with such matters as new contracts, arbitration, discipline, floor broker qualification, rules, and public relations.

The physical layout of the exchange floor is dominated by what are called the pits or rings. These are the arenas for the buying and selling of contracts. A pit has several wooden steps rising from the floor and then back to the floor in an even-sided polygonal shape, such as an octagon or hexagon. Exhibit 2-2 shows a pit. A ring is similar to a pit except that a ring or bar is placed in a circle around the center of the pit for the members to lean on and to provide a visually open area to help communication across the ring. In the United States, the rings are used only on the New York exchange. In both pits and rings, traders stand in specified areas according to the commodity and the contract month they are trading. A certain step on a certain side of a pit may mean that the trader is trading June S & P's Index.

One section of each pit or ring (hereafter we will use only the word "pit") has the price reporters. The role of the price reporters is to

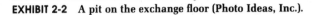

EXHIBIT 2-2 A pit on the exchange floor (Photo Ideas, Inc.).

record and send the prices from the pits into the exchange's computers. The prices are then sent to quotation services around the world and onto the exchange walls.

Circling the exchange floor are numerous booths with telephones and phone clerks. The booths are the communications centers for orders coming into the exchange. Phones, telexes, and wires connect the floor with the incoming orders. Exhibit 2-3 shows the layout of a typical exchange floor and the location of the booths and pits.

Another key feature of the exchange is the huge quotation boards on the walls. Price quotations of the commodities traded at the exchange and at other exchanges and other prices of interest are displayed. In most exchanges, there will be two or three walls for quotations. The other one or two walls are for windows, visitors' galleries, and a restaurant from which members can watch the price action. There are also news and weather service tickers positioned around the perimeter to aid the traders.

The exchange also houses the clearinghouse. The exchange clearinghouse is similar in function to the clearinghouse that matches the checks people write to pay their bills with the banks they are drawn on. The futures clearinghouse facilitates the transfer of money

EXHIBIT 2-3 The layout of a typical exchange floor and the location of the booths and pits (Chicago Mercantile Exchange).

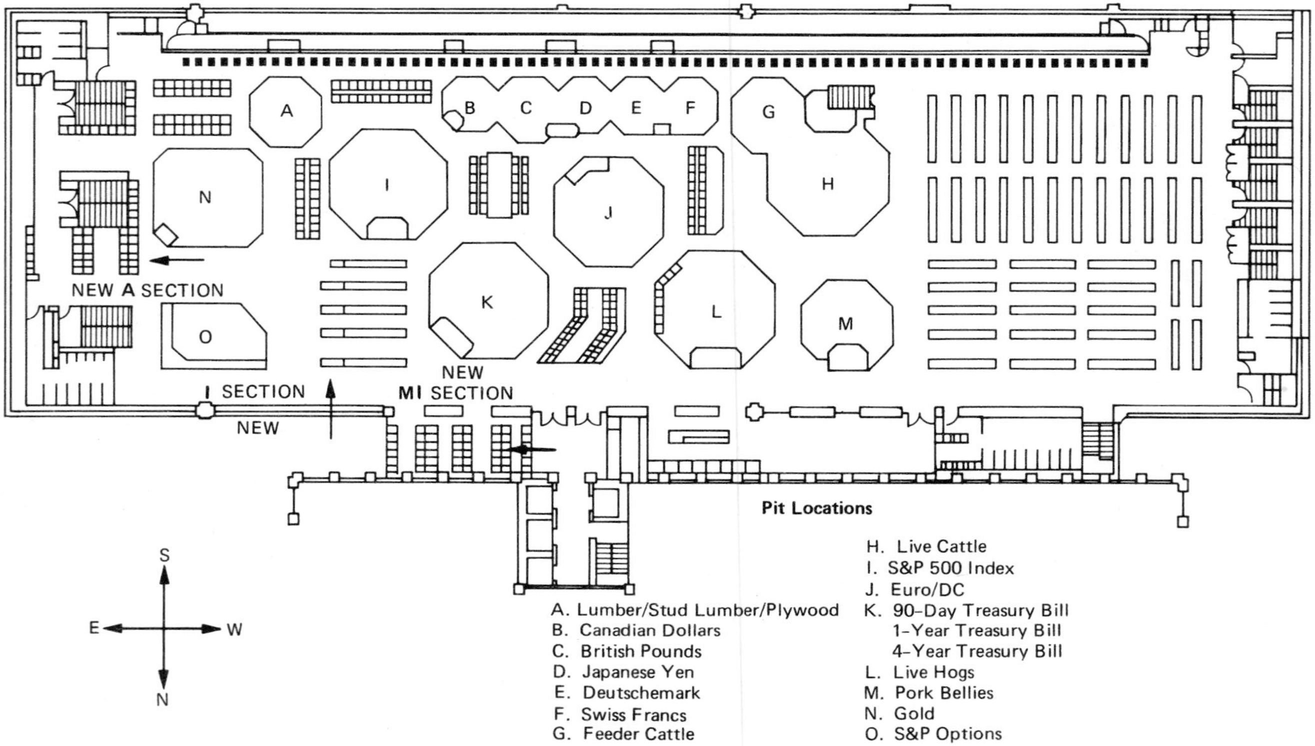
A
B
C
D
E
F
G
H
I
J
K
L
M
N
O
NEW A SECTION
I SECTION
NEW
NEW
MI SECTION
S
E
W
N
Pit Locations
A. Lumber/Stud Lumber/Plywood
B. Canadian Dollars
C. British Pounds
D. Japanese Yen
E. Deutschemark
F. Swiss Francs
G. Feeder Cattle
H. Live Cattle
I. S&P 500 Index
J. Euro/DC
K. 90-Day Treasury Bill
1-Year Treasury Bill
4-Year Treasury Bill
L. Live Hogs
M. Pork Bellies
N. Gold
O. S&P Options

between winner and loser as well as between those making and taking delivery.

The main role of the clearinghouse is to ensure the financial integrity of the futures exchange and its participants. It achieves this by collecting a good faith deposit, called margin, from the buyers and sellers of commodity futures, maintaining high capital and financial standards for its members, and settling daily the changes in margin deposits caused by price fluctuation.

The clearinghouse uses these techniques to back up its position as the opposite side of every futures transaction. The floor trader of a futures contract meets in the pits to engage in open auction with other interested traders. The trade is made when the two parties find a mutually agreeable price. The clearinghouse steps in at this point. It assumes both sides of the trade from the original traders, replacing the person who sold to the buyer. Conversely, the seller has now sold to the clearinghouse. The clearinghouse has effectively become the guarantor of the futures contract. The assets of the clearinghouse are pledged to ensure the integrity of the futures contract.

The assets of a clearinghouse come from its members. Members of a clearinghouse must have large capital and financial resources. Very few exchange members have the financial depth to become clearinghouse members. Clearinghouse members are liable for assessments should a futures contract holder default and the clearinghouse be forced to cover the value of the default. There has been only one default in the 150-year history of United States commodity exchanges. (Compare this track record with the sorry tales of scandals and frauds on the stock exchanges.) There has been no serious threat to the solvency of the commodity clearinghouses.

An additional advantage of the clearinghouse system is the liquidity it provides to the marketplace. If a buyer made a contract with a seller and could only liquidate the contract with the willingness of the original seller, the buyer would be much less likely to enter into the contract. The combination of standardized commodities and the clearinghouse allows the original buyer to find any new buyer to sell to, not merely the original seller. The clearinghouse merely notes that the original obligation of the buyer has been offset.

One of the cornerstones of the clearinghouse system is the use of margin, or good faith deposits. Unlike securities, stocks, or bonds, margin money in commodities does not represent a loan. It is a good faith deposit, or earnest money, to provide token security to the clearinghouse that the buyer or seller has the ability to satisfy the requirements of taking or making delivery of the futures contract. Margin is deposited with the brokerage firm, which then deposits it with the clearinghouse. Some brokerage firms may demand a higher margin deposit than the clearinghouse to provide themselves with more security and/or profit. The client retains ownership and control of the margin money, and it may be withdrawn with suitable notice by the client. If the client has open positions, they may have to be liquidated to release enough funds to cover the amount requested.

Each day, at the end of trading, the clearinghouse settles the value of each contract of each market participant in cash. For each contract that gained in value that day, the clearinghouse credits the dollar gain to the account of the brokerage house, which then credits it to the client. For each contract that lost money that day, additional funds must be posted to cover the loss.

The combination of margin deposits and daily settlement with the capital backing of the clearinghouse members forms a solid underpinning of financial strength for the commodities markets.

In the arena of the commodity futures exchange are the traders of futures. Many traders fill several roles, but, in general, the following categories describe the major types of traders:

- Floor brokers
- Scalpers
- Day traders
- Arbitrageurs
- Speculators
- Hedgers
- Spreaders

The floor broker is the centerpiece of the trading action. Much of the activity of the exchange floor revolves around the floor broker. The floor broker executes the trades sent in by outside brokerage firms and traders. Commission houses, warehousers, growers, processors, and other institutions will send their orders to floor brokers to be initiated or liquidated. Successful floor brokers can execute thousands of trades in a given day. Their fee for executing the trades is only a small part of the commission that the customer pays. The fee typically comes to $2.00 or less for each side of the transaction.

Although floor brokers can trade their own accounts, they rarely do. Their brokerage business usually demands all their time and skill. Any trading done by a floor broker must not conflict with the interests of the broker's customers. Brokers accept fiduciary responsibility for clients' orders and must handle clients' orders before handling their own orders.

The floor broker handles what is called a deck. The deck is composed of cards, similar in size and shape to large playing cards, which list the orders and their prices. The order deck is held in the floor broker's hands or in pockets in the broker's jacket. Market orders are filled as soon as they are received by the floor broker. As the price of the commodity moves higher and lower, the broker monitors the deck to determine whether any of the orders should be executed. When the current price reaches the stop and limit orders the broker will execute the trades immediately.

Floor brokers are important people on the floor. They handle a large percentage of the volume of commodities. Other floor participants vie for places next to the floor broker in order to participate in the order flow from off the floor. It is not uncommon for the big floor brokers to have a set place in the pit where they stand. They regally assume "their" place in the pit and will vigorously defend their "right" to their few square feet. The floor broker has a pecuniary motive beyond the social desire to have a prime location in the pit. From certain locations in the pits the broker can be seen and heard better than from others. The success of the broker is keyed to the ability to execute trades quickly and with a minimum price movement from the previous trade. The floor brokers rightly believe that the prime locations on the floor will result in better executions for their customers. This better service will enable them to attract and keep brokerage business.

The competition to become a floor broker is intense. A successful floor broker in a major commodity futures contract will earn several hundred thousand dollars a year. They usually begin by trading with virtually anyone in the deferred contract months of commodities. For instance, in February the most prominent and widely traded contract month for the NYSE stock index contract is the March contract. The major floor brokers will be handling the deck for the March contract. A person wishing to be a floor broker will probably be trading only the December contract or possibly the March contract one year in the future. Would-be brokers will stand in the pit and trade with as many people as possible to help spread their reputation. They may begin to execute some orders for some of the smaller brokerage houses. They eventually move a contract month (often called an option) closer to the main option traded. Successful brokers will eventually find themselves handling the deck for major brokerage houses in the spot month.

Another common way to become a large floor broker is to become an assistant to a successful floor broker. The big brokers often have assistants to help them in the pits by holding and organizing their decks. The assistant is ultimately given a deck to handle.

This is not to imply that it is easy to become a floor broker. Many have tried and failed. The skills to become a floor broker are not necessarily hard to acquire, but the competition is so intense that the skills need to be developed to a high degree. Small differences in skill become magnified as the competition increases.

The largest group of traders in the pits is the locals. These traders trade only for their own accounts. They can be loosely divided into scalpers and day traders, according to how long they stay in trades and the basic tactics they use to trade. The main attractions to becoming a local are the sharply reduced commissions and being in the middle of the action. Locals most often trade only one commodity. Recently, locals have often traded in the pits of the traditional commodities during their regular trading hours and have moved over the newer commodities after the traditional ones have closed. For example, cattle traders may stay in the cattle pit until it closes at 12:45 p.m. CST and then move over to the S & P Index pit until it closes at 3:15 p.m. CST.

A scalper is a local who is willing to buy contracts at the bid price and sell at the offer price (also called the ask price). The bid and offer prices are the bids and offers in the pit at that particular moment. The bids and offers may be slightly different in different parts of the pit at the same time, but this is relatively short-lived. At any given time, one or more people in the pit will be bidding or offering contracts. The scalper will continually try to buy at the bid price and sell at the offer price. Market makers on securities exchanges have a similar role. Scalpers profit by the liquidity between the bid and offer prices. In a popular commodity, such as the S & P Index contract, the bid and ask will usually be one tick apart. The scalper will thus be looking for only a $25 profit on any given trade in the S & P Index.

The key to the success of the scalper is constant repetition of the buying and selling of minimum ticks. A trader who makes $25 per trade on 100 trades a day will soon be wealthy. In reality, the scalper will not likely have 100 winning trades in a row. The principle of small profits taken many times is what the scalper's success is based upon.

Commodity price action often remains within small trading ranges in a given day before moving to another price level. For example, prices could trade from 137.00 to 137.05 five times before buying pressure pushes prices up to a range of 137.10 to 137.15. The scalper would be trying to buy at 137.00 and sell at 137.05. A successful scalper would be able to complete this process five times before an unprofitable trade. The scalper would be short at 137.05 when the bounce to the new range of, for instance, 137.10 to 137.15 occurred. This bounce would be unprofitable for the scalper and a loss of .05 or .10 would be taken, depending on the final exit price. The new trading range would then be traded by the scalper in the same manner as the previous range.

Scalpers are important for the success of the futures market. Their constant trading provides liquidity to the market and narrows bid/ask spreads as they compete to buy and sell at the bid and ask prices. The scalper's willingness to trade enables other traders, whether speculators or hedgers, to enter the market almost at will. More scalpers in a market ensure a stable market with minimal bid/ask spreads.

The path to becoming a scalper is usually direct. Most become scalpers simply by buying or leasing a seat and trading. Being a scalper does not require the long preparation that a floor broker must have before becoming a success.

This is not to say that a scalper isn't skilled. Scalpers must have the ability to change their minds with lightning speed. When the market lurches to a new trading level scalpers cannot fight the market and assume that it will move back in their favor. Scalpers will typically liquidate a trade if it moves as little as a single tick against them. They must have an aggressive demeanor on the floor to make sure that they are able to buy and sell at the bid and ask prices. When another trader yells out a bid or offer, scalpers will aggressively fight for the attention of the initial trader in order to complete a trade. Scalpers also use the aggressive demeanor to liquidate bad trades quickly. A more low-key approach could cause substantially more losses as the market moves against them while they are trying to liquidate a losing position.

Another type of local is the day trader. Day traders are similar to scalpers, but they hold positions longer. They are called day traders because they, like the scalpers, do not hold positions overnight. This reduces their risk of adverse price movement overnight and means that they do not have to post margin money. This doesn't mean that there is no financial control over their trading. Floor traders may not have to post margin money on day trades, but they do have limits on the amount of trading they are allowed to do on any given size of their account at a clearinghouse.

Day traders and scalpers are similar in trading style. The major differences are that the day trader looks for larger profits and accepts larger losses than the scalper and the day trader does not need to be as aggressive in the pit. Day traders and scalpers probably play different roles more because of personality differences than anything else.

A day trader does not have to be a local, though most are. Many speculators day-trade from off the exchange floor. Few of the non-member speculators make money, because the commission costs usually overwhelm the trading profits.

The largest group of traders is the speculators, who are not on the floor of an exchange. Scalpers and day traders represent just a small number of all speculators. The overwhelming majority of speculators do not trade from the floor. They trade from their homes or offices. As with the day traders and scalpers, they are interested in profiting from changes in price levels of futures contracts.

The speculator aims to profit by assuming the risk that the hedger does not wish to shoulder. The speculator is not concerned with the underlying commodity except as it influences price changes. Making or taking delivery of the underlying commodity is a rarity among speculators. They have no desire to be an owner of the cash commodity, and, in fact, they may not have the financial wherewithal to own it.

The main appeal of commodities to speculators is the lure of investment profits. Most speculators assume that commodity futures are a highly speculative, volatile investment. They are, in fact, a very low-risk investment if traders do not use the leverage available. Commodity prices are more stable than securities prices. It is not uncommon to see a stock move 10 percent or more in a single day. Recently, the stock price of Texas Instruments dropped from over $150 per share to less than $110 per share in one trading day! Commodity prices, on the other hand, will rarely move 10 percent in a day, and commodity futures prices will never move 10 percent in a day.

The image of high volatility of commodity futures comes from the leverage inherent in the futures contract. If an investor were to put up the full value of the contract, there would be substantially less volatility than that in stock prices. The volatility in the customers' equity comes as a result of putting up only 5 to 10 percent of the value of the contract as margin. Most traders utilize leverage to the maximum. They will negotiate with their brokers for the least margin so as to increase their leverage. A move in the December Value Line futures from 150.00 to 165.00 represents a 10 percent increase in the value of the contract. Investors who put down the full value of the contract as margin would gain 10 percent on their investment. The return on investment would be 100 percent if the investors placed 10 percent of the contract value as margin. Therefore, the volatility of commodities is very low, but the volatility of the investor's equity can be very high if the investor uses a lot of leverage.

Speculators come in many varieties and sizes. The majority of speculators are called small speculators because they trade only small quantities. Large speculators can often be trading hundreds or even thousands of contracts at a given time. The Commodity Futures Trading Commission (CFTC) sets limits on the number of contracts that a single trader (or sometimes a group of related traders) can control in most commodities. The CFTC does this in an effort to reduce the potential for manipulation by a single investor or group of investors. The position limit for stock index futures is 5000 contracts. This means that no single individual may control more than 5000 contracts of any single stock index future. The 5000 includes all contract months of the futures contract. It should be noted that this is a net figure; that is, it is a total of all of the long and short positions. For example, if a trader is long one December NYSE Index and, in addition, has a long March/short June spread, the trader is assumed to be net long one position. The spread is considered a scratch for purposes of speculative limits. The CFTC also sets limits on the number of net contracts a trader may hold without reporting the position to the CFTC. A trader holding 25 or more contracts in a single stock index futures contract must report the position to the CFTC.

Speculators can also be divided according to the length of time they hold a position. Day traders hold positions for less than a day, and position traders hold their investment for a longer time. One is considered a position trader if the trade is initiated and expected to be held for several days to many months. Position traders typically do not trade from the trading floor as they find the continual action distracts them from their analysis.

It is relatively easy to become a speculator in stock index futures. The financial requirements are enough money to open an account and a good credit rating. Reputable brokerage houses will examine the financial situation of the prospective speculator in an effort to determine his or her suitability for investing in futures. Because most speculators use the maximum leverage available, it is important to ensure that the money invested is truly speculative capital and will not be needed by the individual for other purposes. Private investors are cautioned to use only money that can be completely lost and not affect the investors' lifestyle. Reputable brokerage firms will examine the net worth and income levels of the prospective speculator and will discourage prospects who may be trading beyond what is a suitable and prudent level.

One type of speculator is the spreader. Spreads, sometimes called "switches" or "straddles" in New York, are a major part of commodity trading. A spread is the simultaneous purchase and sale of different contracts. The contracts may be in different commodities, such as long Value Line and short S & P, or they may be in the same commodity, such as long March NYSE Index and short June NYSE Index. The profitability of a spread comes through the changes in the differences between the two contracts. For example:

September 1

Initiate the spread by:

Buying December NYSE Index at 81.00 and selling March NYSE Index at 82.00. Spread is a 1.00 premium the March contract.

September 23

Liquidate the spread by:

Selling December NYSE Index at 82.30 and buying March NYSE Index at 82.60. Spread is at .30 premium the March contract.

The net effect of the trade is

December NYSE Index = $650 profit (82.30 − 81.00 = 1.30 times $500 per 1.00)

March NYSE Index = $300 loss (82.60 − 82.00 = −.60 times $500 per 1.00)

Total profit = $350

A different type of spreader is the arbitrageur. Arbitrageurs initiate spreads between the various exchanges and between the futures and the cash. The arbitrageurs will, for example, be buyers of the Value Line Index and sellers of the S & P 500 Index if they feel that the spread relationship is out of line. Stock index futures do not have the feature of arbitrage between the cash and futures because there is no cash commodity, as there is with more traditional commodities. However, we will show later in this book a way that proxies for the cash index may be invented, thus allowing something close to arbitrage.

The final main category of participant in the futures market is the hedger. We have already seen in this chapter the ways that a hedger can use the stock index futures market. We have seen the development of the futures market as an aid to the hedger in reducing the risk of inventory. The individual, pension fund, and mutual fund can all use stock index futures to reduce the risk of holding their inventory. The only requirements to become a hedger are owning something or expecting to own something in the future and having the financial ability to hedge. This means that even individuals can be considered hedgers if they own enough of the cash commodity. For example, investors holding $85,000 of a diversified mutual fund could hedge by using one contract of the S & P 500 Index.

The focus of the rest of the book will be on investors and hedgers, not floor traders. We will be touching on the issues and information that help investors profit and reduce their risks in the market.

chapter 3

The Mechanics of Trading

There are several subjects that are necessary for the novice trader to understand before trading commodity futures, including the basics of commissions, margins, and orders. There are other topics as well that a trader should have a grounding in before beginning to trade.

Commissions and Margins

Commissions and margins are subjects dear to the heart of a brokerage firm. Commissions are the fees paid by customers to brokerage houses to execute their trades. Margins are the good faith deposits paid by the customer into trust with the brokerage house.

Commissions represent the cost of trading for both speculators and hedgers. Payment is typically made by customers to the brokerage house at the completion of each trade. In other words, commissions are paid at the liquidation of a trade, not at both the trade initiation and the trade liquidation, as it is in the stock market. When the commission is paid at the end of a trade and not at the beginning, this is called a round turn. There are increasing numbers of brokerage houses that are charging half of the commission going into a trade and the other half of the commission going out of a trade. They do not charge any more than the brokers charging a round turn commission but split the commission into two parts.

Commission rates vary with commodity and brokerage houses. Exhibit 3-1 shows a commission sheet, with additional information, for a major Wall Street brokerage house. Stock index futures tend to have

EXHIBIT 3-1 A commission sheet for a major Wall Street brokerage house.

COMMODITY	GTE SYMBOL	TRADING HOURS NY TIME	CONTRACT SIZE	MINIMUM FLUCTUATION IN PRICE	EQUALS/ CONTRACT	ROUND TURN	DAY TRADE	SPREADS
BROILERS (FRESH)	2 IB	CBT 10 10-2 00	30,000 lbs	2½/100¢ per lb	$ 7 50	$ 65 00	$ 52 00	$ 80 00
CATTLE (FEEDER)	1 FC	CME 10 05-1 45	44,000 lbs	2½/100¢ per lb	$11 00	$ 70 00	$ 56 00	$ 86 00
CATTLE (LIVE)	1 LC	CME 10 05-1 45	40,000 lbs	2½/100¢ per lb	$10 00	$ 70 00	$ 56 00	$ 86 00
CATTLE (LIVE)		MACE 10 05-2 00	20,000 lbs	2½/100¢ per lb	$ 5 00	$ 50 00	$ 40 00	$ 62 00
Certificate of Deposit	2 BC	CBT 8 30-3 00	$1,000,000	01	$25 00	$ 75 00	$ 68 00	$ 80 00
Certificate of Deposit	1 DC	CME 8 30-3 00	$1,000,000	01	$25 00	$ 75 00	$ 68 00	$ 80 00
COCOA	1 CC	CSC 9 30-3 00	10 metric tons	$1 00/metric ton	$10 00	$ 90 00	$ 72 00	$110 00
COFFEE	1 C	CSC 9 45-2 28	37,500 lbs	1/100¢ per lb	$ 3 75	$100 00	$ 80 00	$124 00
Commercial Paper (90-day)	2 P	CBT 9 30-2 35	$1 million	1/100 of 1%	$25 00	$ 80 00	$ 64 00	$ 98 00
Commercial Paper (30-day)	2 RP	CBT 9 30-2 45	$3 million	1/100 of 1%	$25 00	$ 80 00	$ 64 00	$ 96 00
COPPER	1 CP	CMX 9 50-2 00	25,000 lbs	5/100¢ per lb	$12 50	$ 80 00	$ 64 00	$ 98 00
COTTON	1 CT	CTN 10 30-3 00	100 bales 50,000 lbs	1/100¢ per lb	$ 5 00	$ 90 00	$ 72 00	$110 00
CURRENCIES		IMM						
British Pound	1 BP	8 30-2 24	25,000	5 points	$12 50	$ 80 00	$ 64 00	$ 98 00
Canadian Dollar	1 CD	8 30-2 26	100,000	1	$10 00	$ 80 00	$ 64 00	$ 98 00
Deutschemark	1 DM	8 30-2 20	125,000	1	$12 50	$ 80 00	$ 64 00	$ 98 00
Dutch Guilder	1 DG	8 30-2 30	125,000	1	$12 50	$ 80 00	$ 64 00	$ 98 00
French Franc	1 FR	8 30-2 28	250,000	5	$12 50	$ 80 00	$ 64 00	$ 98 00
Japanese Yen	1 JY	8 30-2 22	12,500,000	1	$12 50	$ 80 00	$ 64 00	$ 96 00
Mexican Peso	1 MP	8 30-2 18	1,000,000	1	$10 00	$ 80 00	$ 64 00	$ 98 00
Swiss Franc	1 SF	8 30-2 16	125,000	1	$12 50	$ 80 00	$ 64 00	$ 98 00
ENERGY								
Crude Oil	2 CP	CBT 9 30-3 30	42,000 gals	01	$10 00	$ 94 50	$ 68 50	$ 98 00
	1 CL	NYME 9 30-3 30	42,000 gals	01	$ 0 00	$ 94 50	$ 68 50	$ 98 00
GASOLINE	2NL	CBT 9 30-3 30	42,000 gal	025	$10 50	$ 80 00	$ 64 00	$ 98 00
GASOLINE (New York)	1 HR	NYME 9 30-3 30	42,000 gal	01	$ 4 20	$ 75 00	$ 60 00	$ 92 00
Heating Oil	2 TO	CBT 9 30-3 30	42,000 gals	01	$ 4 20	$ 75 00	$ 60 00	$ 92 00
HEATING OIL	1 HO	NYME 10 00-2 45	42,000 gals	01	$ 4 20	$ 75 00	$ 60 00	$ 92 00
INDUSTRIAL FUEL OIL	1 IO	NYME 10 00-2 45	42,000 gals	01	$ 4 20	$ 75 00	$ 60 00	$ 92 00
EURODOLLAR	1 ED	CME 8 30-3 00	$1,000,000	01	$25 00	$ 80 00	$ 64 00	$ 98 00
GNMA (CDR)	2 M	CBT 9 00-3 00	$100,000	1/32 of a point	$31 25	$ 80 00	$ 64 00	$ 98 00
GNMA (CFT)	2 MC	CBT 9 00-3 00	$100,000	1/32 of a point	$31 25	$ 80 00	$ 64 00	$ 98 00
GOLD								
CBT	2 KI	9 00-2 30	32 15 oz	10¢/oz	$ 3 22	$ 65 50	$ 52 50	$ 79 00
CMX	1 GC	9 00-2 30	100 oz	10¢/oz	$10 00	$100 00	$ 80 00	$124 00
IMM	1 GD	9 00-2 30	100 oz	10¢/oz	$10 00	$100 00	$ 80 00	$124 00
MACE		9 00-2 40	33 2 oz	2¢ oz/oz	83¢	$ 50 00	$ 40 00	$ 62 00
NYME (kilo)	1 GL	9 00-2 30	32 15 oz	20¢/oz	$ 6 43	$ 30 00	$ 30 00	$ 37 00
NYME	1 GN	9 00-2 30	400 oz	5¢/oz	$20 00	$150 00	$120 00	$185 00
GRAINS		CBT						
Corn	2 C	10 30-2 15	5000 bu	1/4¢/bu	$12 50	$ 65 00	$ 52 00	$ 80 00
Oats	2 O	10 30-2 15	5000 bu	1/4¢/bu	$12 50	$ 65 00	$ 52 00	$ 80 00
Soybeans	2 S	10 30-2 15	5000 bu	1/4¢/bu	$12 50	$ 70 00	$ 56 00	$ 86 00
Wheat	2 W	10 30-2 15	5000 bu	1/4¢/bu	$12 50	$ 65 00	$ 52 00	$ 80 00
MACE Grains		MACE						
Corn		10 30-2 30	1000 bu	1/4¢/bu	$ 2 50	$ 40 00	$ 32 00	$ 49 00
Soybeans		10 30-2 30	1000 bu	1/4¢/bu	$ 2 50	$ 40 00	$ 32 00	$ 49 00
Wheat		10 30-2 30	1000 bu	1/4¢/bu	$ 2 50	$ 40 00	$ 32 00	$ 49 00
Wheat	1 MW	MPLS 10 30 - 2 15	5000 bu	1/4¢/bu	$12 50	$ 60 00	$ 48 00	$ 74 00
Sunflower Seed	1 SS	10 25 - 2 20	100,000 lb	0001/lb	$10 00	$ 60 00	$ 48 00	$ 74 00
Wheat	1 KW	KCBOT 10 30-2 15	5000 bu	1/4¢/bu	$12 50	$ 65 00	$ 52 00	$ 80 00

higher than average commissions because of the large contract size. Typical commissions for stock index futures are around $90 per trade. Please note that this is not $90 when initiating a trade and $90 when exiting but $90 as the total commission bill. The commodity industry uses a flat-rate commission rather than a percentage of the value of the investment as is done in the stock market. Even if the value of the stock index future were to double, the commission cost would remain stable. Commission costs as a percentage of the value of the contract are typically less than .5 percent. This is substantially less than that

Commodity	Code	Exchange / Hours	Contract Size	Price Unit				
Rye	1 WR	WPG 10 30-2 15	20 metric tons	10c/metric ton	$ 2 00	$ 15 00	$ 12 00	$ 15 00
Barley	1 WB	10 30-2 15			$ 2 00	$ 15 00	$ 12 00	$ 15 00
Oats	1 WO	10 30-2 15			$ 2 00	$ 15 00	$ 12 00	$ 15 00
Flaxseed	1 WF	10 30-2 15			$ 2 00	$ 15 00	$ 12 00	$ 15 00
Rapeseed	1 RS	10 30-2 15			$ 2 00	$ 15 00	$ 12 00	$ 15 00
HOGS (Live)	1 LH	CME 10 10-2 00	30,000 lbs	2 1/2/100c per lb	$ 7 50	$ 65 00	$ 52 00	$ 80 00
HOGS (Live)		MACE 10 10-2 15	15,000 lbs	2 1/2/100c per lb	$ 3 75	$ 50 00	$ 40 00	$ 62 00
LUMBER Random Lengths	1 LB	CME 10 00 2 05	130,000	10/100 bd ft	$13 00	$ 65 00	$ 52 00	$ 80 00
NYSE COMPOSITE INDEX	1 X	NYFE 10 00-4 15	500 times the NYSE Composite Index	05	$25 00	$80 00	$ 64 00	$ 98 00
NYSE FINANCIAL INDEX	1 YF	10 00-4 15	1000 Times NYSE Financial Index	01	$10.00	$ 80 00	$ 64 00	$ 98.00
ORANGE JUICE (Frozen)	1 OJ	CTN 10 15-2 45	15,000 lbs	5/100c per lb	$ 7 50	$ 75 00	$ 60 00	$ 92 00
PALLADIUM	1 PA	NYME 9:00-2 20	100 troy ounces	10c per troy ounce	$10 00	$ 75 00	$ 60 00	$ 92 00
PLATINUM	1 PL	NYME 9 10-2 30	50 troy ounces	10c per troy ounce	$ 5 00	$100 00	$ 80 00	$120 00
PLYWOOD (Western)	2 WP	CBT 10 00-2 00	76 032 sq feet	10c per 1000 sq feet	$ 7 60	$ 65 00	$ 52 00	$ 80 00
PORK BELLIES	1 PB	CME 10 10-2 00	38,000 lbs	2 5/100 per lb	$ 9 50	$ 70 00	$ 56 00	$ 86 00
POTATOES Round White	1 PT	NYME 10 00-2 00	50 000 lbs	1c per 100 lbs	$ 5 00	$ 70 00	$ 56 00	$ 86 00
POTATOES Russet	1 P	CME 10 00-2 00	80,000 lbs	1c per 100 lbs	$ 8 00	$ 60 00	$ 48 00	$ 74 00
PROPANE GAS	1 LG	CTN 10 45-3 15	42,000 gals	1/100c per gal	$ 4 20	$ 60 00	$ 48 00	$ 74 00
SILVER	1 S	CMX 9:05-2 25	5 000 troy ounces	10/100c per ounce	$ 5 00	$100 00	$ 80 00	$124 00
SILVER	2AG	CBT 9:05-2 25	1 000 troy oz	10/100c per ounce	$ 1 00	$ 51 00	$ 36 00	$ 54 00
SILVER	2SI	9:05-2 25	5,000 troy oz	per ounce	$ 5 00	$100.00	$ 80.00	$124.00
SILVER		MACE 9:05-2 40	1,000 troy ounces	10 oz	$ 1 00	$ 50 00	$ 40 00	$ 62 00
SOYBEAN MEAL	2 SM	CBT 10 30-2 15	100 tons	10c per ton	$10 00	$ 70 00	$ 56 00	$ 86 00
SOYBEAN OIL	2 BO	CBT 10 30-2 15	60 000 lbs	1/100c per lb	$ 5 00	$ 70 00	$ 56 00	$ 86 00
STANDARD & POOR'S 500	1 SP	CME 10 00-4 15	500 times the value of the S&P 500 index	05	$25 00	$ 80 00	$ 64 00	$ 98 00
SUGAR #11 (World)	1 SE	CSC 10 00 1 45	50 tons 112,000 lbs	1/100c per lb	$11 20	$ 90 00	$ 72 00	$110 00
TEN YEAR TREASURY NOTES	2 TY	CBOT 9 00-3 00	$100,000	1/32 of a point	$31 25	$ 80 00	$ 64 00	$ 98 00
U.S. TREASURY BILLS (3 mos)	1 TB	IMM 9 00-3 00	1 Million Dollars	1 basis point	$25 00	$ 80 00	$ 64 00	$ 98 00
U.S. TREASURY BILLS (1 Year)	1 YR	IMM 9 00 2 35	$250,000	1 basis point	$25 00	$ 80 00	$ 64 00	$ 98 00
U.S. TREASURY BILLS (90 day)		MACE 9 00-3 10	$500,000	1/10 basis point	$12 50	$ 61 00	$ 40 00	$ 94 20
U.S. TREASURY BONDS	2 US	CBT 9 00-3 00	$100,000	1/32 of a point	$31 25	$ 80 00	$ 64 00	$ 98 00
U.S. TREASURY BONDS		MACE 9 00-3 15	$ 50,000	1/32 basis point	$15 62	$ 61 00	$ 40 00	$ 94 20
U.S. TREASURY NOTES—4-6 Yrs	2 SN	CBT 9 00-3 00	$400,000	1/128 of a point	$31 25	$ 80 00	$ 64 00	$ 98 00
VALUE LINE	1 KV	KCBOT 10 00-4 15	500 times Value Line index	05	$25 00	$ 80 00	$ 64 00	$ 98 00

charged by stockbrokers for executing a securities trade. However, this fact is somewhat misleading. The leverage of commodities usually means that the investor is placing a minimal amount of money as margin. Traders will rarely invest the necessary funds for the total value of the contract. Their commission cost therefore becomes a much larger percentage of the actual invested capital represented by the margin. For example, if commissions are $100, margin is $6000, and the value of the contract is $60,000, then commissions are 1.6 percent of the value of the actual invested dollars instead of .16 percent of the value of the contract.

Prior to 1978, the commodity industry did not have negotiated commissions. Since that time, individual speculators and hedgers have been able to negotiate with their brokers on commissions. As a practical matter, large hedgers and speculators can push listed commission costs significantly below the listed rate. Reductions of 50 percent or more can be achieved by negotiation. There are now several brokerage houses, called discount brokerage houses, that consistently offer reduced commissions. Whereas a typical discount brokerage house may charge $90 to execute a trade, the discount brokerage house may only charge $30.

Technically, commissions are charged to investors for the service of executing trades. As a practical matter, brokerage houses provide many additional services. Brokerage houses rely on commodity research to compete with one another in the offering of services to their customers. The discount brokerage houses rarely provide any service other than simple execution of the trade. They will not provide research reports, trade ideas, or trading information about commodities. Investors who make their own trading decisions may save a lot of commission dollars through the use of a discount broker. Most investors find the additional support from the broker worth the extra payment. The majority of investors need to use the broker for information and trade concepts. Another factor in favor of full-service brokerage houses is that they tend to be larger and have a larger capital base, and they are therefore more secure from bankruptcy. To sum up, discount houses are good for investors who make their own decisions and can get the information they need to trade themselves, whereas regular brokerage houses are better for traders who prefer personalized service, need information, like trade ideas, and want to deal with larger, better-capitalized firms.

Slightly larger commission costs occur with spreads. Remember, spreads are the simultaneous buying and selling of two separate contracts. One would think that commissions might be doubled, but in most cases they are only 10 to 20 percent greater than if only one position had been initiated. The exception to this is when traders spread between two different markets. For example, one could buy the S & P 100 futures and simultaneously sell the NYSE Index futures. In this case, both markets require full commissions. Double commissions are also charged on spreads between different contracts on the same exchange. For example, a spread between one contract each of the S & P 100 and 500 contracts would cost the sum of the commissions of the two contracts.

Commissions are reduced for day trades. These are trades initiated and liquidated within a single day's trading session. Day-trade commissions can also be applied to trades that are liquidated and then initiated on the same day. This is a twist on the usual day trade, which initiates and then closes. An example of a normal day trade would be to purchase one Value Line contract at the opening and liquidate that contract on the close. An example of the far less frequent type of day trade would be to close out an existing long position on the close. Traders must be alert to mention this to their brokerage houses, as most brokers will not connect the two trades and will charge normal commissions on each trade.. This small technique is used mainly when they are long (or short) going into a day but wish to be short (or long) if prices break a certain level. For example, a trader who is long one contract of S & P 100 and wishes to go short on a break down through a particular price level can place an order to sell two contracts at the specified price level. This type of trade can often qualify as a day trade.

When a trade is liquidated, the client will receive a notice in the mail several days later giving the entry and exit price of the trade as well as the commission charged on the trade. This notice is called trade confirmation if it notifies the client only of the initiation of a trade and is called the purchase and sale (P&S) if it notifies the client of the closing of a trade. Both give the account balance at the beginning of the day of the trade, a list of the trades initiated, the price, and the commission charge. The P&S gives both the entry and exit points of the trade as well as the net profits and total commissions. The broker will typically receive this the day after the trade through the firm's internal wire system. This notification through the mails is a way clients ensure that commission costs are what they expect or negotiated.

Each trader also receives a monthly commodity statement that shows all closed and open positions. Net profits or losses for each trade as well as the commissions charged are listed. Open trade equity on open accounts is listed and combined with the closed equity to give the total account value at the market on the last day of the month. Each of these forms takes several days to arrive from the accounting offices of the brokerage firms to the client. Most brokerage houses have a daily run that outlines the account's position to the broker. The written confirmations, P&Ss, and monthly statements are to be used as backup and confirmation of the broker's numbers as well as the trader's own accounting. Errors in the forms should be reported immediately to the brokerage house as a delay may reduce the possibility of correction.

Commodity exchanges set minimum initial and maintenance margin levels for each commodity. The Federal Reserve Bank is also providing some input in the setting of margins for stock index futures.

EXHIBIT 3-2 A sample margin sheet showing margins for various types of accounts.

July 22, 1983

COMMODITY	SPECULATIVE (2) + (9)		SPREAD		MINIMUM (3)		SPREAD		HEDGE (1)	
	Init	Maint	Init	Maint	Init	Maint	Init	Maint	Init	Maint
Barley (WPG)	200	150	30	30	100	80	30	30	80	80
Broilers	750	600	200	100	500	400	150	100	400	400
Cattle (Feeder – CME)	1350	900	750	500	900	600	500	350	700	600
(Feeder – CME) – SPOT	2500	2500	1800	1300	1500	1200	900	700	1500	1200
Cattle (Live – CME)	1350	900	750	500	900	600	500	350	700	600
(Live – CME) – SPOT	2500	2500	1500	1500	1500	1200	900	700	1500	1200
Cattle (Live – MIDAM)	600	450	150	100	450	300	100	100	300	300
Cocoa	2250	1875	450	338	1875	1500	300	225	1000	700
Cocoa – SPOT	2550	1875	450	338	2550	1875	450	338	1125	844
Coffee C	10000	7500	2000	1000	7500	5000	1500	1000	2250	1687
Coffee – SPOT	20000	20000	20000	20000	20000	20000	20000	20000	2750	2062
Commercial Paper (CBOT)	4500	3375	600	400	3000	2250	400	300	1200	1200
Copper (COMEX)	2250	1687	270	270	1500	1125	180	180	500	375
Corn (CBOT)	900	750	300	200	600	500	100	100	500	500
Corn (MIDAM) 1000 bu.	2250	1500	60	40	1500	1125	40	30	750	750
Cotton	1600	1200	750	500	1000	750	500	375	500	500
CURRENCIES (IMM)										
British Pound	2000	1500	150	100	1800	1350	100	100	1500	1000
Canadian Dollar	2000	1500	150	100	1500	1000	100	100	900	700
Deutschmark	2000	1500	150	100	1800	1350	100	100	1500	1000
Euro-Dollar	3500	2625	600	400	3000	2250	500	300	1500	1200
Japanese Yen	2000	1500	150	100	1800	1350	100	100	1500	1000
Mexican Peso	3500	3000	3500	3000	3500	3000	3500	3000	3500	3000
Swiss Franc	2500	1875	150	150	2000	1500	100	100	2000	1500
French Franc	2000	1500	150	100	1800	1350	100	100	1200	900
Italian Lira	2000	1500	500	300	1800	1350	500	300	1500	1200
Dutch Guilder	2000	1500	150	100	1800	1350	100	100	1200	900

	SPECULATIVE (2) + (9)		SPREAD		MINIMUM (3)		SPREAD		HEDGE (1)	
COMMODITY	Init	Maint	Init	Maint	Init	Maint	Init	Maint	Init	Maint
Flaxseed (WPG) 20 MT	300	250	30	30	250	180	30	30	160	160
Gasoline (NYME)	3700	2900	200	140	2500	1875	200	140	2000	1400
Gasoline (CBOT)	3000	2250	200	140	2500	1875	200	140	1000	1000
GNMA & CD (CBOT)	3000	2250	600	400	2000	1500	400	300	2000	2000
GOLD CBOT	6000	4500	300	250	4000	3000	250	250	1000	1000
COMEX	6000	4500	300	250	4000	3000	250	250	1200	900
IMM	6000	4500	300	250	4000	3000	250	250	1000	1000
MIDAM	2000	1500	150	100	1300	1000	100	100	400	400
KILO (CBOT)	2000	1500	200	100	1300	1000	100	100	400	400
Heating Oil (NYME)	4500	3375	200	140	3000	2250	200	140	1500	1050
Heating Oil (CBOT)	4500	3375	200	140	3000	2250	200	140	1000	1000
Hogs (CME)	1200	750	800	500	800	500	500	300	700	500
Hogs (CME) – SPOT	2000	1500	1500	1000	1200	900	900	600	1000	900
Hogs (MIDAM)	600	500	200	150	400	300	150	120	240	240
Lumber (CME)	1500	1050	900	600	1200	800	600	400	500	300
Lumber (CME) – SPOT	2000	1500	1200	900	2000	1500	1200	900	1200	900
Oats (CBOT)	500	375	150	100	400	300	150	100	400	400
Oats (MIDAM)	150	100	25	25	100	75	10	10	70	70
Orange Juice	2500	1875	650	425	1875	1350	350	225	500	500
Orange Juice – SPOT	2500	1875	1250	1250	1875	1350	1250	1250	1500	1500
Palladium (NYME)	2250	1687	400	300	1500	1125	300	200	750	525
Platinum (NYME)	3000	2250	300	250	2000	1500	200	140	1250	875
Plywood (CBOT)	1050	700	200	100	700	400	100	100	400	400
Pork Bellies (CME)	2200	1500	1000	750	1500	1300	1000	700	1400	1200
Pork Bellies (CME) – SPOT	3000	2500	2000	1500	2000	1500	1200	900	2000	1500
Potatoes (NYME)	500	350	250	175	500	350	250	175	500	350
Potatoes (NYME) – SPOT	1250	1050	1250	1050	1250	1050	1250	1050	750	525
Rapeseed (WPG) 20 MT	350	275	100	100	300	220	100	100	180	180
Rye (WPG)	150	100	30	30	100	80	30	30	80	80
Propane	4000	3000	600	600	2000	1500	300	200	750	563
Lt Crude (NYME)	4500	3375	200	140	3000	2250	200	140	1500	1050
Bot Crude	4500	3375	200	140	3000	2250	200	140	1000	1000

EXHIBIT 3-2   A sample margin sheet showing margins for various types of accounts. (Continued)

COMMODITY	SPECULATIVE (2) + (9)		SPREAD		MINIMUM (3)		SPREAD		HEDGE (1)	
	Init	Maint	Init	Maint	Init	Maint	Init	Maint	Init	Maint
SILVER (CBOT) – 5000 oz.	10000	7500	600	450	7500	5625	440	350	2500	2500
(CBOT) – 1000 oz.	2000	1500	150	100	1500	1125	100	100	500	500
(COMEX) – 5000 oz.	10000	7500	600	450	7500	5625	440	350	3300	2475
(MIDAM) – 1000 oz.	2000	1500	150	100	1500	1125	150	100	450	450
Soybeans (CBOT)	2250	1500	400	300	300	1000	300	200	1000	1000
Soybeans (MIDAM)	450	300	125	100	300	200	100	100	200	200
Soybean Meal (CBOT)	1500	900	250	200	1000	600	200	150	600	600
Soybean Oil (CBOT)	900	600	200	150	600	400	150	100	400	400
Sugar #11, #12	3000	2250	750	563	2000	1500	750	563	625	438
T Bills (IMM)	3000	2250	600	400	2000	1500	400	300	1500	1200
T Bonds (CBOT)	3000	2250	600	400	2000	1500	400	300	1500	1500
T Notes (CBOT)	4500	3375	600	400	3000	2250	400	300	600	600
WHEAT (CBOT)	1500	1000	300	200	1000	750	100	100	600	600
(Kan City)	1500	1000	300	200	1000	750	100	100	600	600
(Minn) (1,000 Bu.)	360	240	100	50	260	190	50	50	120	120
(MIDAM) (1,000 Bu.)	360	240	100	50	260	190	50	50	120	120
Value Line Index (K.C.)	6500	3250	650	650	6500	3250	400	200	2500	1500
S&P 500 Index	6000	3000	400	200	6000	3000	400	200	3000	2500
NYSE Index	3500	1750	200	100	3500	1750	200	100	1500	1200
BOT CD	4500	3375	600	400	2000	1500	600	400	1500	1500
10 YR NOTE (CBT)	4500	4250	600	400	3000	2250	400	300	2000	2000
NYSE FINANCIAL INDEX	8500	4250	400	250	8500	4250	400	250	2500	1300
S&P 100 INDEX	3300	1650	300	200	3300	1650	300	200	1500	1200

The margins levied by the commodity exhange are usually related to the recent volatility and price level of the commodity. Commodity exchanges will tend to set higher margin requirements when the daily range of a commodity becomes wider and the price moves up. In general, margins will be somewhere between 2 and 10 percent of the value of the contract.

Commission houses are allowed to charge higher margins to their customers than the exchange minimums. Exhibit 3-2 presents a sample margin sheet showing margins for various types of accounts. The commission houses can increase both initial and maintenance margins. They will increase margins over exchange minimums if they believe that the exchange margin level provides inadequate protection for the brokerage house or if they believe that they can increase the profitability of the commission house by having higher margins. Higher margins provide increased protection to the commission house because the increased money protects them from debits. One of the major risks that a commission house runs is account debits. There are instances when an account has lost more money than is in the account. The client is liable to the house for these debits. As a practical matter, virtually all debit accounts are cleared up to the mutual satisfaction of the client and the commission house. However, on occasion, the commission house will have to cover the debit to the clearinghouse because the client won't or can't make the payment. The commission house is liable to the clearinghouse for all margin due at the level of the exchange minimums. Commission houses will often increase margins in an effort to provide an additional buffer before a particular trade uses up the margin. The commission house must post daily the margin necessary to cover its customers' positions to the clearinghouse. Any monies above the amount deposited to the clearinghouse can be used to earn interest for the company. If a customer's account size is large enough, typically over $15,000, the money can be invested in treasury bills, which are accepted as margin money. An account with $15,000 would therefore have approximately $10,000 in T-bills and $5000 in cash. The client earns the interest on the $10,000. The extra $5000 usually earns interest for the broker. Thus, the broker increases its interest income by increasing margins because clients must keep higher money balances on deposit.

The CFTC requires that the brokerage firms segregate the customer's margin monies from commission house assets, margins on the other house accounts, and margins on commodities that are not subject to U.S. regulations. This has the effect of reducing the risk of customer loss through brokerage house failure. If the brokerage house goes bankrupt, the client's account is held separate from the house's money and will not go to settle any brokerage house debts. This is not the way it is in the securities industry, where stocks can be held in a street name as the property of the security house, though the security may be owed to a customer. In the commodity futures industry, all monies are separated and remain totally under the control of the client.

The commission house takes the exchange minimum margins and deposits these with the clearinghouse. Only the largest, most financially secure brokerage houses deal directly with clearinghouses. Smaller commission houses rely on the services of a clearinghouse member to provide the necessary interaction with the clearinghouse. The smaller commission house will open an omnibus account with the clearinghouse member. This omnibus account is carried on the books of the clearinghouse member as a single account even though it represents many accounts with the smaller commission house. Commissions charged by non-clearinghouse members are the same as those charged by members of the clearinghouse. They may, of course, charge higher commissions than exchange minimums, just as the clearinghouse members can.

Margin is an important consideration in the commodity futures industry. It is the good faith deposit, or earnest money, that helps guarantee the ability of the clearinghouse and commission house to make or take delivery should that be necessary. It also reduces the possibility of defaults and helps ensure the integrity of the futures industry. This is the reason that commission houses devote so much time to ensuring that margin is always kept at a sufficiently high level.

Price Limits

Two limits are set on price movements on most futures by the exchanges. The exchanges limit the amount of daily price movement to prevent panic buying or selling. Prices are allowed to move to a certain level during a given day, at which point no further trading is allowed. If there was, for example, a tremendous amount of buying pressure in the market and a lack of sellers, the market could shoot extremely high in a short time period. A government announcement or other event may trigger the panic. The exchanges set limits on the amount that the market can move higher or lower on a day to allow market participants to digest and understand the news overnight. It is thought that they will be more calm when they come to trade the next

EXHIBIT 3-3   A chart of daily price limits (Paine Webber).

	ABOVE OR BELOW PREVIOUS CLOSE		BETWEEN HIGH AND LOW	
Boneless Beef	1½¢	per pound	3¢	per pound
Broilers	2¢	per pound	4¢	per pound
Cattle (Feeder)	1½¢	per pound	3¢	per pound
Cattle (Live)	1½¢	per pound	3¢	per pound
Cocoa	$88	metric ton	$176	per metric ton
Coffee	4¢	per pound	8¢	per pound
Commercial Paper	50	points	100	points
Copper (N.Y.)	5¢	per pound	10¢	per pound
Corn	10¢	per bushel	20¢	per bushel
Cotton	2¢	per pound	4¢	per pound
CURRENCIES: (IMM)				
British Pound	500	points	1000	points
Canadian Dollar	75	points	150	points
Deutschemark	100	points	200	points
Dutch Guilder	100	points	200	points
French Franc	500	points	1000	points
Japanese Yen	100	points	200	points
Mexican Peso	150	points	300	points
Swiss Franc	150	points	300	points
ENERGY				
Crude Oil	$1	barrel	$2	barrel
Gasoline (CBT)	3¢	gallon	6¢	
NY	2¢	gallon	4¢	
Heating Oil	2¢	gallon	4¢	
GNMA	64/32	per 32nds	128/32	
Gold (IMM)	$50	per ounce	$100	per ounce
Gold (CMX)	$25	per ounce	$50	per ounce
Hogs (Live)	1½¢	per pound	3¢	per pound
Lumber	$5	per 1000 bd ft	$10	per 1000 bd ft
NYSE Composite Index	No Limit			
Oats	6¢	per bushel	20¢	per bushel
Orange Juice	5¢	per pound	5¢	per pound
Palladium	$6	per ounce	$12	per ounce
Platinum	$20	per ounce	$20	per ounce
Plywood (Western)	$7	per 1000 sq ft	$14	per 1000 sq ft
Pork Bellies	2¢	per pound	4¢	per pound
Potatoes (NY)	50¢	per 100 lbs	$1	per 100 lbs
Propane	2¢	per gallon	4¢	per gallon
Silver (NY)	50¢	per ounce	$1	per ounce
Silver (Chi)	50¢	per ounce	$1	per ounce
Soybeans	30¢	per bushel	60¢	per bushel
Soybean Meal	$10	per ton	$20	per ton
Soybean Oil	1¢	per pound	2¢	per pound
S&P 500	no limit			
Sugar	1¢	per pound	2¢	per pound
U.S. Treasury Bills (IMM)	60	basis points	120	basis points
U.S. Treasury Bonds (CBT)	64/32		128/32	
Value Line	No Limit			
Wheat (Chicago)	20¢	per bushel	40¢	per bushel
Wheat (Minneapolis)	20¢	per bushel	40¢	per bushel
Wheat (Kansas City)	25¢	per bushel	50¢	per bushel
Winnipeg Grains:				
Barley	$5	per metric ton	$10	per metric ton
Oats	$5	per metric ton	$10	per metric ton
Rye	$5	per metric ton	$10	per metric ton
Flaxseed	$10	per metric ton	$20	per metric ton
Rapeseed	$10	per metric ton	$20	per metric ton

day and that the additional time may find participants willing to take the opposite side of the market. Exhibit 3-3 shows a chart of price limits.

The amount that the price can move from the previous day's close is called the daily limit. The maximum range that a commodity can trade is the daily range. The daily range will be double the daily limit. For example, the daily limit in soybeans is 30 cents. This means that the price of soybeans can rally and/or drop 30 cents from the previous day's close. If it were to rally up the daily limit and then move down to one daily limit below the previous night's close, there could be a daily range of 60 cents.

Trading does not stop because prices have moved to the daily limit. There are no constraints on the amount of trading that can occur at the daily limit. However, no trades may be made beyond the limit.

The daily limit is not always in effect or may be changed on occasion. The daily limits are usually eliminated during the delivery month and are often eliminated several days or even weeks before the delivery month. This is done to ensure that the futures market can converge with the cash market on the last trading day. It would otherwise be possible for the cash market to move significantly in one direction and for the futures market never to be able to catch up in price. Exchanges will also usually have provisions for expanding the daily limits should prices continue to move by the daily limit in one direction for several days. A typical example is this: If a commodity moved the daily limit for 2 straight days, then the daily limit would be 150 percent of the normal daily limit for the third day. It is best to maintain contact with your broker for current information on daily limits and changes in daily limits.

A locked-limit day is a day in which there is so much buying or selling pressure that the market moves to the daily limit and trading ceases. As was mentioned above, there is no limit to the amount of trading that can take place at the daily limit. On some occasions, however, buying or selling pressure is so great that no one wishes to go against the trend and trading ceases. In a selling panic, the sellers who are trying aggressively to sell contracts will have a hard time finding someone to buy at the daily price limit. It is not a requirement of the exchange that trading cease at the limits, but it does occasionally occur.

Many novice commodity traders are afraid of the prospect of being locked into their position by a locked-limit day. There is no doubt that being on the wrong side of a market when it goes locked-limit can make a trader uncomfortable. Nonetheless, the trader should remember that the alternative would be to have potentially unlimited losses in just a single day. These would be a far more uncomfortable situation than that created by the current procedure of commodity exchanges, which is to try to provide a semblance of order and calm when news items may be moving the market dramatically. It should also be noted that traders can often offset their locked-limit position by initiating a spread. Another alternative is to put on an opposite position in a related commodity.

Stock index futures are the only futures contracts with no price limits. When stock index futures were first listed, they had limits of from 300 to 500 points, depending on the contract. However, by early 1983 all exchanges carrying stock index futures dropped the price limits and the daily range. This occurred mainly because of competitive pressures between exchanges. Initially, only the NYSE Index had no limits. Whenever the market had a limit move on the Chicago and Kansas City exchanges, orders would shift to the New York exchange, which had no limits. Thus, on days with large price moves, the New York Futures Exchange would have a large volume of trades at the expense of the other exchanges.

Orders

All traders not on the exchange floors must initiate and exit trades by giving orders to their brokers. These orders are relayed to the floor where they are given to floor brokers for execution.

The most common and basic order is the market order. This order simply gives the amount of the commodity that the customer wants to buy or sell. The market order instructs the floor broker to initiate the transaction at the current market value. The brokers are instructed to get the best possible price, but, as a practical matter, the floor broker will take the bid price if trying to sell and take the offer price if trying to buy. Only on exceptionally large trades and only if given discretion will the floor broker actively try to seek out a better price. The market order is best used when speed is important. The market order is filled essentially on entering the pit. It can be useful for a fast-moving market where the trader needs to get in or out quickly to initiate or exit a trade. Traders may also use a market order when prices have reached a level where they wish to initiate a trade. Exhibit 3-4 gives an example of a market order.

The market order is the simplest and easiest order to enter. The

EXHIBIT 3-4 An example of a market order.

ORDER NUMBER					
	C.B.T. ☐	C.M.E. ☐	N.Y.C.E. ☐	OTHER ☐ _____	

BUY/SL/SPREAD/CXL BUY/ CX SL/CXL SPREAD	QUANTITY	COMMODITY
buy	*10*	*Sep S+P 100*

PRICE & CONDITIONS

Market

EXECUTED PRICE

CLIENT ACCOUNT NUMBER		INVESTMENT BROKER NUMBER
OFFICE SYMBOL	NUMBER	
X X	1 2 3 4 5	99

RC 60 REV. 1/78 6/81 00672

1 - TRANSMISSION COPY

CLIENT NAME (DO NOT TRANSMIT)

BRANCH MANAGER'S APPROVAL

customer states, for example, "Buy one December Value Line at the market." It is the basis from which all other orders flow, elaborating and setting limits on the basic market order.

A price limit order instructs the floor broker to execute the trade at the stated price or better. For example, "Buy one December Value Line at 162.00 limit" means to buy the December Value Line contract at 162.00 or better. This ensures that the client will receive a price of 162.00 or less in the purchase of the December Value Line. Traders should note that it is quite possible that the price of the commodity may hit or even move through the limit price level specified and yet not be filled on the order. Although this is not common, the price of the commodity can be slightly different on different sides of the pit. It is therefore possible that the floor broker was unable to accomplish the price level specified. The limit order is always placed under the market if it is a buy order and above the market if it is a sell order. It is usually used to initiate positions rather than exit them. It is particularly useful in trying to initiate trades in illiquid markets. A limit order is shown in Exhibit 3-5.

A first cousin of the limit order is the "fill or kill" order. This is a limit order that is sent to the pit that must be executed immediately

EXHIBIT 3-5 An example of a limit order.

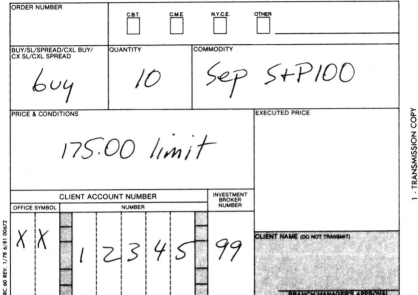

or it is canceled. In other words, if the price is not at or below the limit at the time the order is received, the order is immediately canceled and the client notified.

A stop order is a market order when a specified price level is reached. The stop order is often confused with the limit order. The difference between a stop order and a limit order is that a stop order is placed above the market on the buy side and below the market on the sell side. Traders wishing to buy a contract could use either the limit or the stop order. If the current price were 155.00, traders would enter a limit order as "Buy one June NYSE Index at 154.90 limit" or "Buy one June NYSE Index at 155.10 stop." When the stop level is reached, the stop order becomes a market order. This means that the actual fill on the order may be significantly different from the price mentioned in the stop order. An example of a stop order is shown in Exhibit 3-6.

The most common use of limit orders is to enter the market, and the most common use of stop orders is to protect investors' positions. Investors usually seek to find the best price before entering an order. This is why they use the limit order to enter positions. On the other hand, traders already in positions do not want them to become losers,

41

EXHIBIT 3-6 An example of a stop order.

ORDER NUMBER					
	C.B.T. ☐	C.M.E. ☐	N.Y.C.E. ☐	OTHER ☐ ___	

BUY/SL/SPREAD/CXL BUY/ CX SL/CXL SPREAD	QUANTITY	COMMODITY
buy	*10*	*Sep S+P 100*

PRICE & CONDITIONS

175.00 stop

EXECUTED PRICE

1 - TRANSMISSION COPY

OFFICE SYMBOL	CLIENT ACCOUNT NUMBER / NUMBER	INVESTMENT BROKER NUMBER
X X	1 2 3 4 5	99

CLIENT NAME (DO NOT TRANSMIT)

BRANCH MANAGER'S APPROVAL

RC 60 REV. 1/78 6/81 00672

and, therefore, as the position moves against them, they use stop orders to exit a position.

A combination of the stop and the limit order is the stop limit order. With this hybrid, the stop order becomes a market order when hit, but the price to be entered at must be at the stop level or better. This is often a difficult order to execute as it means the price must stay at the stop level or become more advantageous to be filled. If the price just keeps moving through the stop level, then the order will not be filled. A stop limit order is used more for entry than for exit because of this situation.

The market if touched (MIT) order is similar to the stop order. A MIT order is executed as a market order when the price reaches the level specified in the order. For example, "Buy one March S & P 500 Index at 125.00 MIT" is a market order when the market floor's board shows a price of 125.00.

Orders may be limited by time as well as price. Unless otherwise mentioned, all orders are considered day orders; this means they are canceled at the end of the trading session if not filled. An alternative to the day order is the good till canceled (GTC) order. This is shown

EXHIBIT 3-7 An example of a good till canceled (GTC) order, also
called an open order.

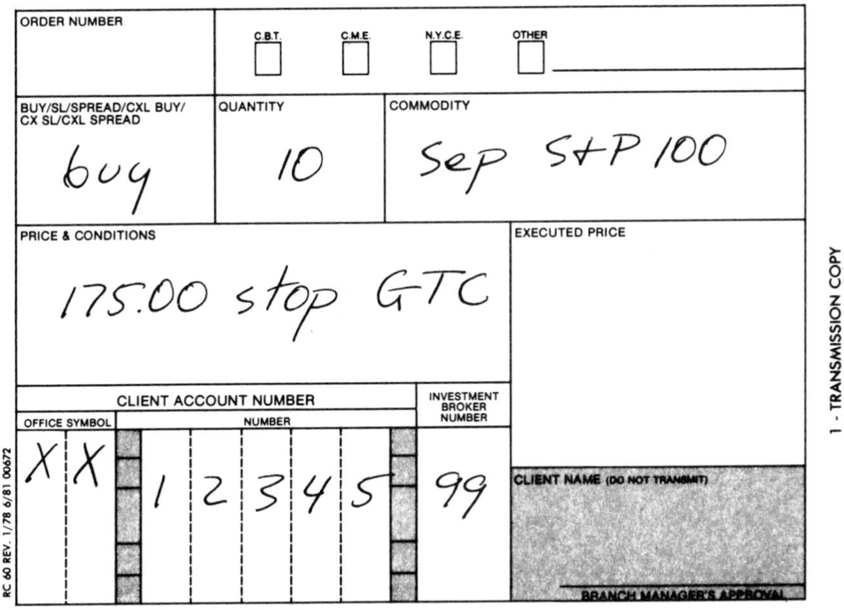

in Exhibit 3-7. Another term for this order is "open order." The GTC
order is considered always in force until either filled or canceled or
until the contract month expires. Brokerage houses are leery of GTC
orders because they have often been in the unfortunate position of
having the order become filled when the client has forgotten that the
order is in and no longer wishes to be in the position. Most brokers
will suggest that traders enter a series of day orders as this provides
a constant reminder that the trader wishes to initiate a position. Brokerage houses will typically send a written notification in the mail
when their clients enter GTC orders.

The time limit order is another order limited by time rather than
price. This can be any type of order but is canceled when a certain
time is reached during the trading session. An example is "Buy 10
June S & P 100 at 168.00 stop, noon."

Two very popular orders are the market on open (MOO) and the
market on close (MOC) orders. Exhibit 3-8 shows a MOC order. These
are market orders that are executed on the open or close. MOO will
be executed in the first 30 to 60 seconds of trading and must be within
the opening range. A MOC order will be executed in the last 30 or 60

EXHIBIT 3-8   An example of a market on close (MOC) order.

ORDER NUMBER				
	C.B.T. ☐	C.M.E. ☐	N.Y.C.E. ☐	OTHER ☐ _____

BUY/SL/SPREAD/CXL BUY/ CX SL/CXL SPREAD	QUANTITY	COMMODITY
buy	*10*	*S+P 100*

PRICE & CONDITIONS	EXECUTED PRICE
M.O.C.	

CLIENT ACCOUNT NUMBER — INVESTMENT BROKER NUMBER

OFFICE SYMBOL — NUMBER

X X   1 2 3 4 5   99

CLIENT NAME (DO NOT TRANSMIT)

BRANCH MANAGER'S APPROVAL

1 - TRANSMISSION COPY

RC 60 REV. 1/78 6/81 00672

seconds of trading and must be within the closing range. Many people believe that the opening and closing are the most significant prices of a trading session. Academic theory suggests that these are important because they represent the accumulated concepts of market participants as they adjust to overnight factors on the opening or as they try to predict what may happen overnight on the close. Many technical and mechanical trading systems use MOO and/or MOC orders. They do this because the opening and closing prices are recorded, whereas intra-day prices are often not recorded except when they are the high or low.

At most exchanges, orders initiated within 15 minutes of the opening or close are on a "not held" basis. This means that stop and limit orders are not necessarily guaranteed. A floor broker will try but will not guarantee the fills. For example, a limit order placed in the middle of the trading session must be filled at the specified price or better. If the order comes back at a price worse than specified, then either the floor broker or brokerage house will correct the problem with the customer. If the same order was placed within 15 minutes of the open or close, then the client does not have recourse to the brokerage house or floor broker and must accept the order fill as received.

EXHIBIT 3-9   An example of a canceled order.

ORDER NUMBER		C.B.T. ☐	C.M.E. ☐	N.Y.C.E. ☐	OTHER ☐ _____
BUY/SL/SPREAD/CXL BUY/ CX SL/CXL SPREAD *buy*	QUANTITY *10*	COMMODITY	*Sep S+P 100*		

PRICE & CONDITIONS

mkt

cancel

EXECUTED PRICE

1 - TRANSMISSION COPY

OFFICE SYMBOL	CLIENT ACCOUNT NUMBER NUMBER	INVESTMENT BROKER NUMBER
X X	1 2 3 4 5	99

RC 60 REV. 1/78 6/81 00672

CLIENT NAME (DO NOT TRANSMIT)

BRANCH MANAGER'S APPROVAL

Traders use the cancel order to eliminate a previous order. The two types of cancel orders are the straight cancel order and the cancel former order. The latter order is also sometimes referred to as a cancel and replace order. The straight cancel order does exactly what it says—it cancels the previous order. For example, if an order had been placed to buy the mini-Value Line contract on a stop, the trader could cancel the order by telling the broker to cancel the order. The cancel former order (or cancel and replace order) cancels the previous order but replaces it with new instructions. A canceled order is shown in Exhibit 3-9.

A relatively rare order is the combination, or contingency, order. This order specifies two orders mentioned above, or when one price level is reached in one contract, an order is placed in another contract. These are relatively rare as few exchanges take them.

The final type of order is the spread order. A spread order is an order for the purchase and sale of two different contracts. The contracts may be within the same commodity but may not be in the same month. Alternately, they could be in two separate commodities, in which case they could be within the same month. A spread order is entered in terms of the price level that one contract is over or under

EXHIBIT 3-10 An example of a spread order.

ORDER NUMBER		C.B.T.	C.M.E.	N.Y.C.E.	OTHER	
BUY/SL/SPREAD/CXL BUY/ CX SL/CXL SPREAD	QUANTITY		COMMODITY			

spread
buy — 10 — sep S+P 100
sell — 10 — Dec S+P 100

PRICE & CONDITIONS   EXECUTED PRICE

+ 45 Dec

CLIENT ACCOUNT NUMBER — INVESTMENT BROKER NUMBER
OFFICE SYMBOL — NUMBER

X X   1 2 3 4 5   99

CLIENT NAME (DO NOT TRANSMIT)

RC 60 REV. 1/78 6/81 00672

1 - TRANSMISSION COPY

the other contract or simply as a market order. Stop orders used to be acceptable in combination with spread orders but are now very rare. Two examples of spread orders would be "Buy one March NYSE index and sell one June NYSE index at 35 points premium the March" and "Buy two September NYSE index and sell one September Value Line at 950 points premium the NYSE Index." We will discuss spreads more fully in Chapter 6. Exhibit 3-10 is an example of a spread order.

Although we have described many types of orders, not all orders are taken at all exchanges. The orders that each exchange accepts are largely determined by the floor brokers one is dealing with. For example, the Chicago Board of Trade does not accept spread stop orders but the Chicago Mercantile Exchange does. Nonetheless, it is difficult to enter a spread stop order at the Chicago Mercantile Exchange as there are few floor brokers who are willing to accept it. Contingency orders are also accepted by many exchanges but by few brokers. In the final analysis, it is the floor broker who determines what orders are accepted or not accepted. Traders should keep in contact with their brokers to alert them to changes in acceptable orders for each exchange.

Volume and Open Interest

Volume and open interest are measurements of trading activity. These numbers are compiled by the exchanges for the CFTC and are printed by newspapers and other news sources daily. Exhibit 3-11 shows the listing from the *Wall Street Journal* showing prices, volume on the right side, and open interest below each futures contract. They are typically issued the day following the day the trading applies to;

EXHIBIT 3-11 **A sample listing from *The Wall Street Journal* showing prices, volume on the right side, and open interest below each futures contract. (Reprinted by permission of *The Wall Street Journal,* © Dow Jones & Company, Inc. (1984). All rights reserved.)**

						Lifetime		Open
	Open	High	Low	Settle	Change	High	Low	Interest
S&P 500 FUTURES INDEX (CME) 500 Times Index								
June	161.40	161.85	159.00	159.15	– 2.80	177.10	155.00	28,701
Sept	164.00	164.40	161.60	161.70	– 2.85	178.15	156.80	2,167
Dec	166.30	166.30	163.70	163.70	– 3.10	179.20	158.60	210
Mar85	166.00	166.00	165.70	166.00	– 2.95	180.25	160.50	55
June	....	....	....	167.70	– 3.30	180.70	161.75	6
Sept	....	....	....	169.40	– 3.30	173.40	165.70	5
Est vol 44,806; vol Thur 38,101; open int 31,144, –16.								
S&P 500 STOCK INDEX (Prelim)								
	160.86	161.20	158.93	159.11	– 2.09	....	....	....
S&P 100 FUTURES INDEX (CME) 200 Times Index								
May	157.80	157.80	157.45	156.80	– 2.90	158.90	153.10	6
June	159.60	160.00	157.20	157.40	– 2.90	177.80	152.20	2,822
July	....	....	....	158.05	– 2.90	157.90	154.05	0
Sept	....	....	....	159.95	– 2.95	168.30	154.30	3
Est vol 1,158; vol Thurs 1,002; open int 2,831, –159.								
S&P 100 STOCK INDEX (Prelim)								
	158.81	159.34	156.53	156.78	– 2.56	....	....	....
NYSE COMPOSITE FUTURES (NYFE) 500 Times Index								
June	93.25	93.40	91.70	91.85	– 1.60	103.00	82.30	6,715
Sept	94.50	94.65	93.10	93.15	– 1.55	103.10	89.25	1,207
Dec	95.75	95.85	94.15	94.80	– 1.55	103.55	91.35	579
Mar85	97.00	97.10	95.45	95.65	– 1.55	103.80	93.00	173
June	98.25	98.25	98.25	96.90	– 1.55	105.00	94.25	81
Sept	99.50	99.50	99.50	98.15	– 1.55	99.75	96.00	28
Est vol 13,945; vol Thur 8,969; open int 8,783, –21.								
NYSE COMPOSITE STOCK INDEX								
	92.75	92.78	91.67	91.75	– 1.08	....	....	....
KC VALUE LINE FUTURES (KC) 500 Times Index								
June	184.40	185.10	181.55	181.70	– 3.10	212.00	176.15	3,153
Sept	187.20	187.20	184.00	184.00	– 3.20	213.50	178.45	113
Dec	....	....	....	186.50	– 3.20	210.00	182.20	3
Est vol 4,532; vol Thur 3,001; open int 3,269, –126.								
KC VALUE LINE COMPOSITE STOCK INDEX								
	183.14	183.20	181.66	181.81	– 1.32	....	....	....

thus the volume and open interest for December 13 will be reported on December 14. This time lag is necessary to compile and verify the data.

Open interest is the number of contracts outstanding. The open interest is the same as the number of longs and the number of shorts but not the number of longs and shorts combined. This is because one long and one short create one contract, not two, as would be the case if both the long and short were counted.

The open interest rises and falls as contracts are entered into or exited. If a trader goes long one contract, the open interest increases by one, and when that contract is liquidated, the open interest will be reduced by one. This is the simplest situation. The real world is slightly more complicated. It is possible that traders may initiate a

EXHIBIT 3-12 Chart of the December 1983 S & P 500 contract (*CRB Futures Chart Service,* a weekly publication of Commodity Research Bureau, Inc., 75 Montgomery St., Jersey City, N.J. 07302.)

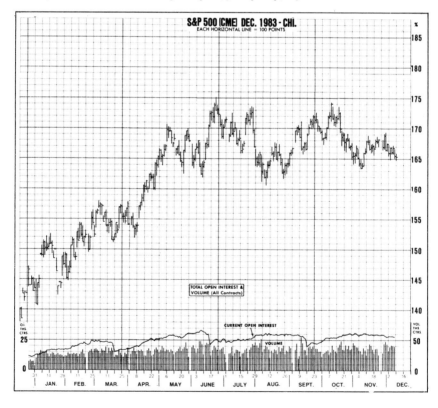

position, increasing open interest by one, but their liquidation of the long contract may go to a person who is also initiating a long contract. In this case, the net effect is as if the first trader handed a contract over to the second trader. This means that the open interest would neither rise nor fall as no new contracts were actually initiated or exited.

The volume for a given day is the number of contracts traded that day. If the trader were to initiate the trade in the morning and liquidate it at the end of the day, then the volume would be two contracts. This is because the trader is a participant in two separate transactions. Exhibit 3-12 shows the volume and open interest of the futures contract across the bottom of the chart. Notice the fluctuations of both the volume and the open interest. It is also interesting to note that the volume often is as great as the open interest. This usually occurs when floor traders are very active.

Traders should note that the volume on a given day can actually be larger than the open interest. This is because many traders may scalp or day-trade contracts throughout the day but end the trading session with no open contracts. The net effect is to increase the volume substantially without increasing the open interest at all.

Delivery

In the futures market all open positions must be closed out by the last trading day of the contract. Most contracts in commodities are liquidated before the delivery time period. They are liquidated by simply offsetting the open position. That is, the owner of a long will liquidate the long contract by selling one contract, and the owner of a short contract will liquidate it by going long one contract. In other commodities it is possible actually to make or take delivery of the cash commodity. Thus, on the last day of trading a trader may have to make or take delivery of 5000 bushels of corn should the trader own a long or short contract.

Stock index futures use a unique and simplified procedure in futures trading: cash settlement. This means that the value of the futures contract of the last day of trading will equal the actual spot index value for the stock index that is the underlying index for that particular contract. All open contracts are "marked to the market," and cash is used as the settlement vehicle. The longs and shorts are notified by the clearing corporation of the settlement price of the last day, and they are required to transfer by wire to the clearing corporation any money owed to it. This cash settlement feature ensures that there is no manipulation, squeezes, or corners. It also ensures that the futures and cash price converge on the last day of trading. For more information on cash settlement, see the previous chapter.

Much of the information outlined in this chapter is subject to change by exchanges or brokerage houses. It is highly recommended that readers keep in close contact with their brokers to ensure the accuracy of the information.

The Contracts

chapter 4

The basics of stock index futures are straightforward but nonetheless important. It would be difficult to trade stock index futures without knowing some basic information such as contract specifications and the way that the indexes are calculated. Each of the stock index futures contracts has unique characteristics. An understanding of these characteristics is necessary before trading stock index futures. The intercommodity spread strategies outlined in this chapter and the next chapter are built upon on understanding of the differences between the major contracts.

Each index is based upon a corresponding cash index. The name of the futures contract refers to the underlying cash index. The NYSE Index futures contract is a futures contract based on the NYSE Index, which is computed by the New York Stock Exchange. The typical cash index existed for decades before the advent of the futures contracts.

Indexes

Indexes are a simplification of an aggregate of information. They simplify reality and ease analysis and understanding. It would be difficult to analyze the market without stock indexes. They provide a short-hand method for understanding movements of the market as a whole. They can be constructed in a number of different ways. The indexes underlying the stock index futures are derived in two different ways, and the Dow Jones Industrial Average uses another method. The differences can be used to discover profitable trading opportunities. The various techniques of averaging will be outlined later in this chapter.

EXHIBIT 4-1 Major attributes of the main stock index futures contracts.

	S&P 500	S&P 100	NYSE	Value Line	Mini Value Line
Contract size	$500 times the value of S&P 500 Stock Index	$200 times the value of S&P 100 Stock Index	$500 times the value of NYSE Composite Index	$500 times the value of the Value Line Index	$100 times the value of the futures price
Delivery	Cash settlement Mark to market No physical delivery	Cash settlement Mark to market No physical delivery	Cash settlement Mark to market No physical delivery	Cash settlement Mark to market No physical delivery	Cash settlement Mark to market No physical delivery
Exchange	Chicago Mercantile Exchange	Chicago Mercantile Exchange	New York Futures Exchange	Kansas City Board of Trade	Kansas City Board of Trade
Trading hours	9:00 a.m. to 3:15 p.m. CST	9:00 a.m. to 3:15 p.m. CST	9:00 a.m. to 3:15 p.m. CST	9:00 a.m. to 3:15 p.m. CST	9:00 a.m. to 3:15 p.m. CST
Last trading day	Third Thursday of contract month	Third Friday of contract month	Third Friday of contract month	Last business day of contract month	Last business day of contract month
Settlement day	Last trading day	Last trading day	Last trading day	Last trading day	Last trading day
Minimum fluctuation	.05 points ($25)	.05 points ($10)	.05 points ($25)	.05 points ($25)	.05 points ($5)
Price Limits	None	None	None	None	None
Contract months	March, June, September, December	March, June, September, December	March, June, September, December	March, June, September, December	March, June, September, December
Margins	Contact your broker	Contact your broker	Contact your broker	Contact your broker	Contact your broker
Commissions	Contact your broker	Contact your broker	Contact your broker	Contact your broker	Contact your broker

The major attributes of the main stock index futures contracts are outlined in Exhibit 4-1. Many of the features are identical, but several features, such as the method of averaging the stocks included, are very different. We will go through the list feature by feature and go into detail about the meaning and significance of the attributes of the index futures.

Each of the futures contracts is based upon some multiple of the cash index. For example, the S & P 500 futures contract represents a dollar value of $500 times the index. It is well to remember that the S & P 500 futures contract is worth $500 times the futures index, not the cash index. The futures index will likely be trading at a price significantly different from the cash index. If the S & P 500 futures contract is selling for 150.00, the value of the contract will be $75,000, which is $500 times the index value of 150.00.

There is a relationship between the cash and futures contracts. This relationship forms the basis for Chapter 6. For now, let us merely state that there is a reasonably close relationship between the cash and futures indexes. This relationship becomes tighter as the expiry date comes closer. On the last day of trading, the cash and futures indexes will be identical.

Contract Size

Three of the stock index futures contracts currently trading have a value of $500 times the index. The S & P 100 contract is worth $200 times the futures index. The Kansas City Board of Trade carries two versions of the Value Line contract. The so-called Value Line contract is worth $500 times the index, while the mini-Value Line contract is worth $100 times the index because it is one-fifth the size of the regular contract.

The New York Futures Exchange has also obtained permission from the CFTC to offer a jumbo NYSE Index contract worth $1000 times the index. The current NYSE contract has a much smaller value than the S & P 500 and Value Line contracts. The index has a value that is worth about half that of the two other contracts. Originally, the New York Futures Exchange felt that the smaller contract size would help build volume by attracting smaller speculators. The New York exchange had its back to the wall before starting the New York Stock Exchange Index contract. It had tried to compete with the bigger and better-capitalized Chicago exchanges with essentially the same products being offered in Chicago. The NYFE had tried several contracts, including a treasury bond contract. All of them had failed or appeared ready to fail because of declining volume and open interest. The New York Futures Exchange took the position that having a smaller contract would help differentiate the product in the eyes of the investing public and aid in producing a viable contract. It had previously been criticized for not having introduced a unique product, the critics contending that the NYFE could not succeed as an exchange until it produced a product that was significantly different from what was being offered in Chicago. This was the setting in which the NYFE made its decision to have a smaller contract value that the S & P 500 and Value Line contracts.

The NYFE then appears to have become worried that the smaller contract value would not be able to compete with the larger contract values in Chicago and Kansas City. It applied for and received permission to trade the jumbo NYSE Index contract, worth $1000 times the index. This contract has never traded because the original concept of the NYFE appears to have been correct. The NYSE Index contract has become very popular and there has been no need to issue the jumbo contract. In fact, the NYSE Index has been so popular that the two most recent futures contracts introduced, the S & P 100 and the mini-Value Line, are the same size as the NYSE Index contract or smaller.

One reason the NYSE Index caught up with the S & P 500 contract and far surpassed the Value Line contract is that it was the only contract with no price limits for several months. There were probably two basic reasons for the lack of a price limit. The first reason was that the New York Stock Exchange founded the New York Futures Exchange. The stock exchange was used to dealing in securities that have no limits. The securities markets have never had price limits similar to the limits at the commodities exchanges. The NYFE also wanted to make the contract useful to the specialists on the floor of the New York Stock Exchange. If the cash stock market was plunging, the specialists would not be able to protect themselves as well by shorting the NYSE Index futures contract if there was a price limit. The price protection feature of the futures market would be less useful to the specialists if the limits prevented them from continuing to short the futures market as the cash market moved to levels that would cause the futures market to hit the bottom price limit. In addition, the NYFE found that many traders and hedgers were switching to the NYSE Index contract on days when the other two contracts went to a price limit and stopped trading. This factor appears to have helped the volume of the NYSE Index tremendously during the first few months of trading. The volume of the NYSE Index was very high on those days when the other contracts had a limit move.

The second reason was that the smaller contract size limited the risk inherent in trading the stock index futures compared with the two larger contracts. The dollar value of a market move will be less with the smaller contract than with the S & P 500 and Value Line. This means traders will be able to control their dollar risk better in volatile markets. NYFE apparently felt that the smaller contract size would lessen the need for price limits as a protective measure.

Cash Settlement

All contracts use a cash settlement that is marked to the market on the last day of trading. This statement contains several important concepts. The first is that the prices of the futures and cash indexes must be equivalent. The futures exchanges have defined the settlement price of the futures contract on the last day always to equal the final cash quote of the cash stock index. This is a major tie keeping the futures prices in line with the cash price.

Cash settlement is different from settlement with traditional commodities, such as corn. The settlement price on the last day of trading in traditional commodities is set by the supply and demand for the futures contracts on the last day of trading. This means that the futures contract can settle at a price far away from the cash price. This rarely happens, though it is theoretically possible. It is rare because of the actions of arbitrageurs and commercial interests who continually evaluate the relative value of the cash and futures prices. When that difference is out of line, the arbitrageurs and commercials will buy the side of the transaction that is undervalued and sell the side of the transaction that is overvalued. For example, if the futures price is undervalued relative to the cash, the arbitrageurs and commercials will likely buy the futures and sell the cash commodity. This process takes place continually during the life of the contract but takes on a more serious aspect after the futures contract comes into the delivery month. The delivery month in a traditional commodity is the time period, typically several weeks before the final trading day, in which the cash commodity can be delivered against the futures contract. It is during these last few weeks of trading that the futures and cash are virtually interchangeable.

One of the main reasons that the futures and cash prices can differ is that there can be many cash prices. For example, corn is deliverable in Chicago, Toledo, and St. Louis. There will be three cash prices during the delivery period. It is difficult for the futures market to find a final selling price that adequately takes into account all three cash prices. In addition, there is more than one grade of corn that is deliverable. The corn contract calls for the delivery of number 2 grade corn, but grades 1 and 3 are also deliverable. Other grades have price adjustments made before they are delivered in an effort to reduce the attractiveness of delivering grades other than grade 2. The three grades of corn combined with the three delivery points make a total of nine different cash prices for the futures market to contend with. The fact that the system has worked so well for over 100 years is a tribute to the soundness of the futures market.

The settlement of the stock index futures is a substantially easier task. There is only one cash price to deal with. It is also virtually impossible for anyone to manipulate the cash price of the cash stock index. It would take billions of dollars to move the market sufficiently to manipulate the cash price to profit on the futures contract. One of the reasons the traditional commodities have so many options for delivery, including grade and location, is to reduce the chance of manipulation of the deliverable supplies and the cash price.

The settlement by cash is a feature that has an advantage over the traditional delivery methods. It makes it easier to build the speculator liquidity that is crucial for the success of a new contract. In the traditional commodities, speculators often worried that they would have insufficient funds available if the underlying commodity were delivered to them. In traditional commodities, people taking delivery must pay for the value of the commodity contract delivered to them within several days or resell the commodity but with the penalties of extra commissions and carrying costs. This is a relatively rare occurrence for the speculators; it happens only when speculators or their brokers are not paying attention. It seems that everyone has heard the old stories of speculators coming home to find 38,000 pounds of pork bellies dumped on their front lawns. No matter how absurd the stories are, speculators tend to shy away from delivery. This is probably a wise decision, as there are few speculators willing or able consistently to come up with the $15,000 or $125,000 necessary to pay for a contract of the traditional commodities. Speculators do not trade commodities to worry about taking delivery.

The speculator's worry has the effect of reducing the speculative influence during the last month of trading and creating more volatility than would otherwise occur. The fewer participants, the greater the volatility. This is particularly true in most commodities, including stock index futures, when the vast majority of commercials are hedging on the short side. Prices become very volatile when the majority of the traders only want to sell the market. The speculators' trading has the effect of smoothing price volatility by providing greater liquidity and evening the balance between longs and shorts.

The cash settlement feature eliminates the worry of acquiring large sums of cash or credit to pay for a delivery. In cash settlement, the futures contract is marked to the market on the last day of trading. This procedure is identical to any other trading day. On all trading days any given account, whether speculative or hedging, will be making or losing money. Positions that are showing a positive equity and making money can have a check drawn against them. This check can be sent from the brokerage house to the investor or hedger who is carrying the profitable position. The check can be for the amount of equity over the amount of margin. For example, a position showing a profit of $2000 after the margin deposit of $6000 could have a check written against it for $2000. One the other hand, owners of positions that are losing money must post enough additional funds to move the margin money back up to the maintenance margin level. The "mark-to-the-market" method used everyday to determine margin payments is the same for the last day of trading. If the contract is worth $60,000, traders do not have to post $60,000 on the last day of trading. They instead post the profit or loss just as outlined above. For example, speculators who bought Value Line futures at 160.00 would have to pay $500 to take delivery of the contract if the settlement price on the last day of trading was 159.00 Notice that they do not actually take delivery of anything. They simply pay the mark-to-the-market margin adjustment. In a traditional commodity they would have had to put up the full value of the contract, which would have meant posting tens of thousands of dollars. This reduction in the possible liability of the trader will help increase liquidity in the final month of trading for a given contract.

The Exchanges

The S & P 100 and S & P 500 contracts were traded at the Index and Options Market (IOM), a subsidiary of the Chicago Mercantile Exchange (CME) in Chicago, Illinois. The Chicago Mercantile Exchange is the second largest commodity exchange and still growing fast. The Chicago Mercantile Exchange is also called the Chicago Merc. The Chicago Merc was the inventor of financial futures when it instituted currency futures in 1973. The concept of financial futures has exploded and now dominates the older agricultural commodities. In addition to the S & P contracts and the currencies, the Merc has agricultural commodities such as hogs and cattle as well as gold. The currencies and gold are traded on the International Monetary Market (IMM), which is also a subsidiary of the CME. The agricultural commodities are traded on the Chicago Mercantile Exchange itself. A member of the Chicago Mercantile Exchange has the right to trade on all of the subsidiary exchanges, but members of the IOM or IMM are not allowed to trade on the CME.

The New York Stock Exchange Index is traded on the New York Futures Exchange (NYFE), in New York City. The NYFE is an affiliate of the New York Stock Exchange and was set up to trade interest rate futures in the late 1970's. This was unsuccessful, and the interest rate futures are no longer being traded on the NYFE. The NYFE was unable to compete effectively with the larger, better-organized, and better-capitalized Chicago exchanges. The New York Futures Exchange became almost dormant. The advent of trading on the New York Stock Exchange Index in 1982 brought new life to the NYFE, and it now is a vibrant success. One of the main features of the NYFE is that it has tremendous participation by the specialist firms from the New York Stock Exchange. The specialists are using the NYSE Index futures as a method of hedging the portfolios of stocks that they must carry as part of their occupational responsibility. In addition, they have apparently used the futures contract to profit when they felt the market was due for a correction.

The Value Line Index and the mini-Value Line contracts are traded on the Kansas City Board of Trade (KCBOT) in Kansas City, Missouri. The KCBOT is the leading exchange for trading hard red winter wheat, though its volume is dwarfed by that of the wheat contract at the Chicago Board of Trade. Nonetheless, the KCBOT is an important wheat market both for cash and for futures. This was the first financial futures contract that the exchange initiated, and it has been a major success, leading the way to other index futures. The volume of the Kansas City Value Line contracts is currently far smaller than that of the S & P 500 and NYSE indexes, but is still very successful for a new contract at a small exchange. The volume is high enough to permit excellent trading and hedging opportunities. The big contract is not growing very much any more but is not showing signs of failure. The mini-Value Line contract is doing well and may provide additional volume to the KCBOT.

Subindexes

The New York Financial Index was traded on the NYFE for several months but never really got off the ground and eventually failed as a contract. It was a subindex of the NYSE Index and was composed of about 30 financial services companies. The list of companies included banks and insurance companies. One problem was that it had a larger contract value than the other contracts by about a third. It was the only contract that was 1000 times the index in value. It was also introduced hard on the heels of the NYSE Index. It is possible that the market had yet to reach the level of sophistication and volume necessary to support a subindex. Other criticisms of the contract were that the index was poorly designed and than it was too broadly based. The various components of the index were not closely correlated in price movement, and it was difficult to analyze or use it.

If the New York Financial Index had been a success, there would probably be other subindexes trading today. The Chicago Merc has gotten permission from the Commodity Futures Trading Commission to trade a consumer staples subindex of the S & P 500. They do not plan to trade the subindex until their new premises are built and they have the room to trade it. In addition, they appear to be shying away from expanding too fast after the experience of the NYFE with the New York Financial Index.

In spite of the failure of the financial subindex and the reluctance of the Chicago Merc to issue the subindex of the S & P 500, the wave of the future is subindexes. These will expand the market for stock index futures and provide even more opportunities for investment profits and hedging. Hedgers and investors will be able to fine-tune their hedging or investing precisely to the industry in which they have an interest.

Trading Hours

The trading hours for all markets are 10:00 a.m. to 4:15 p.m. EST. The futures markets stay open longer than the underlying cash market for a couple of reasons. The first reason is that the futures exchanges wanted to provide something to differentiate the futures market from the cash market. It was felt that the additional 15 minutes of trading in the futures market would give an excellent indication of the opening on the cash market the following day. This is because the market participants who have an opinion on the market and have the money to back it up will continue to trade on the futures markets after the close of the cash markets.

Originally the close on the stock index futures was to be 5 minutes after the money supply figures were released on Friday afternoons. At the time, money supply figures were released by the Federal Reserve Bank of New York at 4:10 p.m. EST. This would give traders 5 minutes to react to the news before the market would close. The extra few minutes would allow traders who had positions in the cash market to hedge them in the futures market if they were losers or to initiate new positions if the trend of the market appeared to be changing. The money supply figures had become a major market influence for Monday's trading. It was hoped that the extra 5 minutes of trading would give the futures market some additional trading and publicity. This worked very well for the exchanges for about 10 months. The Federal Reserve Bank finally responded to the futures market by rescheduling the release of the money supply figures until 4:15 p.m. EST on Friday so that the futures markets could not respond to the announcement until Monday morning. This could be considered a backhanded compliment by the Federal Reserve Bank to the futures exchanges. It shows that the mighty Fed was swayed by the desire to reduce speculation on the numbers it releases.

Last Trading Day

The last days of trading differ slightly for the various futures contracts. The S & P 500 contract has its last trading day on the third Thursday of the contract month. In other words, if we are talking about the March contract, the last trading day will be the third Thursday in March. The NYSE ends trading on the next to the last business day of the contract month, and the Value Line expires on the last business day of the contract month. This difference looks trivial at first glance. However, this small difference has some far-reaching consequences for inter-index and intra-index spread traders as well as for those who follow the basis. We will go into this in much greater detail in Chapter 6. In brief, the difference in delivery dates will affect the valuation of the various contracts because of the timing of dividend flows into the cash market. The cash market is a competing investment for the futures contracts and affects the value of the futures.

Minimum Fluctuation

The minimum price fluctuation is .05, except for the mini-Value Line contract, which has a minimum fluctuation of .01. In other words, the NYSE Index can go from 80.00 to 80.05 even though the underlying cash index can go from 80.00 to 80.01. Originally, the large Value Line Index futures traded in increments of .01. This was dropped when it became cumbersome. Most traders were already trading with a minimum fluctuation of .05. The .01 minimum tick was confusing to the floor brokers and inhibited their effectiveness in making trades for their customers. When the market was volatile, the floor brokers were too busy searching their stacks of orders for price orders at numbers that were not "rounded off" to the nearest .05. The KCBOT finally made official what was already happening on the floor. The KCBOT is trading the mini-Value Line with a contract size of $100 times the index. This is one-fifth the size of the big Value Line contract, the S & P 500 contract, and the NYSE Index and one-half the size of the S & P 100 contract. The mini-Value Line has a minimum tick of .01. For the large contract, however, experience has shown that the .05 minimum tick is a workable minimum that does not need changing.

Price Limits

The daily price limits are identical at all exchanges. No contract currently being traded has a price limit. This means that the price can move to any level during the day. There are no theoretical limits as to how far the price can go up in a day, and the only limit on the downside is that stock indexes cannot sell for less than zero. However, it should be noted that prices have usually traded within several hundred points of the previous night's close.

These are the only commodity futures contracts that never have a price limit. All other commodity contracts have price limits, though these are often waived for the contract nearest to expiry. The traditional commodities have used price limits to limit the amount the price can move either up or down from the previous night's settlement price. The commodity exchanges felt that a lack of price limits could increase risk because it could impair liquidity whenever a panic buying or selling wave occurred. The price limits were instituted to help induce a more rational outlook by forcing traders to wait overnight before trading again.

The exchanges did not want to keep a price locked in a limit situation forever. Typically, the price limits on traditional commodities have been expanded after several trading sessions of limit price moves. This gave traders a couple of sessions to cool down and take a more rational look at the market but at the same time it permitted the futures price to adjust to the new market value quickly.

This combination of price limits and subsequent expansion of price limits in extraordinary circumstances was found by the exchanges to reduce volatility over the long run. A reduction in volatility was found to be of greater service to market participants.

This feature was eliminated after several months of trading of stock index futures by the exchanges. The NYSE Index was originally the only contract without price limits. The small size of the NYSE Index was one reason that the NYFE did not include a limit on its price. The NYFE apparently felt that the small size would enable traders to control the dollar risk of holding a position during a sharp market movement. The NYFE is a subsidiary of the New York Stock Exchange, and the stock exchanges have never put limits on the price of a stock. They will, however, stop trading when they feel there is an imbalance of buy and sell orders. This takes the place of the more formal commodity exchange rules governing price limits. Thus, the NYFE carried its tradition of no price limits into the commodity arena. This innovation was picked up fairly quickly by the Chicago and Kansas City exchanges.

Some people also thought that an index would be less volatile than a futures contract based on a single entity. For example, they felt that a single stock might be having a sharp move but that the average move of all the stocks would be much less susceptible to sharp movements. Individual stocks could often move 10 percent in a single day but it would be very unlikely that a stock index would move as much in the same length of time.

Contract Months

Each of the exchanges has its stock index futures expiring in March, June, September, and December. This quarterly cycle originated with the International Monetary Market. Currency futures commenced trading in 1973, with the contracts being traded on a calendar quarter cycle. It was felt that the four quarters would be able to provide enough contracts in a year to achieve good hedge and speculative opportunities. The calendar quarter concept was designed also to coincide with the calendar quarters used in corporate bookkeeping. Many businesses must make dividend and other types of payments on a quarterly basis. Thus, corporations would be better able to hedge their needs if the contract expired at the end of a quarter than at any other time in the quarter.

The quarterly settlement of futures contracts continued with the beginning of trading of interest rate futures contracts in the mid-1970s. GNMAs, treasury bills, and treasury bonds use the same contract cycle as the stock index futures.

Margins

Margins are a tricky subject to deal with because they are usually different from brokerage house to brokerage house. It was explained in an earlier chapter that the exchanges set minimum margins but that the brokerage houses can charge a higher margin if they wish.

For example, the exchange minimum for the S & P 500 may be $6000 but a brokerage firm could charge, for example, $8000 to its clients. It should be noted that the brokerage firm can charge any amount over the minimum margin set by the exchange.

The S & P 500 has at the time of this writing a minimum margin of $6000, the Value Line index is at $6500, and the NYSE Index is at $3500. Hedgers have had to pay $2500 for the S & P 500, $3250 for the Value Line, and $1500 for the NYSE Index. The maintenance margin has been $2000 for the S & P 500 and Value Line and $1500 for the NYSE Index. It should be stressed that readers should consult their brokers for the latest margins as they may have been changed since the time of this writing.

Margin is a completely different animal from the margin that most securities traders are used to. When securities traders buy a stock on margin they are borrowing money from the brokerage house to pay for some portion of the total transaction cost. For example, traders may wish to purchase IBM stock at $100 and buy 100 shares. Investors could pay $10,000 for the shares or they could borrow part of the cost from the brokerage house. The current Regulation T maximum margin, as specified by the Federal Reserve Bank, is 50 percent. This means that the clients need to put up 50 percent of the value of the security and the brokerage house will lend them the other 50 percent. The brokerage houses are not constrained to do this and may refuse if they so choose. The client must have opened a margin or general account before trading on margin can occur. Opening a margin account is analogous to obtaining a line of credit from a bank.

The margin money that is borrowed from the brokerage house must be paid back, and the brokerage house will charge an interest rate on that margin money lent. Thus, while a client has borrowed margin money, interest must be paid on that money to the brokerage house. This interest is a major part of the income and profitability of brokerage firms. It is a relatively low-risk loan from the brokerage house to the client, as the brokerage house holds the collateral of the underlying shares that have been bought on margin. It is a very profitable transaction for brokerage houses, and they are always eager to lend margin money. The interest on the margin money can be deducted from taxes as long as the margin money has not been used to buy municipal bonds, which are tax-free. Many investors shy away from buying on margin because they do not wish to pay the interest costs associated with the loan.

Margin in the commodities world is significantly different. Firms are not lending customers any money, and there are no interest charges on margin money to customers. In fact, in many cases clients may receive interest for the margin money they have deposited.

Clients earn the revenue because commodity exchanges allow customers to post T-bills as margin. They do not allow T-bonds or stocks or certificates of deposit but only T-bills of any maturity. It typically makes sense for the investors to use T-bills whenever possible. Traders should use a 6-month or longer-maturity T-bill to reduce the eating up of the profits by commissions.

Commodity firms will allow the T-bill to be used as margin, but they will typically not allow the full face value of the T-bill. Although the T-bill may be worth $10,000 on expiry, the brokerage firms will generally only allow 80 to 90 percent of that value to be posted as margin. This is a protective device on their part to ensure that the client has margin above and beyond what he or she is showing.

T-bills are denominated in $10,000 amounts and thus are suitable only for larger traders to use as margin. In addition, most brokerage firms prefer to have several thousand dollars of cash sitting in the account above and beyond the amount of money for the T-bill. For example, the commodity brokerage firm may require that the account have $14,000 in it before it will purchase a T-bill for the account. A commodity brokerage firm does this for two basic reasons. The first is that if the value of the margin in the account should drop below the value of the T-bill, it will have to liquidate the T-bill, forcing the client to pay an additional commission as well as creating extra work for itself. This creates some ill feelings between the customer and the brokerage house and so brokerage houses prefer to avoid the problem. The second reason is that placing client funds into T-bills reduces the amount of profit that the brokerage firm accrues. A brokerage firm's income is largely dependent upon the interest that it receives on the free credit balances of customers. Many brokerage firms will derive 40 percent of their total revenue from interest earnings. If a speculator opens an account for $5000 the brokerage house will lend that money out and receive interest on it. If the clients have placed that money in T-bills then they have taken a major source of highly profitable income from the brokerage firm. By requiring several thousand dollars above and beyond the T-bill for margin, the brokerage house is trying to retain some of that interest revenue.

It can be seen that there are significant differences between margin on stocks and margin on commodity stock index futures. The margin on stocks is a loan from the brokerage house to the customer for up to 50 percent of the value of the underlying security. The brokerage house charges interest to the customer for the use of the brokerage house's money. Futures margin, on the other hand, is a good faith deposit, or earnest money, to show that the customer is willing and potentially able to make or take delivery of the underlying commodity. It therefore can receive interest if T-bills are posted in lieu of cash.

It is a truism that margins increase as the value of the contract increases and vice versa. In general, commodity brokerage houses and exchanges like to keep the value of the margin at some percentage of the value of the contract. Thus, as the price of the commodity increases, margin levels will be increased a similar amount but at a later date. For example, the price of the futures may increase by 10 percent and the margin not increase at all. The futures may then increase another 10 percent for a total of up 20 percent and the margin may increase 10 percent at that point. Margin thus lags behind prices both on the upside and on the downside.

Exchanges and brokerage houses look at several factors to determine the margin level. We have just explained that the price level is often used as a factor in determining margin levels. An additional factor is recent volatility. The higher the volatility of the futures contract the higher the margin will be.

Brokerage houses have two conflicting impulses when it comes to margins. The first and foremost consideration is to satisfy the requirements of the clearinghouse. The clearinghouse is mainly concerned with ensuring that enough good faith money is on deposit to cover any potential defaults and to discourage any potential defaults. This system has been a clear success, as there has been only one default in the more than 125 years of organized futures trading in the United States. The brokerage houses must respond to this demand of the exchanges. In addition, the brokers wish to protect themselves against the possibility of default by clients. Clients who post a lot of margin will be less susceptible to margin calls than clients who post a low margin. If a sudden price shock should move the market tremendously, then the brokerage houses with the most amount of margin will be least likely to suffer debit balances. One of the major costs of doing business as a brokerage firm is debit balances. These are balances that occur when clients have positions go against them by so much that all of the margin is used up in their accounts and they owe the brokerage house additional money. This nasty situation occurs more frequently than is desirable, and both the brokerage house and the client start pointing fingers and placing blame. Clients will often sue brokerage firms and accuse them of unauthorized trading or churning while the brokerage houses turn around and say that the client made the decision and they are owed the money for the additional margin. Brokerage firms always strive for a high margin as a means of protecting themselves. Thus, the brokerage houses have an impetus to move margin rates as high as possible.

There is a conflicting impulse that the brokerage house feels. A high margin has the effect of reducing the amount of trading in an account. Commissions are the lifeblood of the brokerage house, and higher margins decrease the revenues of the company. Commission houses therefore prefer to have the margin as low as possible as a means of encouraging customers to trade more. For example, if margin rates were $10,000 for one NYSE Index contract, then a $10,000 account would be able to initiate only one position. On the other hand, if the margin was at $5000 then the client would be able to initiate two positions. This would double the brokerage house's commissions on the transaction by reducing the margin requirements, not by increasing the commission charge. There is a direct relationship between the price of margin and the amount of trading in an account. The exchanges also like to keep margin low as a means of luring additional participants and increasing the liquidity and therefore the usefulness to market participants.

One of the interesting features of the setting of the margin on stock index futures is that the Federal Reserve Bank has been involved. The Federal Reserve Bank has even contended that it should have the authority to set margins rather than the exchanges, which are regulated by the Commodity Futures Trading Commission. The Federal Reserve Bank has the authority to set margins on securities and feels that stock index futures fall under its purvey. It justifies this on the grounds that it can set the margin for other capital investment, such as stocks and bonds, and that stock index futures will play a role in the formation of new capital. The Federal Reserve believes that investors will buy stock index futures rather than stocks and will thus diminish the ability of companies to raise capital. Many analysts, however, contend that the exact opposite is true. They believe that institutions will be more likely to invest in stocks than in bonds as they will be able to protect themselves more easily against price declines. With the current situation, investing in stocks means having to take a large risk. Stock index futures will allow them to buy stocks, but to hedge easily against price declines.

As of this writing, the exchanges have set their own margins and have retained the authority of margin setting in spite of pressure from the Federal Reserve Bank. They have kept one eye on the Federal Reserve Bank and have not cut margin to as low a level as the exchanges would like for fear that the Federal Reserve Bank will force the issue and take control away from them. This has had the effect of keeping margins relatively high compared to those of other commodity futures contracts. This can be easily seen when you consider that the initial margin of the S & P 500 at a major brokerage house is $6000 and the maintenance is $3000. This is an exceptionally wide spread between initial margin and maintenance margin. A typical commodity will have a ratio of maintenance to initial of about 70 to 80 percent. In other words, a commodity having a margin of $6000 would most likely have a maintenance margin of closer to $4500. By setting the maintenance margin at such a low level they are allowing investors to lose up to $3000 before additional margin must be posted. This is not as powerful a technique for lowering margins as the exchanges would have if they could lower the initial margins, but it still helps accomplish their purposes.

Let us go off on a tangent for a moment and explain what maintenance margins are. Until now, we have been discussing initial margins, which are the amount of money that must be posted when a position is initiated. Clients do not have to post additional funds until the position has lost enough money that the equity remaining is below the maintenance margin level. For example, the client would have to post $6000 to buy one S & P 500 futures contract. Additional margin would not have to be posted until the account dropped below $3000, at which point the client would have to post additional margin to bring it up to the $3,000 maintenance margin level.

In response to the exchanges' actions on the setting of margin, the Federal Reserve Bank is taking a wait-and-see attitude, studying the effects of stock index futures on capital formation. They are walking softly but carrying the threat of a big stick as a way of keeping margins relatively high on stock index futures. However, the major bull market in stock index futures beginning in the summer of 1982 has had the effect of lowering the relative margin for stock index futures. In spite of the major rise in the underlying value of the contract, margins were not raised by brokerage firms. This has the effect of lowering margins versus the value of the contract, thus making it more attractive for speculators and hedgers.

Margin is also required on spreads. There are two types of spreads: intracommodity spreads and intercommodity spreads. An intracommodity spread is one that spreads two contracts of the same futures, that is, long September/short December S & P 100 Index. An intercommodity spread is one that spreads two different futures contracts, that is, long June Value Line/short June S & P 100 Index.

Intracommodity spreads are very low. The spread margin on an S & P 500 spread is only $400 to initiate between contract months in a single index futures. The margin for the NYSE Index is running at around $200. Thus a trader can initiate significantly more intracommodity spreads than outright positions. It would be conceivable that the traders could put on 15 intracommodity spreads or 1 S & P 500 Index. This is typically not done simply because the commission costs would be extremely high and eliminate any advantage that would be gained. However, those traders who have low commission cost due to negotiated commissions or the use of a discount brokerage house may find the trading of intracommodity spreads to have greater reward potential compared to the trading of the outright.

Intercommodity spreads are spreads between different futures contracts and typically require that the margin be posted on the greater of the two sides of the spread. For example, if the margin for the Value Line contract is $6500 and the margin for the S & P 500 is $6000, then the spread between the two contracts would be $6500. This is a matter that has been under increasing discussion, and it appears that reduced margins will become widespread. For example, one major wirehouse is currently charging $1100 to initiate this particular spread.

Spread margins are considerably less than outright margins because of the hedged nature of the investment. It is felt by the exchange and brokerage house officials that the reduced risk and volatility are deserving of a lower margin cost. Traders often use this reduced margin to initiate additional positions. Another effect is that it allows traders with limited capital to trade stock index futures through the use of the spreads.

In all of the discussions on margins it is important for readers to remember that they should consult their brokers to find out the latest margin levels and conditions. Margins are subject to change.

How the Averages Are Calculated

The various stock index futures contracts are computed in different ways. Each of the main contracts provides an indication of the market as a whole, but each index has subtle differences. They represent variations on the main theme.

The originators of each index suggest that their index represents the market as a whole. However, there are significant differences betweeen indexes, and these differences can provide many profit opportunities, particularly for spread traders. The composition of the indexes is different, and they are computed in various ways. The main stock indexes that we are concerned about are computed in three ways.

Each style of averaging has its adherents and detractors, its advantages and disadvantages. These advantages and disadvantages have an impact on the nature and action of the indexes. Each index, using a different style of averaging, will have different action in the same market. In general, to unsophisticated viewers, the action will look similar. More sophisticated observers will notice significant differences in the price behavior of the various indexes merely because of the way that they are computed.

The three methods used by the main indexes are the simple average, the geometric average, and the capitalization method. Let us examine each one of these methods in turn so that we can gain some insights into the difference in behavior of the three indexes.

Simple Average

The Dow Jones Industrial Average is a simple average of the prices of the stocks involved. (The other Dow Jones indexes are also simple averages.) At a quick glance, this appears to be ridiculous, as there is no way that the average of the stocks in the Dow Jones can be worth over $1000. This anomaly is caused by the fact that the index is modified whenever stocks are added or deleted from the list of the Dow Jones Industrials and whenever there are stock dividends and stock splits. Thus, it is a very common occurrence for the Dow Jones Industrial Average to be modified during a year. The modification and adjustment to the index because of changes in the composition and numbers of shares do little to detract from the popularity and usefulness of the index. Certainly, the Dow Jones Industrial Average is the most popular stock index for the general public. As of this writing, there is no futures contract on the Dow Jones Industrials, but there is significant pressure to initiate one. The Chicago Board of Trade wanted to develop a stock index futures contract based on the Dow Jones Industrials but has been blocked by legal challenges.

Nonetheless, it is worthwhile examining the way that the Dow Jones Industrials is calculated so that we may show the difference between it and the stock indexes that are traded on futures contracts. Also, many traders analyze the market by analyzing the Dow Jones Industrial Average. Traders who use this average should know how the way it is calculated differs from the methods used on the futures contracts. Traders will then be able to estimate the effect of a price movement in the Dow Jones Industrials on the various stock index futures.

The Dow Jones Industrial Average is a simple average of the prices of the stocks involved after adjustments for stocks splits, stock dividends, and changes in the roster of stocks in the average. For our example, let us assume that the average does not have to be adjusted for the reasons just given.

A simple average is computed as follows. Let us assume a current portfolio of stock ABC, 10 shares selling at $20, stock BCD, 20 shares at $40, and stock CDS, 30 shares at $60. The simple average of these three stocks is $40. This is computed by adding together the prices of the three stocks, $20, $40, and $60, and dividing by three. Notice that the number of shares owned is irrelevant to the average of the price. The fact that the portfolio has 30 shares of the $60 stock does not change the average. The simple average merely adds together the prices of the stocks and divides by the number of stocks.

If the prices of the stocks should change—let us say, stock ABC to $10, stock BCD to $50, and stock CDS to $40—the simple average would drop to $33.33 per share. Once again, this is computed by adding together the prices of the shares $10, $50, and $40, and dividing by the number of stocks, in this case three. The math yields the simple average of $33.33.

The Dow Jones Industrial Average was invented in the early part of this century, and it is possible that at that time more sophisticated math would have required more capabilities and financial outlay than were practical. The major advantage of the simple average is that it is easy to calculate. In general, over the long run, it will have a close correlation to the underlying market. The major disadvantage of the Dow Jones Industrial Average is that it is composed of only 30 stocks, each of which is a major industrialized firm. The average therefore does not take into account the smaller companies. No financial or service industries are represented as well. The Dow Jones Industrial Average is therefore most useful when one is trying to track the price activity of the major large industrial manufacturing firms. Since the time of the invention of the Dow Jones Industrials, the ability to do complex math rapidly has increased dramatically. We now have the ability to use more complicated averages to determine market direction.

The Geometric Average

The geometric average is a method used by the Kansas City Board of Trade Value Line Index contracts. This is an unweighted index, as is the simple average method outlined above. This means that the number of shares that a stock has outstanding is not factored into the average. In the example we are using, the fact that there are 30 shares of stock CDS does not bias the average in any way. This holds true both for the simple average and the geometric average. This has a profound influence on the difference between the geometric average being outlined here and the capitalization method outlined below.

The simple average is the average of the prices of the stocks. The geometric average differs from this in that it is the average of the percentage change in price versus a base period. An arbitrary base value was assigned to stocks in the Value Line average, and the average has been changing as the prices of the stocks change. Notice that the absolute price level change is not what is being measured. It is the percentage change that is the critical factor.

This simply means that a stock that moves from $10.00 to $11.00 is included in the geometric average as an increase of 10 percent rather than as a change of $1.00. The same $1.00 movement in a $100.00 stock will count as only a 1 percent movement. It is these percentage changes that are computed into the geometric average rather than the absolute price changes. In sum, the geometric average is the average of the percentage price changes over a given period.

Let us use the same example with which we elucidated the simple average. The value of the shares and the prices on March 1 and June 1 will stay the same. The information given is sufficient to compute the simple average but is insufficient to compute the geometric average. A geometric average must have a base period from which to establish the current index value. The simple average simply takes a snapshot of prices and averages them. The geometric average provides a more dynamic view of the world and examines changes in prices rather than levels of prices, and this means that a previous set of data be in existence so that one can find out what the current index is. So let us say that on Janaury 1 stock ABC was selling for $25.00, stock BCD for $45.00, and CDS for $55.00.

The computation of a geometric average is significantly more complicated than that of the simple average. It requires mathematical tables or sophisticated calculators or computers. The reason for the complexity is that logarithms and antilogarithms are necessary. The first step is to take the log (logarithm) of each of the prices and find the average of the logs. In our example, the log of $25.00 is $3.22, the log of $45.00 is $3.81, and the log of $55.00 is $4.01. To find the average of these three numbers we add them together and divide by three. This gives a total of $11.03 and an average of $3.68. The next step is to find the exponential value of this average. The exponential value is sometimes called the antilog (antilogarithm). The antilog of $3.68 is $39.55. This level becomes the index value of 100, and all subsequent values are compared to that index.

Let us continue the example through March 1 and June 1. On March 1, the prices of the three stocks were $20.00, $40.00, and $60.00, respectively. The log values of those three prices are $3.00, $3.69, and $4.09, respectively. The average of the log values is $3.59. The antilog of this value is $36.34. We can find the index for March 1 by dividing the value of March 1 by the value of January 1. The value that we are referring to is the exponential and antilog of the average of the logs of the prices on that particular day. In this case the index would be found by dividing $36.34 by $39.55. Once again, this is the antilog on March 1 versus January 1.

On June 1 prices had adjusted somewhat further and the logs of the three companies were $2.30, $3.91, and $3.69. The average of these log values was $3.30 and had an exponential value, or antilog, of $27.15. To find the index on this day we divide the $27.15 by the $39.55 of January 1. The result is $69.69, which means that the index was 69 percent of the base period of January 1.

We have now discovered the geometric index for the three periods, January 1, March 1, and June 1. Let us see how this compares with the simple average. Both averages are considered to be at 100 on January 1. The geometric average had an index value of 92 on March 1 and 69 on June 1. The simple average was $41.67 on January 1 and had dropped to $40.00 on March 1 and $33.33 on June 1. The $40.00

EXHIBIT 4-2 How a geometric average is constructed.

		January 1		March 1		June 1	
Stock	# Shares	Price	Log*	$ Price	Log*	$ Price	Log*
ABC	10	25.00	3.2189	20.00	2.9957	10.00	2.3026
BCD	20	45.00	3.8067	40.00	3.6889	50.00	3.9120
CDS	30	55.00	4.0073	60.00	4.0944	40.00	3.6889
		41.67	11.03	40.00	10.7790	33.33	9.9035
	Average of logs =		3.6776		3.5930		3.3012
	Exponential value =		39.5514		36.3429		27.1452
	Index =		100		92		69

*Log of price.

amount is 96 percent of $41.67, so we can say that prices on the simple average had dropped approximately 4 percent from January 1 to March 1. On the other hand, the geometric had dropped 8 percent in the same time period. The June 1 average price of $33.33 was 80 percent of the average price on January 1. Thus the simple average had dropped 20 percent since January 1. On the other hand, the geometric index was now at 69 percent of its January 1 level.

It can be seen from this simple example that the geometric average will tend to accentuate price movements. In our example, prices were in a bear trend and thus the geometric average accentuated the down movement. The same type of action occurs in an upmove. That is, the geometric average will accentuate price movement higher. This example is summed up in Exhibit 4-2. Traders do not need to learn how to construct geometric averages or how to manipulate logs and antilogs. It is worthwhile to understand why the geometric averaging technique accentuates price movements.

This added volatility will be a very useful tool for traders wishing to invest in stock index futures. We will discuss this in much more detail in the chapter that deals with spreads. Let us just make the quick comment here that the additional volatility of the Value Line Index creates very profitable spread opportunities between it and other indexes.

Capitalization Method

The final method of index construction is called the capitalization, or market value, method. This is the method used by the New York

Stock Exchange Index, the S & P 500 Index, and the S & P 100 Index. This method is more complex than the simple average method. In addition to price behavior, the capitalization method takes into account the number of shares each stock has outstanding and the total market value of the stocks that are being averaged. In effect, the total value of the shares being averaged is computed by multiplying the number of shares outstanding times the current market price and is divided by the same calculations from a prior time period.

The capitalization method suffers from the same problems as the simple average. In particular, new issues, stock splits, stock dividends, and delisted stocks will change the value of the index. This is also why the index value becomes adjusted over time.

The math is relatively simple compared to that of the geometric average but slightly more difficult that the calculations of the simple average. Taking the example from January 1, the number of shares times the price gives the total value. This total value or total capitalization becomes the index. Exhibit 4-3 is the same as Exhibit 4-2 but with a couple of additional figures. Notice that on January 1 the value of ABC stock is $250, that of BCD is $900, and that of CDS is $1650, for a total of $2800 in market value. This becomes the index of 100. To find the index value from March 1 the same procedure is used. Ten shares times $20.00 equals a total market value of $200.00 for ABC stock. The same type of math yields a value of $800.00 for BCD and $1800 for stock CDS for a grand total of $2800 in total market value. Because this total market value is the same as on January 1, we can say that the market capitalization index would stay at 100. Notice that this occurs because there are more shares of CDS than there are of ABC and BCD. Thus the $5.00 increase of CDS is more than enough to offset the $5.00 declines of ABC and BCD. The other two methods, geometric and simple, both suggested that the market had dropped during this time period while the capitalization method said the market was steady.

June 1 represents a different situation. Here the value of ABC has dropped further to $100, BCD has climbed to $1000, but CDS, the most heavily capitalized stock, has dropped to $1200. Total value for the shares on that day is $2300 and represents 82 percent of the original market value on January 1. Thus the index is 82, showing an 18 percent decline from January 1.

Thus, the market capitalization method dropped 18 percent from January to June, whereas the simple average dropped 20 percent and the geometric average 31 percent. The difference between the various indexes is that a stock with the greatest percentage changes was also the stock with the lowest capitalization. We saw stock ABC drop from

EXHIBIT 4-3 How a capitalization average is constructed.

Stock	No. of Shares	January 1 $ Price	January 1 Log*	January 1 $ Value	March 1 $ Price	March 1 Log*	March 1 $ Value	June 1 $ Price	June 1 Log*	June 1 $ Value
ABC	10	25.00	3.2189	250	20.00	2.9957	200	10.00	2.3026	100
BCD	20	45.00	3.8067	900	40.00	3.6889	800	50.00	3.9120	1000
CDS	30	55.00	4.0073	1650	60.00	4.0944	1800	40.00	3.6889	1200
		41.67	11.03	2800	33.33	10.7790	2800		9.9035	2300
Average of logs =			3.6776			3.5930			3.3012	
Exponential value =			39.5514			36.3429			27.1452	
Index =			100			100			82	

*Log of price.

20 to 10 for a loss of 50 percent of its value. The stock with the largest capitalization, CDS, dropped by a third while the second most heavily capitalized stock actually rose by 25 percent. The last two stocks therefore offset the effect of the lesser-capitalized stock. The lesser-capitalized stock, ABC, however, was weighted just as heavily using the geometric average and the simple average as the larger-capitalized shares. The geometric average is therefore weighted in favor of large percentage gains, which tend to occur with less-capitalized and less-expensive shares. The simple and capitalization methods are weighted in favor of those stocks that are heavily capitalized and have more shares outstanding or are higher-priced. The geometric average tends to be more of a proxy of lower-priced secondary stocks than the capitalized and simple methods. Remember, it takes much less buying power to move a $10 stock $1 than it does to move a $100 stock $1. It is also much more difficult to move a stock with 500 million shares outstanding than it is to move one with 5 million shares outstanding. Thus, the net effect is that we can use the Value Line Index, which uses the geometric averaging method, as a better proxy for secondary stocks than the S & P 500 and NYSE indexes. The S & P 500 and NYSE both use the capitalization method and therefore represent larger, better-capitalized, and higher-priced issues.

The Value Line indexes are composed of just under 1700 stocks (as of this writing it was 1683 stocks). These are largely on the New York Stock Exchange but include several American Stock Exchange, over-the-counter, and Canadian issues. The New York Stock Exchange composite index includes all stocks that are listed on the New York Stock Exchange. This represents just over 1500 stocks (as of this writing it was 1512 stocks). The S & P 500 is 500 major industrial companies listed on the New York Stock Exchange only. The S & P 100 is composed of 100 large industrial companies listed on the New York Stock Exchange. In the next chapter we will examine how the differences in the composition of these various contracts can open up interesting and profitable investment opportunities.

Statistical Information

There are three ways to analyze a relationship between an individual stock and the stock market average. They are beta, r^2, and standard deviation. The beta is the most common figure of the three. It is derived from the capital asset pricing model, which we will explain in some detail in the next chapter. It is an attempt to measure the risk in a given stock in terms of the risk of the market as a whole. The beta is an index of systematic risk. That is, it measures the amount of risk in holding an individual stock that is derived from the market as a whole. The beta is constructed by using statistical techniques called regression analysis and correlation analysis to relate the individual stock's price performance with that of the market as exhibited by the major stock indexes.

The risk in holding a stock is divided into two parts: the systematic and unsystematic risks. The systematic is the risk associated with the rising and falling of the market as a whole. The unsystematic risk is associated with changes that are connected with the particular stock. Systematic risk could be associated with Federal Reserve Bank policy, the economy, oil price hikes, and so on. Unsystematic risks would be associated with changes in management, introduction of new products, new competition, and the like. One of the endeavors of market analysis for many years has been to try to differentiate between systematic and unsystematic risks. It has often happened that an analyst has correctly identified an existing company for investment but has bought it just as the market as a whole was going into a decline. This unfortunate circumstance can result in a loss in the investor's portfolio in spite of correct analysis. The opposite can also occur. The poor analyst can select a number of bad stocks but select them at a time when the market begins to move higher. Although the analyst is poor, changes in the market as a whole will reward the analysis.

The beta for a stock tries to identify how much of the change in the stock price is attributable to changes in the market. A beta of 1.00 means that the volatility of the stock has been equivalent to that of the market over a long period of time. If a beta is larger than 1.00, the stock is more volatile than the market and is considered an aggressive stock. A beta of less than 1.00 implies a defensive stock and one that is less volatile than the market. For example, a beta of 1.56 indicates that the return to that individual stock will tend to increase 56 percent more than the return of the market average when the market is rising. When the market falls, the individual stock's return will tend to fall 56 percent more than the decrease in the market as a whole.

Each of the stock index futures claims to have a beta of approximately 1.00 over the long run. For example, the Value Line Index has been shown to have a beta of 1.01, which is close to 1.00. Over the short run, however, there are significant differences in changes in price level. We will look at these later in the chapter and will also show how to determine the beta of a portfolio. In another chapter we will discuss how to utilize that information profitably.

Exhibit 4-4 (courtesy of the Kansas City Board of Trade) shows the

EXHIBIT 4-4   Table of Value Line Index components with beta, R^2, and standard deviation. (Reprinted with permission of the Kansas City Board of Trade.)

MONTHLY DATA, JANUARY 1977-DECEMBER 1981

Stock	Regression Est. of Beta	R^2	Sta. Deviation of Price (%)	Stock	Regression Est. of Beta	R^2	Sta. Deviation of Price (%)
ACF Industries	.98	.54	6.44	Allright Auto Parks	.98	.28	8.96
AMF Inc.	.84	.32	7.22	Alpha Portland	1.26	.42	9.44
AM Int'l.	1.68	.29	15.04	Aluminum Co. of Amer.	.92	.39	7.16
APL Corp.	1.09	.26	10.25	Amalgamated Sugar	1.07	.22	11.13
ARA Service	.75	.29	6.70	Amarex Inc.	1.24	.18	14.12
ASA Ltd.	.69	.09	11.20	Amax Inc.	1.13	.30	10.03
AVX Corp. (3)	2.03	.42	17.51	Amdahl Corp.	1.48	.24	14.79
Abbott Labs	.86	.37	6.83	Amerace Corp.	1.16	.42	8.58
Acme Cleveland	1.53	.46	10.93	Amerada Hess	1.28	.35	10.49
Acton Corp.	1.24	.23	12.82	Amer. Airlines	1.44	.29	12.89
Adams Drug Inc.	1.24	.42	9.24	Amer. Bakeries	1.08	.31	9.30
Adams Express	.65	.42	4.90	Amer. Bankers Ins. Grp.	.73	.12	10.34
Adams-Millis Corp.	.90	.19	10.03	Amer. Brands	.73	.39	5.67
Adams-Russell (3)	1.18	.32	11.10	Amer. Broadc. Cos.	1.02	.40	7.77
Adv.Micro Dev. (2)	1.75	.39	14.99	Amer. Bldg. Maint.	.84	.30	7.45
Aetna Life & Cas.	.76	.30	6.74	Amer. Can	.76	.28	6.96
Ahmanson (H.F.)	.99	.28	9.07	Amer. Century Trust	1.44	.22	14.80
Aileen Inc.	1.58	.37	12.52	Amer. Cyanamid	.71	.23	7.07
Airborne Freight	1.26	.39	9.85	Amer. District Telegr.	1.34	.54	8.83
Air Florida Sys. (3)	1.74	.35	16.33	Amer. Elec. Power	.24	.78	4.16
Air Products & Chem.	1.16	.49	7.95	Amer. Express	.89	.35	7.24
Akzona Inc.	1.16	.33	9.72	Amer. Family Corp.	.67	.18	7.68
Alagasco, Inc.	.41	.20	4.45	Amer. Gen'l. Bond (2)	.34	.12	5.33
Alaska Airlines (3)	1.47	.42	12.47	Amer. Gen'l. Corp.	.94	.42	7.05
Alaska Interstate	1.12	.24	11.01	Amer. Greetings	.84	.33	7.11
Albany Int'l. (1)	1.33	.33	11.92	Amer. Heritage Life	.86	.26	8.21
Alberto-Culver Co.	1.37	.36	11.08	Amer. Hoist & Derrick	1.28	.42	9.59
Albertson's, Inc.	.86	.37	6.86	Amer. Home Products	.65	.29	5.89
Alcan Aluminium	.83	.23	8.37	Amer. Hospital Supply	.97	.39	7.45
Alco Standard	.78	.40	5.98	Amer. Int'l. Group	.72	.30	6.40
Alexander & Alexander	.98	.35	8.01	Amer. Maize-Prod.	1.31	.31	11.25
Alexander & Bldwn (1)	1.42	.54	9.81	Amer. Medical Int'l.	1.41	.42	10.51
Alexander's Inc.	1.17	.24	11.46	Amer. Microsyst. (3)	1.61	.28	16.36
Algoma Steel (1)	.61	.23	6.65	Amer. Motors	1.16	.30	10.33
Alleghany Corp.	1.40	.54	9.28	Amer. Natural Res.	.65	.29	5.86
Allegheny Int'l.	1.28	.41	9.62	Amer. Quasar (1)	.98	.15	12.61
Allegheny Power Sys.	.38	.13	5.24	Amer. Seating	.96	.25	9.31
Allen Group Inc.	.95	.44	6.91	Amer. Ship Building	1.39	.44	10.21
Allied Bancshares (3)	.86	.40	7.64	Amer. Standard	1.23	.52	8.23
Allied Corp.	1.05	.43	7.82	Amer. Sterilizer Co.	1.42	.41	10.71
Allied Maintenance	.86	.31	7.46	Amer. Stores	.96	.33	8.13
Allied Products	.58	.12	8.11	Amer. Tel. & Tel.	.27	.14	3.45
Allied Stores	.68	.26	6.41	Amer. Water Works	.38	.14	4.99
Allied Supermarkets	1.31	.08	22.66	Ameritrust	.83	.44	5.99
Allis-Chalmers	1.00	.33	8.38	Ameron Inc.	.97	.37	7.63

Stock	Regression Est. of Beta	R^2	Sta. Deviation of Price (%)	Stock	Regression Est. of Beta	R^2	Sta. Deviation of Price (%)
Ames Dept. Stores (1)	1.39	.43	10.99	Baldwin United	1.12	.34	9.28
Ametek Inc.	1.04	.48	7.24	Ball Corp.	.95	.44	6.93
Amfac Inc.	1.25	.49	8.60	Bally Mfg.	1.87	.31	16.13
Ampco-Pitts Corp.	.89	.21	9.49	Balt Gas & Elec.	.46	.21	4.84
Amp Inc.	.70	26	6.62	BankCal Tri-State	.97	.22	9.94
Amrep Corp.	1.96	.31	16.95	Bandag, Inc.	1.26	.54	8.29
Amstar Corp.	1.26	.42	9.46	Bangor Punta Corp.	1.62	.39	12.50
Amsted Industries	.97	.47	6.79	Bankamerica Corp.	.53	.19	5.88
Analog Devices (3)	1.05	.22	12.59	Bank Amer. Realty Inv.	1.29	.41	9.74
Anchor Hocking	.63	.35	5.10	Bankers Trust N.Y.	.73	.38	5.68
Anderson Clayton	.94	.45	6.76	Bank of New York	.77	.39	5.98
Angelica Corp.	1.29	.40	9.79	Bank of Virginia	.72	.41	5.50
Anglo Amer. So. Afr.	.67	.10	10.05	Banner Inds. (1)	1.48	.21	16.43
Anglo Amer. Gold Inv.	.62	.07	11.18	Barber-Greene (2)	1.33	.37	11.70
Anglo Energy Ltd.	1.63	.38	12.74	Bard (Cr.) Inc.	1.29	.48	8.99
Anheuser-Busch	.76	.24	7.44	Barnes Group	.72	.21	7.64
Anixter Bros.	1.86	.56	11.99	Barnett Banks of Fla.	1.19	.55	7.73
Apache Corp.	1.61	.34	13.32	Barry R.G. (1)	1.72	.37	14.73
Applied Magnetics	1.27	.18	14.34	Barry Wright	1.47	.52	9.84
Arcata Corp.	.89	.24	8.71	Bausch & Lomb	.80	.17	9.34
Archer Daniels	1.12	.38	8.79	Baxter Travenol Labs	.69	.24	6.82
Arden Group Inc.	1.66	.27	15.53	Bay State Gas (1)	.73	.41	5.69
Arizona Public Serv.	.31	.10	4.68	Bayuk Cigars	.41	.04	9.68
Arkansas Best	1.32	.38	10.41	Bearings Inc.	.54	.19	6.09
Arkla Inc.	.79	.35	6.47	Beatrice Foods	.69	.32	5.88
Arlen Realty & Dev.	1.41	.17	16.54	Beckman Instruments	.82	.27	7.64
Armada Corp.	.83	.20	9.06	Becton Dickinson Co.	.66	.26	6.19
Armco Inc.	.99	.37	7.87	Beker Industries	1.79	.30	15.63
Armstrong Rubber	1.00	.21	10.55	Bekins Co. (3)	2.06	.41	17.80
Armstrong World Inds.	.97	.47	6.84	Belco Petroleum Corp.	1.02	.24	10.08
ARO Corp.	.63	.24	6.22	Belding Heminway	.70	.31	6.15
Arrow Electronics (1)	1.41	.31	13.07	Bell & Howell	1.37	.48	9.53
Artra Group (1)	1.57	.47	11.95	Bell Industries (1)	1.58	.44	11.97
Arvin Industries	1.06	.35	8.70	Bell Tel. of Canada	.22	.07	4.19
Asamera Inc. (2)	1.33	.42	10.83	Bemis Co.	.61	.22	6.32
Asarco, Inc.	1.57	.34	12.92	Bendix Corp.	.92	.37	7.31
Ashland Oil	.73	.16	8.86	Beneficial Corp.	.91	.36	7.36
Assoc. Dry Goods	.86	.29	7.78	Benguet Corp.	1.41	.12	19.36
Athlone Inds.	.85	.35	6.97	Bentley Labs. (1)	1.08	.19	12.34
Atlanta Gas Light	.47	.29	4.26	Berkey Photo	1.33	.17	15.78
Atlantic City Electric	.41	.15	5.14	Best Products	.84	.14	10.67
Atlantic Richfield	.53	.12	7.43	Bethlehem Steel	1.07	.39	8.32
Atlas Consol. "B"	1.42	.17	16.57	Betz Labs.	.92	.36	7.41
Atlas Corp.	1.54	.33	13.03	Beverly Enterprises (1)	1.87	.64	12.13
Augat, Inc. (1)	1.39	.57	9.30	Bic Pen	1.20	.30	10.57
Automatic Data Proc.	.89	.35	7.30	Big Three Ind.	1.07	.49	7.38
Avco Corp.	1.76	.58	11.16	Binney & Smith	1.55	.37	12.39
Avery Int'l.	1.01	.31	8.75	Bird & Son (1)	.98	.33	8.82
Avnet Inc.	1.47	.55	9.58	Black & Decker	1.05	.47	7.36
Avon Products	.75	.38	5.83	Blair (John) & Co.	1.15	.34	9.57
Aydin Corp. (2)	1.37	.32	13.01	Bliss & Laughlin	.89	.36	7.11
BBDO Int'l.	.90	.40	6.89	Block (H & R) Inc.	.79	.36	6.39
Bairnco Corp.	1.14	.43	8.37	Blue Bell Inc.	.89	.30	7.85
Baker Int'l. Corp.	.99	.33	8.41	Blyvoor Gold Mng.	.78	.07	14.35
Baldor Electric Co. (2)	1.13	.32	10.77	Bobbie Brooks Inc.	1.64	.36	13.27

Stock	Regression Est. of Beta	R^2	Sta. Deviation of Price (%)	Stock	Regression Est. of Beta	R^2	Sta. Deviation of Price (%)
Bob Evans (2)	.84	.29	8.20	Canadian Pacific	.93	.34	7.69
Boeing	1.14	.31	9.91	Canal-Randolph Corp.	.59	.07	10.90
Bohemia Inc.	1.61	.54	10.60	Cannon Mills 'A'	.64	.11	9.37
Boise Cascade Corp.	1.27	.55	8.30	Canon Inc. (ADR) (1)	.55	.08	10.04
Borden Inc.	.44	.20	4.75	Capital Cities Comm.	.97	.47	6.79
Borg-Warner	.89	.46	6.31	Capital Holding	.67	.23	6.78
Borman's Inc.	1.37	.30	12.16	Carling O'Keefe Ltd.	1.23	.32	10.57
Boston Edison	.23	.07	4.18	Carlisle Corp.	1.50	.40	11.45
Braniff Int'l. Corp.	1.27	.29	11.34	Carnation Co.	.68	.28	6.14
Brascan Ltd.	.89	.33	7.43	Carolina Freight	1.05	.23	10.60
Briggs & Stratton	.59	.22	6.06	Carolina Power & Light	.25	.05	5.46
Bristol-Myers	.81	.39	6.31	Carpenter Technology	.86	.27	8.02
British Petroleum	.41	.05	8.45	Carson Pirie Scott	.80	.19	8.82
Brockway Glass Co.	.66	.23	6.69	Carter Hawley Hale	1.01	.44	7.39
Broken Hill Pty. (2)	1.03	.36	8.94	Carter-Wallace	1.15	.39	8.89
Brooklyn Union Gas	.38	.12	5.30	Cascade Natural Gas	.30	.08	5.17
Brooks Fashion	1.47	.31	12.93	Castle & Cooke	.99	.44	7.25
Brown & Sharpe	1.46	.49	10.12	Caterpillar Tractor	.79	.43	5.81
Brown-Forman Dist. B	1.01	.50	6.91	Ceco Corp.	1.13	.47	7.95
Brown Group Inc.	.90	.41	6.77	Celanese Corp.	.79	.37	6.36
Browning Ferris	1.39	.53	9.25	Cenco Inc.	1.68	.29	15.21
Brown (Tom) Inc.	1.52	.27	14.12	Centex Corp.	1.41	.46	10.04
Brunswick Corp.	1.42	.52	9.47	Cen. & South West	.23	.06	4.55
Brush Wellman	1.41	.52	9.51	Cen. Hudson G & E	.33	.13	4.53
Bucyrus-Erie	.97	.31	8.40	Cen. Illinois Light	.33	.13	4.51
Burlington Inds.	.77	.30	6.83	Cen. Illinois Pub. Ser.	.31	.11	4.41
Burlington-Northern	1.23	.37	9.76	Cen. Maine Power	.46	.25	4.44
Burndy Corp.	1.14	.53	7.59	Cen. Soya	1.22	.36	9.90
Burns Intl. Sec. Ser.	1.51	.54	9.98	Cen. Tel. & Util.	.41	.16	4.94
Burns (R.L.) Corp.	1.61	.23	16.24	Centronics Data Corp.	1.21	.14	15.57
Burnup & Sims (3)	1.67	.47	12.99	Certain-Teed Prod.	.80	.24	7.99
Burroughs	.63	.18	7.09	Cessna Aircraft	1.14	.25	11.10
Butler Intl.	1.31	.38	10.56	Champion Home Bldrs.	1.43	.24	14.15
Butler Mfg.	.47	.13	6.35	Champion Intl. Corp.	1.20	.48	8.40
Buttes Gas & Oil	1.47	.35	12.10	Champion Spark Plug	.76	.30	6.78
CBI Industries	.71	.20	7.74	Charming Shoppes	1.54	.36	12.71
CBS Inc.	.85	.38	6.72	Charter Co.	1.15	.11	16.67
CCI Corp.	1.99	.52	13.40	Chart House	1.34	.39	10.41
CFS Cont'l. (3)	1.16	.50	9.52	Chase Cv. Fd. Boston	.64	.45	4.64
CLC of America	1.32	.27	12.35	Chase Manhattan Corp.	.65	.30	5.81
CNA Finl.	1.49	.49	10.26	Chelsea Inds.	.1.25	.39	9.63
CPC Intl. Inc.	.66	.43	4.87	Chemed Corp. (3)	.58	.26	6.06
CP Nat'l. Corp. (1)	.45	.14	6.13	Chemical New York	.77	.38	6.02
CPT Corp. (3)	1.53	.51	11.43	Chesapeake Corp. Va.	.90	.23	9.12
CSX Corp.	1.00	.43	7.36	Chesebrough-Ponds	.67	.30	5.93
CTS Corp.	1.29	.46	9.22	Chicago Milwaukee	1.87	.20	20.45
Cabot Corp.	1.28	.49	8.82	Chicago & N.W.Tran. (2)	1.23	.16	16.13
Cadence Ind. Corp.	1.37	.21	14.43	Chic. Pneu. Tool Co.	1.11	.48	7.73
Caesars World Inc.	1.59	.16	19.40	Chieftain Develop. (1)	1.45	.28	13.82
Callahan Mining Corp.	.88	.11	12.72	Chock Full O Nuts	1.37	.25	13.34
Cameron Iron Works (1)	.99	.23	10.70	Chris-Craft	1.29	.23	13.11
Campbell Red Lake	.72	.10	10.75	Chromalloy Amer. Corp.	1.45	.56	9.38
Campbell Soup	.48	.25	4.69	Chrysler Corp.	1.32	.34	10.91
Campbell Taggart	.91	.37	7.17	Chubb Corp.	.34	.06	6.98
Canadian Pac. Enterp. (3)	1.01	.35	9.33	Church's Fr. Chicken	1.26	.44	9.19

Stock	Regression Est. of Beta	R^2	Sta. Deviation of Price (%)	Stock	Regression Est. of Beta	R^2	Sta. Deviation of Price (%)
Cincinnati Bell	.37	.18	4.22	Consol. Edison	.27	.07	4.89
Cincinnati Gas & Elec.	.32	.08	5.38	Consol. Foods	.55	.24	5.47
Cincinnati Milacron	1.47	.51	9.95	Consol. Freightways	1.22	.40	9.31
Citicorp	.80	.29	7.20	Consol. Natural Gas	.57	.23	5.80
Cities Service	.73	.13	9.76	Consolidated Oil & G.	1.78	.44	12.94
Citizens & So. Ga.	.92	.29	8.23	Consolidated Paper	1.06	.38	8.50
Citizens Util. 'B' (3)	.67	.32	6.71	Consumers Power	.39	.14	5.08
City Investing Co.	1.24	.43	9.17	Cont'l. Air Lines	1.38	.24	13.72
Clark Equipment	.96	.39	7.38	Cont'l. Copper	1.01	.22	10.48
Clark (J.L.) Mfg. (1)	.83	.34	7.38	Cont'l. Corp.	.51	.24	4.99
Cleveland-Cliffs	1.00	.57	6.43	Cont'l. Group Inc.	.81	.45	5.86
Cleveland Electric	.32	.09	5.19	Cont'l. Illinois Corp.	.76	.28	6.88
Clevepak Corp.	1.42	.42	10.63	Cont'l. Telephone	.46	.20	5.00
Clorox Co.	.82	.30	7.20	Control Data	1.34	.50	9.14
Cluett Peabody	1.28	.42	9.58	Conwood Corp.	.84	.37	6.72
Coachmen Inds.	1.95	.46	13.98	Cook United Inc.	1.93	.48	13.51
Coastal Corp. (The)	1.53	.23	15.44	Cooper Industries	.86	.35	7.00
Cobe Labs.	1.10	.29	10.02	Cooper Laboratories	1.01	.15	12.45
Coca Cola	.60	.29	5.41	Cooper Tire & Rubber	.84	.13	11.03
Coherent (3)	.99	.21	12.08	Coors (Adolph)	1.25	.51	8.52
Coldwell, Banker & Co.	1.25	.26	11.91	Copperweld Corp.	.57	.13	7.62
Coleco Ind.	1.75	.23	17.49	Cordis Corp.	1.91	.39	14.78
Coleman Co. Inc.	.93	.31	8.10	Cordura Corp.	1.21	.23	12.12
Colgate-Palmolive	.69	.26	6.48	Core Industries	1.14	.46	8.06
Collins & Aikman	1.10	.50	7.59	Core Labs (3)	1.44	.57	11.05
Collins Foods	1.64	.48	11.49	Corning Glass Works	.86	.38	6.72
Colonial Penn. Group	1.16	.33	9.81	Corroon & Black	1.00	.41	7.57
Color Tile (2)	1.23	.24	13.50	Cowles Communicate	1.24	.50	8.46
Colt Industries Inc.	.79	.21	8.31	Cox Broadcasting	.78	.28	7.10
Columbia Gas	.48	.17	5.70	Craig Corp.	1.05	.25	10.25
Columbia Pictures	.82	.17	9.61	Crane Co.	1.17	.36	9.42
Combined Int'l. Corp.	.58	.25	5.55	Crawford & Co. (1)	.99	.34	8.76
Combustion Eng.	.95	.28	8.72	Cray Research (2)	1.37	.37	11.80
Comcast 'A' (3)	1.45	.45	11.54	Credithrift Fin.	1.02	.22	10.47
Cominco Ltd.	.86	.24	8.50	Criton Corp. (2)	1.21	.38	10.47
Commerce Clear House	.70	.17	8.33	Crocker Natl. Corp.	.64	.25	6.19
Commercial Metals (3)	1.20	.30	12.16	Crompton & Knowles	1.10	.45	7.90
Commodore Int'l. (3)	2.20	.36	20.42	Cross & Trecker	1.42	.45	10.22
Commonwealth Edison	.35	.13	4.70	Cross (A.T.) (1)	.92	.39	7.44
Commonwealth Energy	.47	.18	5.29	Crown Central Petr. (2)	1.20	.14	16.77
Commonwealth Oil	1.65	.12	23.57	Crown Cork	.98	.47	6.88
Communic. Inds. (3)	.97	.20	11.58	Crown Zellerbach	1.10	.40	8.39
Comm. Satellite Corp.	1.11	.40	8.55	Crum & Forster	.94	.42	7.01
Community Psych.	1.60	.53	10.84	Crystal Oil (3)	1.11	.16	15.09
Compo Inds. (3)	1.48	.37	13.01	Cubic Corp. (2)	1.72	.50	12.87
Compugraphic Corp.	1.31	.22	13.41	Culbro Corp.	.91	.19	10.23
Computer Sciences	1.80	.45	13.06	Cummins Engine Co.	1.23	.42	9.11
Computervision (1)	1.76	.40	14.11	Curtiss-Wright	1.07	.20	11.55
Conagra Inc.	.89	.25	8.53	Cyclops Corp.	1.37	.43	10.08
Conair Corp. (3)	1.67	.33	16.67	DMG Investors	1.69	.26	15.91
Condec Corp. (3)	1.41	.32	13.24	DWG Corp.	1.40	.28	12.88
Cone Mills	.95	.33	7.93	Damon Corp.	1.71	.46	12.19
Conn Gen'l. Corp.	.84	.33	7.13	Dana Corp.	.68	.20	7.27
Conn. Natural Gas (1)	.40	.13	5.88	Daniel Inds. (1)	1.39	.37	11.52
Conrac Corp.	1.48	.49	10.20	Dan River Inc.	.99	.26	9.44

Stock	Regression Est. of Beta	R^2	Std. Deviation of Price (%)	Stock	Regression Est. of Beta	R^2	Std. Deviation of Price (%)
Dart & Kraft Inc.	.43	.25	4.19	Dunkin Donuts	1.51	.42	11.29
Data General Corp.	1.05	.25	10.30	Du Pont	.91	.41	6.91
Datapoint Corp.	1.50	.43	11.12	Duquesne Light	.36	.14	4.76
Dataproducts Corp.	1.76	.47	12.43	Duriron (2)	.84	.28	8.42
Data Terminal Sys.	1.22	.13	16.93	Dynalectron Corp. (2)	1.78	.29	17.71
Dayco Corp.	1.01	.46	7.18	Dynamics Corp. Amer.	1.36	.38	10.70
Dayton Hudson Corp.	.95	.43	6.99	EG & G Inc.	1.27	.46	9.03
Dayton Power & Lt.	.39	.15	4.89	E-Systems Inc.	1.43	.44	10.36
Dean Witter Reynolds	1.52	.37	12.04	Eagle-Picher Inds.	.71	.16	8.53
DeBeers Consol. Mng.	.98	.26	9.35	Easco Corp.	1.06	.42	7.95
Deere & Co.	.71	.30	6.31	Eastern Air Lines	1.68	.42	12.54
Dekalb Ag. Research	1.20	.31	10.51	Eastern Gas & Fuel	1.30	.44	9.54
Delmarva Pwr. & Lt.	.43	.18	4.87	Eastern Util. Assoc.	.28	.10	4.30
Delta Air Lines	1.04	.33	8.70	Eastman Kodak	.74	.23	7.42
Deltona Corp.	2.40	.56	15.50	Eastmet Corp.	1.09	.27	10.20
Deluxe Check Print	.81	.35	6.57	Eaton Corp.	.92	.45	6.59
Denison Mines, Ltd.	.74	.17	8.77	Echlin Mfg. Co.	.92	.26	8.69
Dennison Mfg.	.85	.35	6.90	Eckerd (Jack) Corp.	.79	.29	7.11
Denny's Inc.	.98	.25	9.41	Economics Laboratory	1.13	.40	8.63
Dentsply. Intl. Inc.	.90	.29	8.17	Edison Bros. Stores	.92	.38	7.25
De Soto Inc.	1.11	.38	8.63	Edwards (A.G.) & Son	1.67	.52	11.17
Detroit Edison	.33	.19	3.66	Elcor Corp. (2)	1.08	.32	10.29
Dexter Corp.	.66	.18	7.48	Electronic Assoc.	2.50	.54	16.51
Dial Corp.	.64	.09	10.47	Electronic Data Sys.	1.40	.52	9.40
Diamond Internatl.	1.12	.35	9.17	Electronic Memories	1.86	.53	12.41
Diamond Shamrock	1.24	.43	9.09	Elgin National Ind.	1.32	.34	11.00
Diebold Inc.	1.13	.32	9.77	Elixir Ind.	1.37	.24	13.58
Di Giorgio Corp.	1.01	.21	10.73	El Paso Co.	1.10	.39	8.60
Digital Equip.	1.01	.40	7.75	El Paso Electric	.28	.11	4.11
Dillon Cos.	.51	.10	7.59	Emerson Electric	.72	.38	5.69
Disney (Walt) Prod.	1.06	.38	8.34	Emery Air Freight	.83	.30	7.34
Diversified Inds.	1.75	.26	16.61	Emhart Corp.	1.16	.57	7.44
Dr. Pepper	.99	.34	8.15	Empire Dist. Elec.	.35	.14	4.48
Dollar General	1.31	.47	10.27	Empire Inc.	.92	.11	13.15
Dome Mines	.86	.16	10.46	Ennis Business Forms	1.19	.36	9.58
Dome Petroleum	.88	.13	11.59	Enserch Corp.	.99	.31	8.54
Dominion Stores (1)	.64	.27	6.38	Enterpr. Developm.	.51	.02	17.66
Dominion Textile (1)	.68	.25	7.14	Entex, Inc.	1.08	.43	7.93
Domtar Inc.	.87	.27	8.12	Envirotech Corp.	1.59	.41	11.97
Donaldson Co.	.97	.35	8.08	Equifax, Inc.	.67	.30	5.97
Donaldson, Lufkin	1.78	.46	12.72	Equimark Corp.	.85	.25	8.24
Donnelly RR & Sons	.84	.46	6.04	Equitable Gas	.98	.38	7.70
Dorchester Gas	1.41	.36	11.32	Equitable Life Mtg.	.89	.29	7.92
Dorsey Corp.	1.21	.33	10.25	Equitable Sav. & Loan	1.65	.37	13.10
Dover Corp.	.75	.36	6.02	Esmark Inc.	.85	.23	8.60
Dow Chemical	1.01	.49	6.97	Esquire Inc.	1.25	.36	10.11
Dow Jones	.91	.42	6.86	Essex Chemical	.94	.21	9.84
Doyle Dane Bernbach	.80	.23	8.03	Esterline Corp.	1.96	.51	13.28
Dravo Corp.	.73	.22	7.57	Ethyl Corp.	.77	.30	6.85
Dresser Industries	.94	.28	8.64	Evans Products	1.03	.39	8.00
Drexel Bond-Deb.	.35	.16	4.20	Ex-Cell-O	1.42	.57	9.12
Dreyfus Corp.	1.13	.26	10.75	Executive Inds.	.80	.04	19.08
Driefontein	.61	.06	11.72	Exxon Corp.	.55	.27	5.09
Duke Power	.24	.05	5.18	FMC Corp.	1.03	.55	6.70
Dun & Bradstreet	.81	.47	5.70	Faberge Inc.	1.35	.33	11.34

Stock	Regression Est. of Beta	R^2	Sta. Deviation of Price (%)
Fabri-Centers (1)	1.08	.27	10.77
Facet Enterprises	.76	.14	9.75
Fairchild Inds. Inc.	1.49	.43	11.50
Falconbridge Nickel	1.49	.29	13.33
Falstaff Brewing	.87	.10	13.41
Family Dollar Stores (2)	1.07	.36	9.62
Farah Mfg. Co.	1.23	.17	14.31
Farmers Group	.87	.31	7.61
Farm House Foods (3)	.90	.18	11.34
Far West Financial	1.08	.33	9.07
Fedders Corp.	1.62	.33	13.59
Federal Co.	.85	.35	6.92
Federal Express (2)	1.51	.41	12.49
Federal-Mogul	.85	.34	7.05
Federal Nat'l. Mtg.	.60	.14	7.76
Federal Paper Board	.92	.26	8.83
Federal Resources	1.67	.31	14.56
Federal Signal Corp.	.99	.23	9.84
Federated Dept. Stores	.82	.33	6.88
Ferro Corp.	1.24	.40	9.58
Fidelcor Inc.	1.08	.23	10.97
Fidelity Fin'l.	1.62	.34	13.50
Fidelity Union Banc.	.44	.25	4.28
Fieldcrest Mills	.72	.19	8.12
Figgie Int'l.	1.49	.55	9.75
Filmways Inc.	1.58	.23	16.08
Fin'l. Corp. Amer.	1.40	.26	13.21
Fin'l. Corp. St. Barbara	1.19	.30	10.48
Financial Federation	1.22	.22	12.44
Financial General	.38	.06	7.67
Firestone Tire	.74	.24	7.34
First Bank System	.62	.29	5.56
First Boston Inc.	1.33	.40	10.20
First Charter Financ.	1.06	.23	10.72
First Chicago Corp.	1.06	.42	7.93
First City Banc Tex.	.81	.42	6.03
First City Properties	1.02	.25	9.85
First Int'l. Bancshrs.	.80	.41	6.04
First Interstate Bank	.74	.29	6.66
First Mississippi	1.34	.23	13.62
First Nat'l. (Boston)	.59	.27	5.57
First Nat'l State Bank	.73	.36	5.84
First Penn. Cp. (Phil.)	.91	.34	7.57
First Penn. Mtg. Tr.	1.61	.25	15.58
First Union Bankcorp	.68	.37	5.39
First Un. Real Est.	.70	.32	5.95
First Va. Bankshares	.57	.20	6.23
First Wisconsin Corp.	.67	.26	6.32
Fischbach Corp.	.86	.33	7.19
Fisher & Porter Co.	1.50	.46	10.67
Fisher Foods	.94	.21	9.89
Fleetwood Enterprise	1.63	.48	11.42
Fleming Co. Inc.	.72	.37	5.70
Flexi-Van Corp.	1.47	.31	12.75
Flightsafety Int'l. (1)	1.29	.45	9.95
Florida East Coast	.86	.21	9.14
Florida Power	.48	.17	5.62
Florida Power & Light	.45	.20	4.86
Florida Steel Corp.	1.41	.35	11.58
Flow General (2)	2.03	.40	16.70
Fluke (John) Mfg. (1)	.91	.26	9.20
Fluor Corp.	.82	.18	9.37
Foote Cone & Belding	.63	.17	7.40
Ford Motor	.81	.31	7.04
Foremost-McKesson	.70	.27	6.43
Forest Labs. (3)	1.60	.29	16.35
Forest Oil	1.16	.31	10.14
Fort Howard Paper	1.00	.53	6.65
Foster Wheeler	1.25	.31	10.85
Fotomat	1.20	.15	14.85
Four-Phase Sys.	1.83	.37	14.57
Foxboro Co.	.92	.39	7.14
Franklin Electric (1)	.71	.14	9.79
Freeport McMoran	1.19	.34	9.87
Free State Geduld	.74	.06	14.92
Fremont Gen'l. (3)	1.38	.50	10.74
Frigitronics Inc.	1.36	.18	15.65
Frontier Airlines (1)	1.91	.44	14.91
Fruehauf Corp.	.94	.41	7.09
Fuji Photo Film	.49	.07	8.70
Fuller (H.B.) (1)	1.02	.40	8.38
Fuqua Inds. Inc.	1.21	.36	9.82
GAF Corp.	1.31	.40	10.01
GATX Corp.	1.08	.50	7.39
GCA Corp.	1.98	.42	14.81
G F Business Equip.	1.39	.33	11.80
Galveston Houston (3)	.99	.21	11.55
Gannett Co.	.76	.40	5.83
Gap Stores	1.57	.37	12.54
Gas Service Co.	.56	.16	6.71
Gates Learjet (2)	1.39	.33	12.98
Gearhart Inds.	.94	.20	10.23
GEICO Corp.	1.32	.42	9.83
Gelco Corp.	1.37	.34	11.31
Gemini Fund	1.03	.72	5.86
Gen'l. Amer. Invest.	.87	.38	6.80
Gen'l. Amer. Oil Co.	.73	.16	8.95
Gen'l. Automotive (1)	.46	.10	7.37
Gen'l. Bancshares	.55	.23	5.54
Gen'l. Cinema	1.31	.57	8.38
Gen'l. Dynamics	1.13	.28	10.40
Gen'l. Electric	.74	.55	4.85
Gen'l. Foods	.59	.22	6.04
Gen'l. Host	1.06	.35	8.68
Gen'l. Housewares (3)	1.19	.39	10.23
Gen'l. Instrument	1.52	.55	9.94
Gen'l. Mills	.61	.16	7.36
Gen'l. Motors	.62	.27	5.82
Gen'l. Public Util.	.42	.43	9.73
Gen'l. Refractories	1.50	.32	12.81

(1) 50-59 Observations   (2) 35-49 Observations   (3) Less Than 35 Observations

Stock	Regression Est. of Beta	R^2	Sta. Deviation of Price (%)	Stock	Regression Est. of Beta	R^2	Sta. Deviation of Price (%)
General Re Corp.	.77	.23	7.68	Hajoca Corp.	.97	.24	9.61
Gen'l. Signal Corp.	1.02	.44	7.42	Hall (Frank B) & Co.	.84	.35	6.86
Gen'l. Steel Inds.	.97	.23	9.84	Halliburton Co.	.91	.35	7.43
Gen'l. Tel. & Electro.	.47	.25	4.50	Hamilton Bros. (3)	.69	.12	10.73
Gen'l. Tire	1.10	.34	9.09	Hammermill Paper	1.02	.32	8.70
Genesco Inc.	1.39	.25	13.35	Hancock (John) Inv.	.36	.14	4.57
Genstar Corp.	1.02	.31	8.79	Handleman Co.	1.36	.29	12.31
Genuine Parts Co.	.63	.22	6.49	Handy & Harman	1.31	.26	12.55
Georgia-Pacific	1.23	.57	7.88	Hanna Mining Co.	.86	.35	7.05
Geosource (1)	1.32	.43	10.25	Harcourt Brace/Jov.	.94	.35	7.70
Gerber Products	.81	.23	8.20	Harland (John H.)	.98	.43	7.32
Gerber Scientific (3)	1.84	.36	16.47	Harnischfeger Corp.	1.13	.22	11.62
Getty Oil	.84	.26	8.01	Harris Bankcorp	.82	.31	7.12
Giant Portland Cem.	1.08	.30	9.50	Harris Corp.	1.09	.40	8.34
Gibraltar Financial	1.69	.37	13.47	Harsco Corp.	.51	.24	5.09
Giddings & Lewis	1.47	.44	10.70	Harte Hanks Communic.	1.07	.32	9.15
Gifford-Hill & Co.	1.15	.37	9.16	Hartfield-Zodys (1)	1.25	.28	11.91
Gilbert Assoc.	1.07	.31	9.33	Hart Schaffner & Marx	1.00	.42	7.45
Gillette	.90	.42	6.72	Hawaiian Electric	.17	.03	4.63
Gino's Inc.	1.36	.25	13.28	Hayes-Albion Corp.	1.15	.37	9.18
Girard Company	.65	.31	5.58	Hazeltine	1.34	.41	10.04
Gleason Works	1.68	.50	11.48	Heck's Inc.	1.30	.49	9.02
Global Marine	2.06	.52	13.76	Hecla Mining	1.41	.15	17.33
Golden Nugget (3)	1.33	.25	14.90	Heileman G. Brewing	1.17	.49	8.07
Golden West Fin'l.	.85	.20	9.06	Heinz (H J)	.57	.26	5.44
Goodrich (BF)	.92	.34	7.64	Helene Curtis	1.30	.22	13.36
Goodyear Tire	.65	.27	6.02	Heller Int'l.	1.50	.38	11.77
Gordon Jewelry	.96	.25	9.17	Helmerich & Payne	1.20	.38	9.41
Gotaas-Larsen (3)	1.92	.37	16.73	Hemisphere Fund	1.27	.33	10.72
Gould Inc.	.71	.22	7.43	Hercules Inc.	1.35	.52	9.06
Goulds Pumps (1)	.85	.34	7.51	Hershey Foods	.65	.21	6.82
Grace (W R)	.79	.34	6.55	Hesston Corp.	1.17	.24	11.54
Grainger (W.W.)	.87	.46	6.25	Heublein Inc.	.73	.20	7.83
Graniteville Co.	.91	.40	6.99	Hewlett-Packard	.85	.33	7.15
Graphic Scanning (3)	1.74	.29	17.49	Hexcel Corp. (2)	1.77	.64	11.89
GT Atlantic & Pacific	1.01	.22	10.55	High Voltage Eng.	2.12	.58	13.49
GT Lakes Chemical	.93	.39	7.23	Hillenbrand Inds.	.88	.39	6.78
GT Lakes Int'l.	.56	.08	9.80	Hilton Hotels	1.36	.37	10.81
Gt. Northern Iron	.49	.07	9.20	Hi-Shear Inds. (2)	1.14	.25	12.10
Grt. Northern Nekoosa	.92	.42	6.87	Hitachi, Ltd. ADR	.43	.06	8.46
Gt. Western Financial	.98	.26	9.28	Holiday Inns Inc.	1.66	.58	10.56
Greyhound Corp.	.90	.34	7.45	Holly Sugar	1.01	.11	14.93
Grolier Inc.	.21	.01	25.56	Homestake Mining	.90	.14	11.50
Grow Group, Inc.	.54	.09	8.93	Honda Motor Adr.	.50	.09	8.26
Grumman	1.12	.21	11.83	Honeywell Inc.	.95	.39	7.36
Guardian Industries	1.23	.32	10.42	Hoover Co.	.82	.15	10.25
Gulf Canada Ltd.	.58	.06	11.52	Hoover Universal Inc.	1.06	.39	8.16
Gulf Oil	.41	.09	6.67	Horizon Corp.	2.13	'.33	17.86
Gulf Resources	1.12	.19	12.57	Hormel George A & Co.	.67	.21	7.10
Gulf States Util.	.29	.09	4.64	Horn & Hardart Co.	1.33	.18	15.14
Gulf United	1.03	.34	8.58	Hosp. Corp. of Amer.	1.21	.48	8.39
Gulf & Western Ind.	1.09	.49	7.49	Host International	1.19	.22	12.24
Gulton Industries	1.55	.43	11.46	Houghton Mifflin	.52	.12	7.16
HMW Industries Inc.	1.92	.51	13.04	Household Int'l.	.60	.27	5.51
Hackensack Water	.40	.12	5.58	House of Fabrics	1.14	.36	9.16

Stock	Regression Est. of Beta	R²	Sta. Deviation of Price (%)	Stock	Regression Est. of Beta	R²	Sta. Deviation of Price (%)
Houston Inds. Inc.	.38	.13	5.03	Interstate Bakeries	1.50	.36	12.08
Houston Natural Gas	1.32	.50	9.03	Interstate Power	.31	.08	5.31
Hubbard Real Estate	.42	.26	3.98	Iowa Elec. Lt. & Pwr.	.34	.11	4.88
Hubbell Harvey 'B' (2)	.86	.46	6.81	Iowa-Ill. Gas & Elec.	.28	.10	4.44
Hudson Bay Mining	1.10	.28	10.07	Iowa Public Service	.33	.13	4.40
Hudson Bay Co. (1)	.52	.14	7.30	Iowa Resources	.44	.20	4.76
Huffy Corp.	.31	.02	9.69	Iowa So. Utilities	.44	.17	5.22
Hughes Tool	.97	.32	8.31	Ipco Corp.	1.27	.34	10.51
Humana Inc.	1.54	.45	11.12	Iroquois Brands (3)	1.35	.42	12.19
Hunt (P A) Chemical	1.24	.29	11.19	Irving Bank Corp.	.60	.35	4.92
Husky Oil Ltd.	.73	.17	8.61	Itek Corp.	1.78	.49	12.35
Hutton (E.F.) Group	1.75	.46	12.39	Itel Corp.	1.39	.10	21.45
Hyster Co.	.90	.33	7.59	JWT Group, Inc.	.97	.37	7.63
IC Industries Inc.	1.07	.50	7.33	James (Fred S.) & Co.	1.25	.51	8.45
ICN Pharmaceuticals	1.80	.30	15.78	James River (2)	1.35	.36	12.07
I.M.S. Int'l.	.94	.25	9.17	Jamesway Corp.	1.66	.54	10.97
INA Corp.	.87	.43	6.39	Japan Fund	.55	.16	6.66
I-U. Int'l. Corp.	1.10	.29	9.86	Jefferson-Pilot Corp.	.67	.30	5.93
Idaho Power	.25	.09	4.10	Jerrico, Inc.	1.44	.34	11.95
Ideal Basic	1.32	.52	8.84	Jewel Companies	.76	.30	6.77
Ideal Toy	1.64	.43	12.07	Johnson (E.F.)	2.04	.50	14.02
Illinois Power	.33	.10	5.18	Johnson & Johnson	.65	.29	5.90
Illinois Tool Works	.88	.49	6.08	Johnson Controls Inc.	1.21	.40	9.23
Imperial Corp. Amer.	1.37	.35	11.14	Johnson Products	1.60	.41	12.08
Imperial Group Ltd. (2)	.32	.03	8.98	Jonathan Logan	1.21	.38	9.52
Imperial Oil Ltd. "A"	.67	.12	9.31	Jorgensen (Earle M)	.82	.31	7.13
Inco Limited	1.14	.34	9.50	Jostens Inc.	.79	.31	6.84
Income & Capital Shs.	1.21	.65	7.29	Joy Mfg.	1.16	.45	8.36
Indiana Gas Co.	.75	.33	6.36	Justin Inds.	1.81	.60	12.52
Indianapolis Pwr. & Lt.	.26	.07	4.65	KDT Inds.	.85	.30	7.51
Industrial Nat'l. Corp.	.74	.40	5.63	KLM Royal Dutch	.94	.21	9.96
Inexco Oil	1.25	.28	11.39	K Mart Corp.	.95	.35	7.76
Ingersoll-Rand	.89	.40	6.81	Kaiser Aluminum	1.08	.42	8.11
Ingredient Technology	1.14	.38	9.01	Kaiser Cement	1.51	.50	10.31
Inland Steel	.64	.28	5.86	Kaiser Steel	.49	.06	9.58
Insilco Corp.	1.19	.49	8.18	Kane Miller	.82	.21	8.69
Intel Corp.	1.26	.44	9.15	Kaneb Services	1.12	.29	10.11
Interco Inc.	.73	.43	5.41	Kansas City Pwr. & Lt.	.39	.13	5.21
Interlake Inc.	1.04	.44	7.57	Kansas City Southn.	1.04	.30	9.13
Intermedics (2)	1.45	.34	12.90	Kansas Gas & Elec.	.40	.17	4.75
Int'l Aluminum	1.76	.56	11.61	Kansas-Nebraska	.47	.16	7.16
Int'l. Banknote Co.	1.44	.24	14.27	Kansas Pwr. & Lt.	.42	.21	4.48
Int'l. Business Mach.	.63	.38	4.93	Katy Industries	1.64	.42	12.24
Int'l. Controls Corp. (2)	1.92	.44	15.45	Kaufman & Broad	1.76	.48	12.36
Int'l. Flavors & Frag.	.71	.21	7.43	Keller Industries	1.82	.38	14.27
Int'l. Harvester	1.41	.50	9.67	Kellogg	.68	.28	6.17
Int'l. Minerals	.78	.24	7.67	Kellwood Co.	.91	.32	7.76
Int'l. Multifoods	.81	.35	6.63	Kelly Services (1)	1.15	.45	8.88
Int'l. Paper	1.05	.48	7.37	Kemper Corp. (2)	1.08	.39	9.22
Int'l. Rectifier	1.86	.42	13.86	Kenai Corp. (3)	1.25	.35	11.29
Int'l. Tel. & Tel.	.93	.55	6.09	Kennametal Inc.	1.10	.39	8.57
Internorth, Inc.	.63	.17	7.33	Kentucky Utilties	.35	.14	4.55
Interpace Corp.	.82	.30	7.18	Kerr Glass	1.29	.52	8.70
Interpublic Group	.95	.41	7.18	Kerr-McGee Corp.	.66	.14	8.35
Inter-Regional (3)	1.15	.30	11.20	Keystone Consol. Ind.	1.09	.22	11.13

(1) 50-59 Observations   (2) 35-49 Observations   (3) Less Than 35 Observations

EXHIBIT 4-4 Table of Value Line Index components with beta, R^2, and standard deviation. (Reprinted with permission of the Kansas City Board of Trade.) (*Continued*)

Stock	Regression Est. of Beta	R^2	Sta. Deviation of Price (%)	Stock	Regression Est. of Beta	R^2	Sta. Deviation of Price (%)
Keystone Foods (3)	1.20	.40	11.07	Longs Drug Stores	.74	.26	7.11
Kidde Inc.	.89	.39	6.90	Loral Corp.	1.27	.45	9.19
Kimberly-Clark	.67	.35	5.51	Louisiana Land	.85	.22	8.88
Kloof Gold Mng.	.81	.08	13.48	Louisiana-Pacific	1.37	.60	8.61
Knight Ridder Newsp.	1.03	.49	7.07	Louisville Gas & Elec.	.31	.12	4.32
Kollmorgen	1.47	.48	10.46	Lowenstein (M)	1.16	.15	14.71
Koppers	1.12	.40	8.57	Lowe's Companies	.96	.31	8.40
Kroehler Mfg.	1.07	.14	13.76	Lubrizol Corp.	.75	.30	6.65
Kroger	.69	.24	6.90	Lucky Stores	.66	.31	5.71
Kubota Ltd.	.16	.03	4.58	Lukens Steel	.97	.27	9.07
Kyoto Ceramic (2)	.70	.21	7.89	Lynch Communications	.66	.09	10.50
Kysor Ind'l.	1.09	.35	8.93	M/A-Comm., Inc.	1.55	.56	9.97
LFE Corp.	2.16	.54	14.19	MCA Inc.	.84	.31	7.38
LLC Corp.	1.78	.26	17.03	MCI Communic. (2)	1.35	.25	14.53
LTV Corp.	1.84	.44	13.46	MEI Corp.	.79	.20	8.41
Labatt (John) Ltd. (2)	.56	.31	5.34	MGIC Investment Corp.	1.57	.48	10.99
Laclede Gas	.38	.08	6.56	MacMillan Inc.	1.36	.37	10.82
Lamson & Sessions	1.28	.32	11.05	Macy R H	.86	.40	6.57
Lancaster Colony	1.08	.21	11.40	Madison Fund Inc.	.89	.49	6.14
Lane Bryant	1.39	.39	10.80	Magic Chef	1.36	.42	10.18
Lanier Business (1)	1.27	.45	9.68	Magma Power	1.71	.33	14.47
La Quinta Motor Inns	1.11	.29	9.98	Mallinckrodt Inc.	.62	.22	6.30
Lawson Prod. (3)	.69	.25	7.42	Malone & Hyde	.87	.43	6.47
Lawter Int'l.	1.13	.40	8.63	Management Asst. (2)	-.02*	.00	17.16
Lear Petroleum (2)	1.56	.27	16.03	Manhattan Inds.	1.12	.28	10.28
Lear Siegler Inc.	1.45	.50	9.95	Manitowoc Co. (1)	1.38	.40	11.36
Leaseway Transport	.79	.26	7.49	Manufactrs. Hanover	.66	.27	6.11
Legett & Platt (3)	1.01	.22	11.63	Manville Corp.	1.04	.47	7.30
Lehigh Valley Inds.	1.45	.21	15.20	Mapco Inc.	1.13	.46	8.06
Lehman Corp.	.91	.43	6.75	Marathon Oil	.73	.11	10.81
Lennar Corp.	1.96	.47	13.79	Marine Midland Bank	1.21	.38	9.49
Lenox Inc.	1.21	.61	7.51	Marion Laboratories	.95	.26	9.05
Leslie Fay	1.00	.38	7.86	Mark Controls	1.50	.46	10.69
Leucadia Nat'l. Corp.	1.05	.11	15.33	Marriott Corp.	1.36	.47	9.63
Leverage Fund	1.39	.76	7.70	Marshall Field	.87	.18	9.87
Levi Strauss & Co.	.84	.23	8.54	Marsh & McClennan	.55	.32	4.71
Levitz Furniture	1.10	.31	9.58	Martin Marietta	1.22	.57	7.83
Libbey-Owens-Ford	.56	.29	5.05	Martin Processing	.98	.17	11.57
Liberty Corp.	1.18	.50	8.08	Mary Kay Cosmetics	1.14	.18	12.90
Liberty Nat'l. Ins.	.50	.15	6.22	Maryland Cup Corp.	.91	.22	9.26
Lifemark Corp.	1.30	.31	11.36	Maryland Nat'l. Corp.	.96	.46	6.87
Lilly, Eli	.76	.31	6.62	Masco	1.25	.48	8.70
Limited Stores	1.68	.30	15.05	Masonite	.82	.23	8.39
Lin Broadc. (3)	.82	.33	8.34	Massey-Ferguson	1.01	.17	11.72
Lincoln First Banks	.85	.34	7.12	Mass Mutual Mtg. R'lt.	.61	.30	5.39
Lincoln Nat'l. Corp.	.89	.56	5.74	Matsushita Elec. Adr.	.43	.07	7.97
Lionel Corp.	1.64	.32	14.01	Mattel Inc.	1.89	.42	14.11
Litton Industries	1.07	.37	8.54	May Dept. Stores	.85	.36	6.82
Lockheed	2.25	.48	15.70	Maytag	.63	.31	5.46
Loctite Corp.	1.17	.27	10.90	McCormick & Co.	.28	.02	9.23
Loews Corp.	1.18	.48	8.30	McDermott Inc.	.89	.20	9.51
Lomas Nettleton Fin.	1.29	.48	9.01	McDonald's Corp.	.66	.24	6.46
Lomas & Nettleton Mt.	.95	.37	7.61	McDonnell Douglas	1.06	.19	11.62
Lone Star Inds.	1.19	.54	7.84	McGraw-Edison	.83	.24	8.20
Long Island Ltg.	.28	.13	3.74	McGraw Hill Inc.	.95	.33	7.99

Stock	Regression Est. of Beta	R^2	Sta. Deviation of Price (%)	Stock	Regression Est. of Beta	R^2	Sta. Deviation of Price (%)
McIntyre Mines	1.81	.39	14.06	Montgomery Street	.32	.15	3.99
McLean Trucking	.95	.24	9.29	Mony Mtg. Investors	.60	.30	5.28
McLouth Steel	1.17	.37	9.33	Moog Inc. 'A' (2)	1.54	.34	13.73
McNeil Corp.	.94	.39	7.30	Moore Corp.	.69	.33	5.79
Mead Corp.	1.19	.44	8.66	Moore McCormack Res.	1.40	.51	9.47
Measurex Corp.	1.46	.41	11.04	Moran Energy (3)	1.66	.36	15.00
Media General	1.06	.56	6.88	Morgan (J.P.) & Co.	.44	.16	5.36
Medtronic, Inc.	1.25	.34	10.30	Morrison Inc.	1.10	.34	9.12
Mellon Nat'l. Bk. (Pitt.)	.64	.34	5.29	Morrisson Knudsen	1.43	.42	10.70
Melville Corp.	.85	.35	6.97	Morse Shoe Inc.	1.15	.27	10.66
Mercantile Stores	.53	.24	5.27	Morton-Norwich	.86	.35	7.00
Mercantile Texas (2)	.95	.45	7.60	Motorola	1.02	.36	8.22
Merck & Co.	.65	.28	6.03	Mountain Fuel Supp.	.74	.24	7.27
Meredith Corp.	1.16	.49	7.99	Munford	.56	.06	11.26
Merrill Lynch Pierce	1.57	.65	9.39	Munsingwear	.41	.12	5.63
Mesabi Trust	.60	.23	6.13	Murphy G C	.75	.31	6.46
Mesa Petroleum	1.07	.18	12.32	Murphy Oil Corp.	1.05	.22	10.86
Mesta Machine	1.29	.43	9.46	Murray Ohio Mfg.	.88	.29	7.93
Metpath (1)	.90	.21	9.86	Mutual of Omaha	.37	.18	4.30
Metromedia Inc.	1.22	.49	8.38	Myers (L.E.) Co.	1.34	.29	12.09
Meyer (Fred) 'A'	1.09	.37	8.62	NBD Bancorp	.60	.30	5.28
Michigan Energy Res.	.39	.09	6.29	NCH Corp.	1.24	.39	9.59
Michigan Nat'l. Corp. (2)	.57	.24	6.25	N C N B	.88	.28	7.98
Michigan Sugar	1.33	.24	13.10	NCR Corp.	1.18	.40	8.97
Mid-Cont'l. Telephone	.54	.27	5.01	NL Inds. Inc.	1.14	.42	8.51
Middle South Util.	.36	.12	5.08	NLT Corp.	.99	.26	9.37
Midland-Ross	1.21	.47	8.57	NVF Company	1.38	.28	12.67
Miller (Herman)	1.69	.58	10.99	Nabisco Brands	.61	.31	5.26
Miller-Wohl	.99	.22	10.23	Nalco Chemical	.77	.37	6.08
Millipore Corp.	1.32	.39	10.21	Narco Scientific	1.63	.28	14.92
Milton Bradley	1.62	.45	11.71	Nashua Corp.	1.33	.34	10.99
Milton Roy (1)	.60	.12	9.03	Nat'l. Can	1.20	.44	8.81
Minnesota Gas	.53	.24	5.23	Nat'l. City Corp.	.58	.31	5.11
Minnesota Mining	.69	.33	5.81	Nat'l. Data Corp. (3)	1.40	.41	11.86
Minnesota Pwr. & Lt.	.28	.11	4.13	Nat'l. Distillers	.80	.47	5.61
Mirro Corp. (2)	.68	.17	8.75	Nat'l. Fuel Gas	.42	.13	5.65
Mission Ins. Group	1.06	.35	8.66	Nat'l. Gypsum	1.06	.42	7.85
Missouri Pac. Corp.	.95	.41	7.18	Nat'l. Homes	1.19	.30	10.49
Missouri Pub. Serv.	.28	.06	5.45	Nat'l. Medical Care	1.06	.21	11.07
Mitchell Energy.	1.45	.34	12.03	Nat'l. Medical Enter.	1.63	.46	11.58
Mite Corp. (1)	.60	.12	8.80	Nat'l. Mine Service	1.15	.28	10.46
Mobil Corp.	.40	.07	7.50	Nat'l. Patent Dev.	1.59	.34	13.18
Mobile Home Ind.	1.43	.24	14.11	Nat'l. Presto Ind.	.89	.22	9.19
Modern Merchandising	1.01	.20	10.86	Nat'l. Semiconductor	1.39	.32	12.01
Mohasco Corp.	1.00	.33	8.43	Nat'l. Service Ind.	.83	.53	5.51
Mohawk Data Sciences	2.02	.47	14.27	Nat'l. Standard Co.	.95	.39	7.44
Mohawk Rubber	1.21	.28	11.04	Nat'l. Steel	.79	.40	5.97
Molex Inc. (3)	.96	.35	8.66	Nat'l. Tea	1.00	.16	12.22
Molson Cos. 'A' (2)	.46	.16	6.26	Nat'l. Utilities & Ind.	.48	.07	8.91
Monarch Capital	.88	.20	9.50	Natomas Co.	1.29	.36	10.50
Monarch Mach. Tool Co.	1.68	.50	11.44	Nevada Power	.42	.12	5.95
Monogram Industries	1.45	.44	10.51	New England Elec.	.60	.26	5.67
Monsanto	.87	.39	6.74	Newhall Land & Farm	1.18	.30	10.35
Montana-Dakota Util.	.62	.29	5.56	Newmont Mining	1.47	.39	11.32
Montana Power	.64	.26	6.03	Newpark Resources	1.78	.43	13.33

(1) 50-59 Observations   (2) 35-49 Observations   (3) Less Than 35 Observations

Stock	Regression Est. of Beta	R^2	Sta. Deviation of Price (%)	Stock	Regression Est. of Beta	R^2	Sta. Deviation of Price (%)
New Process	1.24	.28	11.37	Outlet Co.	1.67	.51	11.29
N Y State Elec. & Gas	.33	.15	4.22	Overhead Door	1.03	.45	7.41
New York Times	1.00	.39	7.74	Overnite Transportn.	1.17	.44	8.59
Niagra Mohawk	.33	.11	4.89	Overseas Shipholding	1.52	.50	10.46
Niagra Share	.92	.47	6.46	Owens-Corning	.93	.41	6.98
Nicor Inc.	.63	.34	5.22	Owens-Ill. Inc.	.75	.29	6.71
Nielsen (A.C.) "A"	1.08	.41	8.16	Oxford Inds. (1)	.99	.29	9.42
Noranda Mines	.92	.24	9.09	Ozark Air Lines (2)	1.80	.45	14.32
Norcen Energy Res.	.78	.19	8.60	P H H Group (1)	.86	.30	7.90
Nordstrom Inc.	1.00	.27	9.35	PNB Mortgage (1)	1.16	.41	9.38
Norfolk & Western	.93	.36	7.53	PPG Industries	1.17	.49	8.05
Norlin Corp.	.78	.23	7.90	PSA Inc.	.91	.15	11.28
No. Amer. Coal Corp.	1.27	.28	11.54	Pabst Brewing	.91	.21	9.61
No. Amer. Philips	1.04	.50	7.09	Paccar Inc.	1.06	.49	7.33
Northeast Utilities	.33	.11	4.79	Pacific Gas & Elec.	.17	.05	3.92
Northern Cal. S&L (2)	1.36	.33	12.64	Pacific Lighting	.32	.09	4.98
Northern Ind. P S	.40	.12	5.47	Pacific Lumber	1.02	.40	7.79
Northern Mutual Life	.85	.41	6.35	Pacific Power & Lt.	.41	.25	3.98
Northern States Pwr.	.47	.18	5.29	Pacific Tel. & Tel.	.45	.14	5.89
Northern Telecom	.93	.33	7.86	Pacific Tin Consol.	.86	.11	12.30
Northern Trust Corp.	.74	.39	5.69	Paine Webber Inc.	2.34	.63	14.20
Northgate Explor.	1.22	.19	13.66	Pall Corp.	.96	.37	7.75
Northrop Corp.	1.39	.40	10.68	Palm Beach Inc.	.88	.27	8.19
Northwest Airlines	1.23	.34	10.22	Pan Amer. World Air	1.45	.40	11.18
Northwest Bancorp.	.63	.25	6.09	Panhandle Eastern	.83	.25	7.98
Northwest Energy	.99	.27	9.15	Pantry Pride Inc.	1.54	.16	18.69
Northwestern Steel	.70	.30	6.14	Papercraft Corp.	.99	.38	7.77
Northwest Inds.	.78	.28	7.19	Pargas Inc.	.95	.26	9.04
Northwest Nat. Gas	.74	.34	6.14	Parker Drilling	1.52	.47	10.72
Norton Co.	.82	.32	6.93	Parker-Hannifin	.94	.32	8.0
Norton-Simon	.73	.27	6.85	Parker Pen	1.09	.33	9.18
Nova. An Alberta (1)	.91	.35	8.01	Parsons Corp.	1.44	.37	11.46
Noxell Corp.	1.17	.46	8.36	Patrick Petroleum	1.30	.25	12.70
Nucor Corp.	1.66	.59	10.40	Payless Cashways	1.25	.48	8.70
Oak Inds.	1.55	.32	13.14	Pay Less Drug NW	1.33	.47	9.34
Oakite Products	.59	.22	6.16	Pay'N Save Corp.	1.18	.46	8.36
Occidental Petroleum	1.01	.38	7.92	Peavey Co.	.73	.19	8.22
Ocean Drilling	1.08	.29	9.68	Penn Cent Corp. (2)	1.20	.24	13.11
Offshore Logistics	1.39	.36	11.25	Penncorp. Fin'l.	1.28	.28	11.77
Ogden Corp.	1.19	.49	8.21	Penn-Dixie Ind.	1.83	.17	21.36
Ogilvy & Mather	.97	.42	7.30	Penney (J C)	.72	.23	7.32
Ohio Casualty Corp.	.92	.37	7.33	Penn Power & Lt.	.39	.19	4.32
Ohio Edison	.45	.17	5.35	Pennwalt Corp.	.75	.44	5.47
Oklahoma Gas & Elec.	.32	.11	4.68	Pennzoil Company	.93	.25	9.05
Olin Corp.	.84	.16	10.02	Pentair Inds.	1.13	.34	9.37
Olympia Brewing	.49	.05	10.86	Peoples Drug Stores	1.06	.31	9.17
Omark Industries	1.20	.43	8.84	Pepsico Inc.	.80	.37	6.34
Oneida Ltd.	1.60	.42	11.95	Perkin-Elmer Corp.	1.07	.36	8.66
Oneok Inc.	1.20	.41	9.15	Petrie Stores Corp.	.91	.34	7.56
Opelika Mfg. Co.	.65	.23	6.47	Petrolane Inc.	1.10	.43	8.16
Orange & Rockland Ut.	.22	.04	5.04	Petroleum & Res.	.93	.33	7.82
Orange-Co., Inc.	1.25	.31	10.96	Petro-Lewis (3)	1.40	.18	17.75
Orion Capital	.93	.26	9.07	Petrolite Corp.	.64	.14	8.24
Otter Tail Power	.43	.18	4.91	Pfizer Inc.	.66	.27	6.16
Outboard Marine	1.34	.34	11.16	Phelps Dodge	1.33	.34	10.93

Stock	Regression Est. of Beta	R^2	Sta. Deviation of Price (%)	Stock	Regression Est. of Beta	R^2	Sta. Deviation of Price (%)
Phila. Electric	.41	.16	4.91	Putnam Duofund	1.37	.65	8.21
Phila. Nat'l. Corp.	.65	.35	5.30	Quaker Oats	.77	.34	6.40
Philip Morris	.76	.30	6.64	Quaker State Oil	1.29	.42	9.66
Philips Industries	1.80	.45	12.94	Quanex Corp.	1.20	.30	10.66
Philips N.V. (2)	.62	.29	6.14	Questor Corp.	1.38	.27	12.93
Phillips Petroleum	.78	.20	8.44	RCA Corp.	.91	.42	6.83
Phillips-Van Heusen	1.34	.41	10.10	RLC Corp. (2)	1.70	.62	11.49
Phoenix Steel	1.63	.29	14.71	RTE Corp.	1.16	.37	9.27
Piedmont Aviation (1)	1.94	.45	14.64	Rainier Bancorp.	.58	.22	6.05
Piedmont Nat'l. Gas	.51	.19	5.72	Ralston Purina	.86	.34	7.15
Pier 1 Imports	1.46	.20	15.64	Ramada Inns	1.57	.29	14.22
Pillsbury Co.	.78	.31	6.78	Rampac (3)	.80	.35	7.09
Pinkerton's Inc. 'B'	1.01	.45	7.28	Ranco Inc.	1.06	.26	10.02
Pioneer Corp.	.78	.18	8.95	Ranger Oil (3)	1.19	.20	14.66
Pioneer Electronics	.64	.08	10.81	Rank Organization	.56	.07	10.32
Pioneer Hi-Bred	.81	.24	8.02	Raybestos-Manhattan	1.18	.31	10.31
Pitney-Bowes	1.24	.44	9.04	Raychem Corp. (2)	1.06	.46	8.36
Pittsburgh Nat'l. (3)	.71	.40	6.03	Raymond Int'l.	1.70	.49	11.69
Pittston	1.00	.36	8.10	Raytheon Co.	1.13	.47	8.01
Pittway Corp.	.82	.33	6.93	Reading & Bates	1.62	.42	12.10
Pizza Inn	1.37	.30	12.08	Recognition Equip.	2.13	.40	16.27
Planning Research	1.99	.43	14.67	Redken Labs.	1.62	.33	13.58
Plantronics	1.52	.47	10.72	Redman Industries	1.92	.49	13.30
Playboy Enterprises	1.51	.17	17.53	Reece Co.	.95	.29	8.56
Plessey Plc.	.59	.10	8.85	Reeves Brothers	.60	.22	6.18
Pneumo Corp.	1.47	.42	11.04	Regency Electronics	1.67	.34	13.84
Pogo Producing Co.	1.05	.26	10.00	Reichhold Chemicals	.85	.29	7.69
Polaroid Corp.	1.27	.34	10.42	Reliance Group Inc.	.67	.20	7.23
Ponderosa Systems	1.57	.28	14.36	Republic Airlines	1.61	.35	13.12
Pope & Talbot (1)	1.35	.47	10.23	Republic Corp.	1.67	.50	11.50
Portec Inc.	1.00	.33	8.47	Republic Fin'l. Serv.	.92	.23	9.37
Portland Genl. Elec.	.36	.21	3.88	Republic N. Y. (3)	1.73	.58	12.95
Potlatch Corp.	1.01	.41	7.64	Republic Steel	.85	.32	7.25
Potomac Elec. Power	.27	.08	4.70	Republic Tex. Corp.	.66	.28	6.01
Prec. Metals Hldg. (1)	1.03	.17	12.75	Research-Cottrell	1.37	.44	10.00
Premier Industrial	.57	.23	5.72	Resorts Int'l. "A"	1.37	.14	17.88
Prentice Hall Inc.	.96	.42	7.14	Revco Drug Stores	.92	.28	8.39
Presley Cos. (1)	1.89	.35	16.14	Revere Copper	1.74	.33	14.64
Prime Computer	1.73	.35	14.53	Revlon Inc.	.91	.29	8.11
Procter & Gamble	.45	.20	4.84	Rexham Corp.	1.41	.44	10.35
Prod. Research & Chem.	.81	.16	9.83	Rexnord Inc.	.80	.33	6.74
Proler Int'l.	1.18	.37	9.38	Reynolds & Reyn. (2)	.87	.23	9.38
Publicker Inds.	1.81	.38	14.15	Reynolds Inds.	.67	.28	6.09
Pub. Ser. Elec. & Gas	.30	.09	4.90	Reynolds Metals	1.03	.41	7.76
Public Ser. (Colo.)	.42	.13	5.50	Richardson Co.	.78	.17	9.05
Public Ser. (Indiana)	.33	.08	5.66	Richmond Tank (3)	1.13	.28	12.43
Public Ser. (N H)	.31	.10	4.86	Riegel Textile	.93	.44	6.80
P. S. of New Mexico	.28	.07	5.17	Rio Grande Inds.	1.26	.33	10.67
Pueblo Int'l.	1.21	.31	10.43	Rite Aid	1.22	.50	8.34
Puget Sound P & L	.42	.13	5.52	Rival Mfg.	.84	.23	8.55
Pulte Home (3)	1.87	.53	14.19	Roadway Express	.98	.39	7.63
Purex Inds.	.75	.31	6.44	Robertshaw Controls	1.11	.31	9.63
Puritan Bennett	1.45	.46	10.31	Robertson (H H)	.85	.24	8.30
Puritan Fashions (3)	1.85	.32	17.34	Robins (A H) Co.	.89	.32	7.68
Purolator Inc.	1.16	.39	9.02	Robintech, Inc.	1.07	.17	12.55

(1) 50-59 Observations (2) 35-49 Observations (3) Less Than 35 Observations

Stock	Regression Est. of Beta	R^2	Sta. Deviation of Price (%)	Stock	Regression Est. of Beta	R^2	Sta. Deviation of Price (%)
Rochester Gas & Elec.	.37	.12	5.16	Sealed Air Corp. (3)	1.42	.27	14.78
Rochester Telephone	.39	.12	5.40	Sealed Power Corp.	1.03	.25	9.88
Rockcor Inc.	2.00	.49	13.82	Searle (G D)	.88	.29	7.96
Rockwell Int'l.	.84	.31	7.26	Sears Roebuck	.68	.32	5.88
Rogers Corp. (3)	1.41	.33	13.03	Security Pac Corp.	.90	.35	7.40
Rohm and Haas	1.02	.40	7.82	SEDCO Inc.	1.36	.32	11.69
Rohr Ind. Corp.	1.74	.38	13.74	Service Corp. Int'l. (3)	1.32	.43	11.66
Rollins Inc.	1.17	.40	8.90	Servicemaster (3)	.59	.24	6.69
Rolm Corp.	1.40	.24	13.77	Service Merchandise	1.39	.34	11.51
Ronson	1.32	.22	13.56	Shaklee Corp.	1.55	.33	13.12
Roper Corp.	1.10	.39	8.45	Shapell Ind.	1.51	.59	9.48
Rorer Group (1)	.67	.15	8.91	Shared Medical Sys. (1)	1.10	.42	8.54
Rouse Co. (2)	1.30	.33	12.12	Shell Canada 'A' (2)	.14	.01	9.88
Rowan Cos.	1.15	.26	10.84	Sheller Globe	1.18	.39	9.10
Royal Crown Cos.	.63	.13	8.43	Shell Oil	.70	.16	8.39
Royal Dutch Petr.	.44	.16	5.36	Shell Transport	.46	.11	6.61
Rubbermaid Inc.	.79	.28	7.24	Sherwin-Williams	1.19	.38	9.34
Russ Togs Inc.	.89	.45	6.39	Shoney's Inc.	1.19	.39	9.16
Ryan Homes	1.32	.43	9.71	Showboat	1.03	.19	11.49
Ryder System	1.53	.58	9.72	Sierra Pacific Pwr.	.26	.09	4.33
SCA Services, Inc.	1.97	.49	13.64	Sigmor Corp. (2)	1.29	.26	13.78
SCM Corp.	1.02	.32	8.69	Signal Companies	1.37	.50	9.39
SFN Cos.	1.05	.38	8.29	Signode Corp.	.82	.47	5.74
SPS Tehnologies	1.86	.50	12.81	Simmonds Precision	1.75	.37	13.82
Sabine Corp.	1.22	.32	10.40	Simplicity Pattern	1.02	.31	8.82
Safeco Corp.	.88	.44	6.43	Singer Co.	1.41	.32	12.14
Safeway Stores	.75	.30	6.61	Skyline Corp.	1.50	.48	10.44
Saga Corp.	1.03	.29	9.23	Smith (A O)	1.13	.54	7.45
St. Joseph Lt. & Pwr.	.25	.08	4.36	Smith Int'l. Inc.	.81	.18	9.29
St. Paul Cos.	.56	.18	6.41	Smithkline Corp.	.76	.29	6.85
St. Regis Paper	.88	.45	6.34	Smucker (J M) Co.	.79	.24	7.85
Salant Corp.	.99	.29	8.90	Snap-On Tools	1.13	.43	8.39
Sanders Associates	1.53	.42	11.35	Sony Corp. (ADR.)	.54	.09	8.88
San Diego Gas & Elec.	.33	.10	5.09	Soo Line Railroad	.52	.11	7.62
Santa Fe Industries	.80	.24	7.92	South Atlantic Fin'l.	1.17	.12	16.48
Sargent-Welch Sci.	1.10	.47	7.73	So. Carolina E & G	.42	.16	5.09
Savanna Elec. & Pwr.	.30	.07	5.33	Southdown Inc.	1.25	.30	11.08
Sav-A-Stop	1.50	.34	12.55	Southeast Banking Co.	.92	.38	7.19
Savin Corp.	1.69	.30	14.85	Southeastern Pub. Ser.	.49	.11	7.03
Saxon Industries	1.69	.56	10.92	Southern Cal. Edison	.23	.07	4.16
Scherer (R. P.)	1.43	.42	10.62	Southern Co.	.19	.04	4.77
Schering Plough	.88	.34	7.25	So. Indiana Gas & E.	.44	.16	5.28
Schlitz	.73	.12	10.27	Southern Nat. Res.	.81	.25	7.76
Schlumberger Ltd.	.81	.33	6.84	Southern New Eng. Tel.	.29	.13	3.86
Scientific Atlanta (1)	1.00	.30	9.39	Southern Pacific Co.	1.03	.46	7.36
SCOA Industries	1.06	.31	9.30	Southern Railway	.75	.43	5.51
Scot Lad Foods	1.09	.22	11.16	Southern Union Co.	.92	.25	8.78
Scott & Fetzer & Co.	1.18	.52	7.95	South Jersey Ind.	.66	.32	5.64
Scott Paper	.98	.30	8.65	Southland Corp.	.94	.32	8.01
Scotty's Inc.	1.34	.50	9.13	Southmark Properties	1.82	.12	25.34
Scovill Inc.	.69	.32	5.86	Southwest Airlines	1.72	.46	12.24
Scudder Duo-Vest	1.26	.74	7.06	Southw. Bancshares	.68	.30	5.97
Sea Cont/Seaco	1.66	.37	13.21	Southwestern Pub. Ser.	.15	.02	4.85
SEAFIRST Corp.	.77	.40	5.84	Southwest Forest	1.70	.48	11.94
Seagram Co.	.68	.19	7.58	Sparton Corp.	1.15	.26	10.95

Stock	Regression Est. of Beta	R^2	Sta. Deviation of Price (%)	Stock	Regression Est. of Beta	R^2	Sta. Deviation of Price (%)
Spectra Physics	1.18	.31	10.23	TDK Electron. ADR (2)	.89	.33	8.30
Sperry Corp.	1.19	.57	7.62	Teco Energy	.38	.12	5.42
Springs Mills	1.30	.56	8.37	TRE Corp.	1.71	.45	12.37
Square D	.83	.36	6.64	TRW Inc.	.81	.38	6.41
Squibb Corp.	.73	.20	7.95	Taft Broadcasting	1.20	.52	8.10
Staley Mfg.	1.12	.27	10.56	Talley Inds.	1.01	.31	8.78
Stanadyne, Inc.	.93	.26	8.86	Tampax	.61	.18	7.03
Stand Brands Paint	.91	.31	7.87	Tandem Comp. (3)	1.51	.47	11.71
Standard Motor Prod.	1.50	.47	10.60	Tandy Corp.	1.47	.39	11.34
Standard Oil (Cal.)	.39	.07	7.21	Tandycrafts (3)	1.20	.29	12.01
Standard Oil (Ind.)	.46	.08	7.98	Technicolor	1.27	.24	12.51
Standard Oil (Ohio)	.79	.15	9.79	Tektronix Inc.	.86	.32	7.36
Standard Pacific	1.34	.25	12.93	Telecom Corp. (2)	1.83	.40	15.71
Standard Register	.71	.32	6.05	Teledyne	1.26	.41	9.54
Standex Int'l. Corp.	.93	.34	7.68	Telex Corp.	2.26	.48	15.78
Stanley Works	1.05	.39	8.10	Tenneco Inc.	.76	.38	5.95
Stanwood Corp.	.63	.05	13.39	Teradyne, Inc.	1.70	.50	11.57
Sta-Rite Industries	1.27	.32	10.82	Tesoro Petroleum	1.49	.27	13.86
Starrett (L S) Co.	.77	.23	7.69	Texaco Canada (2)	.85	.11	13.57
Stauffer Chemical	1.10	.39	8.56	Texaco Inc.	.29	.07	5.47
Stelco Inc. 'A'	.59	.28	5.46	Texas Air Corp. (2)	1.69	.44	13.58
Sterchi Bros. Stores	.74	.35	6.01	Texas Commerce Bkshr.	.65	.38	5.12
Sterling Bancorp.	.86	.28	7.84	Texas Eastern Corp.	.93	.31	8.11
Sterling Drug	.75	.23	7.47	Texas Gas Trans.	.98	.41	7.37
Sterndent	.67	.07	12.25	Texas Industries	1.36	.44	9.88
Stevens J P	.99	.53	6.57	Texas Instruments	.98	.43	7.22
Stewart-Warner	1.10	.56	7.15	Texas Int'l. Co.	1.50	.22	15.42
Stokely-Van Camp	.73	.15	9.10	Texas New Mexico (3)	.24	.04	6.86
Stone Container	1.40	.26	13.18	Texas Oil & Gas	.94	.23	9.47
Stone & Webster	.78	.21	8.28	Texas Pac Land	.85	.16	10.40
Stop & Shop Cos.	.60	.20	6.55	Texas Utilities	.29	.08	4.91
Storage Technology	1.35	.27	12.70	Texfi Ind.	1.34	.13	17.82
Storer Broadcasting	1.16	.42	8.64	Textron Inc.	1.12	.59	7.04
Stride Rite Corp.	.72	.19	7.99	Thackeray Corp.	1.41	.26	13.29
Suave Shoe Corp.	1.58	.38	12.33	Thermo Electron (2)	1.37	.53	10.05
Suburban Propane Gas	.78	.19	8.72	Thiokol Corp.	1.25	.51	8.46
Sullair Corp. (3)	1.47	.22	18.17	Thomas & Betts Corp.	.84	.36	6.73
Sun Banks of Fla.	1.14	.48	7.96	Thomas Industries	1.32	.39	10.23
Sunbeam	.90	.23	9.01	Thrifty Corp.	1.29	.39	10.01
Sun Chemical	1.28	.41	9.66	Tidewater Inc.	1.22	.33	10.29
Sun Company	.90	.23	8.98	Tiger Int'l. Inc.	1.50	.45	10.87
Sundstrand Corp.	1.22	.48	8.47	Time Inc.	1.11	.51	7.49
Sun Electric	1.42	.33	11.94	Times Mirror Co.	1.10	.58	6.96
Sunshine Mining	1.19	.16	14.23	Timken Co.	.76	.37	6.03
Super Food Serv. (3)	.57	.18	7.44	Todd Shipyards Corp.	1.51	.33	12.68
Superior Electric	.98	.20	10.42	Tokheim Corp. (1)	1.46	.52	10.28
Superior Oil Co.	.83	.22	8.64	Toledo Edison	.31	.11	4.49
Supermarkets Gen'l.	1.12	.43	8.24	Tonka Corp.	1.70	.44	12.39
Superscope, Inc.	1.72	.37	13.71	Tootsie Roll Inds.	.77	.21	8.08
Super Valu Stores	.96	.44	7.04	Toro Co.	1.34	.34	11.10
Supron Energy	1.12	.20	12.23	Tosco Corp.	1.45	.22	15.12
Swank Inc.	.93	.35	7.68	Total Petroleum	1.09	.19	12.22
Sybron Corp.	.87	.35	7.18	Town & Country M H	1.73	.39	13.36
Syntex	1.16	.47	8.14	Toys-R-Us (2)	1.01	.31	9.71
Sysco Corp.	1.10	.50	8.39	Tracor Inc.	1.77	.57	11.34

EXHIBIT 4-4 Table of Value Line Index components with beta, R^2, and standard deviation. (Reprinted with permission of the Kansas City Board of Trade.) (*Continued*)

Stock	Regression Est. of Beta	R^2	Sta. Deviation of Price (%)	Stock	Regression Est. of Beta	R^2	Sta. Deviation of Price (%)
Trane Co.	1.25	.56	8.08	United Technologies	1.12	.48	7.79
Transamerica	1.04	.52	6.96	United Telecomm.	.45	.15	5.64
Transamerica Rlty. In.	1.40	.39	10.76	Unit. Va. Bankshs. (2)	.55	.27	5.65
Transco Cos. Inc.	.92	.28	8.39	Unitrode	1.46	.43	10.72
Transcon Inc. Calif.	1.45	.36	11.73	Univar Corp.	.99	.26	9.33
Transohio Fin'l.	1.27	.39	9.89	Universal Food	.25	.03	7.38
Transway Int'l. Corp.	.82	.38	6.40	Universal Leaf Tob.	.68	.19	7.62
Trans World Corp.	2.04	.47	14.40	Upjohn Co.	.78	.28	7.19
Travelers Corp.	.85	.39	6.57	USLIFE Corp.	1.17	.46	8.27
Triangle Industries	1.12	.40	8.51	Utah Power & Lt.	.38	.14	4.80
Triangle Pacific	1.71	.50	11.70	VF Corp.	.69	.26	6.59
Tri-Continental	.85	.58	5.35	Valero Energy (3)	1.54	.27	15.83
Trinity Industries	1.35	.32	11.58	Valley Inds.	1.60	.40	12.18
Tri South Investment	.83	.04	19.73	Valley Nat'l. Corp.	.83	.34	6.86
Triton Group	.81	.05	17.48	Varian Associates	1.22	.42	9.17
Tubos De Acero	1.45	.22	16.16	Varo Inc.	1.86	.50	12.65
Tucson Elec. & Pwr.	.30	.08	5.03	Veeco Instr. (3)	1.89	.50	14.34
Tyco Laboratories	1.73	.53	11.50	Vendo	1.72	.47	12.12
Tyler Corp.	1.04	.28	9.60	Vermont America (1)	.98	.32	8.97
Tymshare, Inc.	1.63	.47	11.57	Vernitron (2)	1.67	.48	12.57
Tyson Foods (1)	1.15	.25	12.00	Viacom Int'l.	1.06	.31	9.19
UAL, Inc.	1.42	.38	11.12	Victoria Station	1.30	.22	13.35
UGI Corp.	.85	.28	7.84	Va. Electric & Pwr.	.34	.11	4.95
UMC Industries Inc.	.87	.32	7.45	Va. Nat'l. Banks	.94	.42	6.95
UNC Resources	1.37	.26	13.07	Vista Resources	1.00	.34	8.26
UNR Industries	1.18	.47	8.28	Vornado Inc.	1.70	.32	14.45
USF&G Corp.	.86	.34	7.08	Vulcan Materials	.56	.19	6.17
Unilever Plc.	.32	.04	7.66	Wachovia Corp.	.60	.22	6.23
Unilever Nv. NY.	.35	.16	4.21	Wachovia Realty Inv.	1.55	.36	12.50
Union Camp Corp.	.65	.32	5.56	Wackenhut	1.54	.38	12.09
Union Carbide	.85	.50	5.84	Wainoco Oil Co. (3)	.90	.11	14.96
Union Corp.	1.74	.45	12.56	Walgreen Co.	1.17	.51	7.90
Union Electric	.45	.22	4.63	Wallace Comp. Serv.	.89	.34	7.40
Union Oil (Cal.)	.74	.16	8.87	Wal Mart Stores	1.17	.44	8.52
Union Pacific	.91	.23	9.11	Walter (Jim) Corp.	.99	.41	7.45
Uniroyal Inc.	1.47	.43	10.80	Wang Labs "B"	1.59	.36	12.83
United Asbestos	.81	.03	24.26	Warnaco Inc.	1.28	.32	11.04
United Brands	1.50	.41	11.36	Warner Commun.	1.11	.38	8.66
United Energy Res.	.89	.26	8.49	Warner-Lambert	.84	.37	6.72
United Illuminating	.40	.11	5.68	Washington Gas Lt.	.49	.08	8.43
United Industrial	1.40	.40	10.71	Washington Nat'l. Cor.	1.11	.26	10.50
United Inns	1.81	.58	11.55	Washington Post "B"	.81	.35	6.56
United Jersey Banks	.57	.26	5.39	Washington Water Pwr.	.34	.13	4.61
United Mercants	.98	.06	19.21	Waste Management	1.16	.52	7.80
U.S. Bancorp	.58	.23	5.80	Watkins-Johnson	1.42	.43	10.50
U.S. & Foreign Secur.	.92	.67	5.42	Wayne-Gossard	1.13	.27	10.49
U.S. Air, Inc.	1.58	.31	13.81	Wean United	1.33	.42	9.99
U.S. Gypsum	.96	.47	6.79	Webb (Del E) Corp.	1.80	.24	17.80
U.S. Home Corp.	1.73	.48	12.15	Weis Markets	.36	.15	4.49
U.S. Industries	.99	.26	9.32	Wells Fargo & Co.	.83	.32	7.10
U.S. Leasing Int'l.	1.27	.48	8.81	Wells Fargo Mtg. Eq.	.74	.23	7.41
U.S. Shoe	1.04	.31	8.99	Wendy's Int'l.	1.48	.31	12.87
U.S. Steel	.88	.27	8.25	Westburne Int'l. (3)	1.08	.30	10.95
U.S. Surgical	1.38	.42	10.27	Westcoast Trans.	.60	.24	5.96
U.S. Tobacco	.55	.23	5.57	Western Air Lines	1.70	.49	11.70

Stock	Regression Est. of Beta	R²	Std. Deviation of Price (%)	Stock	Regression Est. of Beta	R²	Std. Deviation of Price (%)
Western Co. No. Am.	1.58	.43	11.68	Wolverine World Wide	1.25	.31	10.81
Western Deep Lev.	.94	.13	12.43	Wometco Enterprises	1.39	.40	10.59
Western Holdings	.56	.04	13.42	Woods Petroleum	1.37	.34	11.39
Western Pacific Ind.	.96	.16	11.61	Woodward & Lothrop	.42	.09	6.93
Western Union	.91	.25	8.79	Woolworth F W	.84	.29	7.56
Westinghouse Elec.	1.11	.48	7.72	World Airways	1.72	.26	16.18
Westmoreland Coal	.97	.20	10.40	Worthington Ind. (3)	.80	.22	9.19
West Pt. Pepperell	.86	.42	6.37	Wrigley Wm. Jr.	.48	.16	5.80
Westvaco Corp.	.91	.42	6.78	Wurlitzer Co.	1.45	.21	15.29
Wetterau Inc.	.83	.21	9.06	Wyle Labs. (1)	1.85	.63	12.02
Weyerhaeuser	1.16	.52	7.76	Wyly Corp.	1.94	.27	17.92
Wheelabrator-Frye	1.13	.45	8.19	Wyman Gordon (2)	1.39	.57	9.89
Wheeling-Pitts Steel	1.61	.39	12.46	Wynn's Int'l. (3)	1.18	.21	14.33
Whirlpool Corp.	.86	.33	7.17	Xerox Corp.	.92	.48	6.40
White Consol, Ind.	1.00	.42	7.41	Xtra Corp.	1.95	.55	12.71
Whittaker Corp.	1.75	.47	12.28	Yellow Freight	.84	.19	9.42
Wickes Cos.	1.25	.50	8.55	Zale	.98	.33	8.27
WICOR Inc.	.39	.15	5.00	Zapata Corp.	1.47	.36	11.84
Wieboldt Stores	.77	.11	11.29	Zayre Corp.	1.61	.50	11.04
Willamette Ind.	1.05	.38	8.18	Zenith Radio	1.51	.43	11.18
Williamhouse Reg. (3)	1.15	.52	9.26	Zimmer Homes	1.73	.41	13.17
Williams Cos.	1.12	.34	9.23	Zions Utah Bancorp.	.65	.19	7.30
Wilshire Oil of Texas	1.51	.47	10.72	Zurn Inds.	1.25	.43	9.25
Winn-Dixie Stores	.28	.08	4.72				
Winnebago	1.95	.32	16.72				
Winter (Jack)	.74	.25	7.10				
Wisconsin Elect. Pwr.	.24	.06	5.03				
Wisconsin Pwr. & Lt.	.14	.02	5.21				
Wisconsin Pub. Ser.	.35	.10	5.39				
Witco Chemical	1.11	.54	7.30				

beta ranges of individual stocks versus the Value Line Index. It is also a list of those stocks that are in the Value Line Index. It can be seen that the range is from approximately 0.00 to 2.50. The vast majority of stocks lie somewhere between .50 and 1.50. This implies that the market is a major determinant of individual price performance of stocks. This information can be used profitably by investors in their investment portfolios.

Another important consideration is the volatility of the individual stock. One measure of the volatility of the stock price is the standard deviation. The standard deviation is a statistical concept that measures the distribution around an average point. The concept is less important than the application. A stock that had no price changes and did not vary would show a standard deviation equal to zero. The higher the standard deviation, the greater the volatility of the stock. Thus, a stock with a standard deviation of 20.00 would have more volatility than a stock with a standard deviation of 15.00. Exhibit 4-5 shows the standard deviations of the stocks within the Value Line Index grouped by each 10 percent of the total. It can be seen that the

---

EXHIBIT 4-5 Decile ratings—standard deviations of VLA.
(Reprinted with permission of the Kansas City Board of Trade.)

INDIVIDUAL STOCK PRICES (IN PERCENT) MONTHLY DATA, JANUARY 1977-DECEMBER 1981

STANDARD DEVIATION OF VLA = 4.839

Decile	Number of Stocks	Standard Deviations		
I	168	25.56	—	13.56
II	168	13.51	—	11.80
III	168	11.77	—	10.62
IV	168	10.61	—	9.60
V	169	9.59	—	8.82
VI	169	8.81	—	8.06
VII	169	8.05	—	7.36
VIII	167	7.35	—	6.66
IX	169	6.65	—	5.57
X	168	5.56	—	3.45
	1683			

average is around 8.80 and that the range is from 3.45 to 25.56. It is worth noting that the standard deviation for the Value Line Index itself is 4.839 percent. For the period in the study, 96 percent of the individual stocks comprising the Value Line Index were more volatile than the index itself. This is to be expected because an average of all those stocks should have less volatility than each individual component. This is because some stocks may be going in opposite directions and may dampen the effects of the individual movements.

A final statistic to keep in mind is the r^2 of the stock. The r^2 is another statistical construct, which is an estimate of the proportion of return variability explained by the market factor as opposed to the variability due to income or yield. This is similar to beta but from a slightly different perspective. For example, ACF Industries has a beta of .98 and an r^2 of .54, while Allright Auto Parts has exactly the same beta of .98, but an r^2 of .28. This basically means that their volatility compared to that of the market is very similar but that the proportion of the return gained by investing in that particular stock is significantly different. Over 50 percent of the return of investing in ACF is attributable to the market as a whole, while less than 30 percent of Allright Auto Parts is derived from the market. Exhibit 4-4 lists the Value Line stocks and their estimated beta, r^2's, and standard deviations.

To determine the exact relationship of a portfolio with the stock indexes, it is necessary to use the three statistics outlined above. In general, though, it is necessary to use only the beta statistic. The first step is to compute the beta for your portfolio. This is done by weighting the portfolio by multiplying the number of shares of the stock times the beta of that stock. The second step is to add all of the sums just computed and divide by the number of shares. This will give the beta for the individual's portfolio. The closer the value is to 1.00, the closer the portfolio is to matching the market's performance. This does not mean that a shareholder can simply buy one stock with a beta of 1.00 and expect it to track identically with the market as a whole. It should be noted that betas are calculated using monthly price action rather than daily price action. Thus, the betas can oscillate around the long-term-average beta. Diversification of the portfolio beyond one stock will further ensure investors that their portfolios, with a beta of 1.00, will track the market as a whole. If the portfolio has a beta of 1.00, then investors can hedge on a straight dollar-to-dollar basis with the stock indexes over a long run. For example, a portfolio worth $650,000 and having a beta of 1.00 could use 10 stock index futures if each stock index future was worth $65,000.

If the beta of this portfolio is something different than 1.00, then the number of stock index futures can be adjusted. For example, a portfolio of a beta of 1.50 can use significantly fewer stock index futures to hedge as it will get more bang from the buck from any given single point move in the stock market. We will discuss hedge relationships further in a later chapter.

Inter-index Relationships

It is worthwhile to examine the relationship between the various stock indexes on a preliminary basis at this point so that one can see the differences and similarities of the various contracts. Obviously,

---

EXHIBIT 4-6 Major stock market indicators*. (Reprinted with permission of the Kansas City Board of Trade.)

ANNUAL CORRELATION COEFFICIENTS, WEEKLY CLOSE 1962-1980

YEAR	R(VL,DJ)	R(VL,SP)	R(VL,NY)	R(DJ,SP)	R(DJ,NY)	R(SP,NY)
1962	.974	.989	.987	.995	.997	.999
1963	.908	.938	.935	.983	.986	.999
1964	.982	.966	.991	.962	.990	.971
1965	.960	.955	.971	.992	.994	.995
1966	.972	.982	.984	.987	.985	.999
1967	.910	.968	.980	.909	.893	.996
1968	.933	.981	.988	.970	.963	.999
1969	.974	.937	.958	.978	.975	.992
1970	.489	.749	.830	.931	.879	.991
1971	.946	.866	.849	.950	.938	.997
1972	-.134	-.284	-.134	.973	.984	.987
1973	.960	.975	.986	.981	.986	.993
1974	.955	.983	.989	.982	.973	.999
1975	.908	.946	.964	.966	.961	.997
1976	.839	.846	.868	.799	.767	.995
1977	.299	.507	.610	.945	.913	.992
1978	.962	.966	.977	.989	.986	.999
1979	.581	.966	.979	.626	.563	.995
1980	.978	.965	.972	.966	.968	.999

*VL = Value Line Composite Average, DJ = Dow Jones Industrial Average, SP = Standard & Poor's 500 Composite Index, NY = NYSE Composite Index.

the following studies were conducted on the cash indexes rather than on the futures indexes, but the relationships will still hold in the carryover to the futures contracts.

Exhibit 4-6 shows the major stock market indicators—Value Line, Dow Jones Industrials, Standard and Poor's 500, and New York Stock Exchange Composite Index—with their annual correlation coefficients based on the weekly closes from 1962 to 1980. In plain English, this means that the correlation between weekly closes was examined and placed in the table on an annual basis. The correlation coefficients are the same as the r^2 mentioned above. They show the correlation between any two numbers. For example, the top left-hand corner of the table shows that the relationship between the Value Line and the Dow Jones Industrials in 1962 was .974. This means that 97.4 percent of the movement in one index was the same as the other index. Note that in 1972 there is a minus sign between the Value Line Index and the Dow Jones, S & P 500, and NYSE. This means that there was a negative correlation. In other words, the Dow Jones, S & P 500, and NYSE indexes were going in one direction and the Value Line was going in an opposite direction. A closer study of Exhibit 4-6 shows that the correlation between the S & P 500 and NYSE is very high. This is to be expected as they are both capitalization-weighted indexes. Five hundred of the largest companies represented by the S & P 500 are the largest components of the NYSE index. The Dow Jones tends to be fairly well correlated with the S & P 500 and NYSE indexes because it is a simple average, but this tends to give a result fairly similar to that of the capitalization technique. The Dow Jones Average, with 30 of the largest companies, tends to be correlated with the S & P 500 rather than with the Value Line, which tends to accentuate the secondary stocks. This accentuation of secondary stocks and the different styles of averaging make the Value Line a significantly different animal. The year 1972 is the most dramatic illustration of this difference. We will examine closely in a subsequent chapter how these differences can be capitalized on, but let it be reiterated that because the Value Line focuses mainly on percentage changes and secondary stocks, it is almost a momentum indicator for the other indexes. Exhibit 4-7 shows a comparison of the major stock market indicators with the cyclical percentage changes at key periods from 1962 to 1980. This table shows that there are occasionally times when the major indexes move in opposite directions. Once again, the period from April 1972 to January 1976 shows the Value Line turning down but the other three indexes moving up. The period from February 1976 to March 1978 shows the Value Line higher but the other three indexes lower.

EXHIBIT 4-7 Comparison of cyclical percentage changes.
(Reprinted with permission of the Kansas City Board of Trade.)

MAJOR STOCK MARKET INDICATORS, 1962-1980*

Cycle Period	VLA	NYSE	S&P	DJIA
6/62- 2/66	82.5%	80.5%	78.1%	83.4%
2/66-10/66	-24.7	-22.7	-22.7	-24.7
10/66-10/67	47.2	37.3	32.9	24.8
10/67- 3/68	-10.7	- 9.3	- 9.1	-11.1
3/68-12/68	35.4	24.3	21.7	18.8
12/68- 7/70	-54.1	-35.0	-32.2	-29.8
7/70- 4/71	43.6	44.5	42.6	36.7
4/71-11/71	-20.3	-11.7	-11.6	-13.3
4/71- 4/72	26.8	21.2	19.5	18.5
4/72- 1/73	- 7.6	6.7	9.1	8.2
1/73-12/74	-58.9	-45.6	-44.0	-42.5
12/74- 2/76	87.7	54.4	52.1	64.0
2/76- 3/78	1.2	-10.9	-14.3	-24.3
3/78- 9/78	31.6	23.8	22.1	21.5
9/78-12/78	-17.8	-11.0	-10.0	-11.3
12/78-10/79	27.8	18.2	15.8	11.5
10/79-11/79	-11.6	- 8.9	- 8.8	-10.2
11/79- 2/80	18.3	17.0	16.2	11.1
2/80- 3/80	-20.1	-15.9	-14.6	-13.2
3/80-12/80	37.9	37.8	35.6	24.3

*Based on week's end closing values.

Exhibit 4-8 shows how the three indexes correlate with each other and with various sectors of the market. This correlation can be a useful aid depending on the structure of the portfolio and your expectations for the future in the business and credit cycle. For example, if the trader believes that consumer nondurables are the best sector to invest in, then he or she would be more likely to invest in the Value Line than in the S & P 500 or NYSE indexes. Conversely, technology issues are more highly correlated with the S & P 500 than with the NYSE or the Value Line.

A major source of difference is the stocks that are included in the index. The stocks included in the Value Line Index are listed in Exhibit 4-4 with their r² and beta. Traders should use this table when

EXHIBIT 4-8   Correlation to sectors (r^2) (Wilshire Associates).

	S&P500	NYSE	V L
CONSUMER NON-DURABLES	89	88	94
CONSUMER DURABLES	79	75	77
MATERIALS & SERVICES	88	88	94
RAW MATERIALS	86	87	92
TECHNOLOGY	89	86	84
ENERGY	86	84	72
TRANSPORTATION	88	86	86
UTILITIES	72	74	72
FINANCE	77	77	82

trying to find r^2s and betas for portfolios. There are no weightings listed in this table because stocks in the Value Line Index are weighted by price change, not market capitalization. Exhibit 4-11 is the S & P 500. This lists all of the stocks in the S & P 500 as of December 31, 1982. The market value and weighting in the index are included. The exhibit also shows the beta in relation to the S & P 500. Hedgers can use this beta or the beta in Exhibit 4-4 for hedging pur-

EXHIBIT 4-9   The 10 most heavily weighted groups*
(Standard & Poor's Corporation).

Group	% of S&P 500
1. Office & business equipment	7.77
2. Oil (integrated international)	6.87
3. Oil (integrated domestic)	6.03
4. Drugs	4.37
5. Electric companies	4.36
6. Foods	3.23
7. Electronic major cos.	2.63
8. Automobiles	2.53
9. Oil well equip. & services	2.36
10. Chemicals	2.22

*Excluding miscellaneous; as of December 31, 1982.

EXHIBIT 4-10 Cumulative market value of stocks comprising the S & P 100 Index and percentage of total S & P 100 (Standard & Poor's Corporation).

Companies on the S&P 100 Stock Index	Market Value* (in millions)	% of 100	Cumulative %
1. American Tel. & Tel.	61919.199	12.15	12.15
2. International Bus. Mach.	59025.409	11.58	23.73
3. Exxon Corp.	26189.139	5.14	28.87
4. General Electric	23459.432	4.60	33.47
5. General Motors	19447.035	3.82	37.29
6. Eastman Kodak	13851.846	2.72	40.01
7. Schlumberger	13231.192	2.60	42.61
8. Standard Oil (Indiana)	11813.119	2.32	44.93
9. Mobil Corp.	11013.215	2.16	47.09
10. Atlantic Richfield	10784.124	2.12	49.21
11. Sears, Roebuck	10039.704	1.97	51.18
12. Hewlett-Packard	9898.063	1.94	53.12
13. DuPont (E.I.)	9453.040	1.86	54.98
14. Johnson & Johnson	9047.259	1.78	56.76
15. Minn. Min. & Mfg.	8834.802	1.73	58.49
16. Coca-Cola	6784.200	1.33	59.82
17. Digital Equipment	6730.791	1.32	61.14
18. Merck & Co.	6343.442	1.24	62.38
19. American Express	6264.522	1.23	63.61
20. Tandy Corp.	5764.008	1.13	64.74
21. Dow Chemical	5573.303	1.09	65.83
22. R.J. Reynolds	5506.746	1.08	66.91
23. Ford Motors	4777.428	.94	67.85
24. Weyerhaeuser	4657.035	.91	68.76
25. Bristol-Myers	4635.213	.91	69.67
26. Citicorp	4451.828	.87	70.54
27. International Tel. & Tel.	4164.300	.82	71.36
28. Texas Instruments	4158.704	.82	72.18
29. Raytheon Co.	4053.232	.80	72.98
30. Halliburton	4044.035	.79	73.77
31. Superior Oil	3916.412	.77	74.54
32. Rockwell-International	3637.883	.71	75.25
33. Commonwealth Edison	3624.411	.71	75.96
34. McDonald's	3539.823	.69	76.65
35. Boeing	3511.533	.69	77.34
36. Monsanto	3394.590	.67	78.01
37. Baxter Travenol Labs	3373.612	.66	78.67
38. United Technologies	3315.723	.65	79.32
39. K mart	3283.451	.64	79.96
40. Norfolk Southern	3281.189	.64	80.60
41. Amer. Electric Power	3258.546	.64	81.24
42. PepsiCo	3285.558	.63	81.87
43. Xerox	3081.435	.60	82.47
44. Teledyne	3062.549	.60	83.07
45. CIGNA Corp.	2962.811	.58	83.65
46. BankAmerica	2915.376	.57	84.22
47. Amer. Hospital Supply	2913.028	.57	84.79
48. AMP	2639.312	.52	85.31
49. Aluminum Co. of Amer.	2593.739	.51	85.82
50. Northern Telecom Ltd.	2585.368	.51	86.33

*As of 1/31/83.

Companies on the S&P 100 Stock Index	Market Value* (in millions)	% of 100	Cumulative %
51. NCR Corp.	2505.838	.49	86.82
52. International Paper	2444.528	.48	87.30
53. Avon Products	2405.333	.47	87.77
54. Merrill Lynch	2393.638	.47	88.24
55. Humana, Inc.	2378.703	.47	88.71
56. Burlington Northern	2355.525	.46	89.17
57. Litton Industries	2280.398	.45	89.62
58. Disney Productions	2242.653	.44	90.06
59. Squibb Corp.	2224.244	.44	90.50
60. General Dynamics	2056.446	.40	90.90
61. Honeywell, Inc.	2004.517	.39	91.29
62. General Foods	1981.044	.39	91.68
63. Ralston Purina	1928.120	.38	92.06
64. Warner Communications	1900.892	.37	92.43
65. Burroughs Corp.	1867.300	.37	92.80
66. Delta Airlines	1829.052	.36	93.16
67. Fluor Corp.	1811.034	.36	93.52
68. Control Data	1667.061	.33	93.85
69. Sperry Corp.	1654.554	.32	94.17
70. Colgate-Palmolive	1618.572	.32	94.49
71. RCA Corp.	1603.589	.31	94.80
72. Upjohn Co.	1531.229	.30	95.10
73. Holiday Inns	1384.887	.27	95.37
74. Gulf & Western Ind.	1313.624	.26	95.63
75. Champion International	1298.241	.25	95.88
76. Tektronix, Inc.	1280.801	.25	96.13
77. Harris Corp.	1270.763	.25	96.38
78. Safeway Stores	1181.839	.23	96.61
79. Hughes Tool	1165.973	.23	96.84
80. Revlon, Inc.	1183.037	.22	97.06
81. Homestake Mining	1051.849	.21	97.27
82. Northwest Airlines	1023.482	.20	97.47
83. International Minerals	1011.151	.20	97.67
84. UAL, Inc.	1005.958	.20	97.87
85. Boise Cascade	993.979	.20	98.07
86. International Flavors	896.087	.18	98.25
87. Polaroid Corp.	893.826	.18	98.43
88. Black & Decker	879.005	.17	98.60
89. Bethlehem Steel	862.720	.17	98.77
90. Esmark, Inc.	829.742	.16	98.93
91. Storage Technology	765.811	.15	99.08
92. Northwest Industries	746.744	.15	99.23
93. Owens-Illinois	734.800	.14	99.37
94. National Semiconductor	675.271	.13	99.50
95. Great Western Financial	628.025	.12	99.62
96. Williams Co.	602.883	.12	99.74
97. Datapoint	446.806	.09	99.83
98. Brunswick Corp.	301.626	.06	99.89
99. Computer Sciences	286.724	.06	99.95
100. Skyline	252.383	.05	100.00
	509744.021		

*As of 1/31/83.

poses depending on which index they intend to hedge. The weightings allow analysts to gauge the effect on the index of projected price changes in individual stocks or industries. In addition, hedgers and arbitrageurs may want to construct hedgeable portfolios with betas of 1.00 and a very large weighting within the index.

Exhibit 4-9 shows the 10 most heavily weighted groups, excluding miscellaneous, in the S & P 500 as of December 31, 1982. These weightings can be used in the same manner suggested for the weightings of the individual stocks.

Exhibit 4-10 highlights the stocks in the S & P 100, their weightings within the index, and the cumulative weightings as of January 31, 1983. Note that the top 11 companies account for over 50 percent of the weighting. Over 75 percent of the weighting comes from the top 32 companies. Thus, relatively few companies account for a relatively large amount of the index. This can simplify the analysis of components of the index.

Exhibit 4-11 highlights the stocks in the S & P 500, their weightings within the index, and their beta.

EXHIBIT 4-11 S & P 500 in alphabetical order (Standard & Poor's Corporation).

Ticker	Company	Market value (mil. $)	% of 500	*Beta
ACF	ACF Inds.	258.365	.02	1.11
AMF	AMF, Inc.	382.749	.03	0.94
AMP	AMP Inc.	2446.301	.27	.99
AMR	AMR Corp.	920.576	.08	1.40
ARA	ARA Services	411.054	.05	.76
ASA	ASA Ltd.	684.000	.06	1.15
AR	ASARCO Inc.	759.667	.10	1.61
ABT	Abbott Labs	4720.486	.45	0.86
AMT	Acme-Cleveland Corp.	78.989	.01	1.14
AET	Aetna Life & Casualty	3420.960	.35	0.66
AHM	Ahmanson (H. F.) & Co.	685.425	.07	1.84
ACV	Alberto-Culver	70.135	.01	1.64
AL	Alcan Aluminium	2341.584	.25	1.28
ALD	Allied Corp.	1065.105	.20	1.25
ALS	Allied Stores	793.763	.08	0.69
AH	Allis-Chalmers	122.655	.02	1.03
AA	Alum. Co. of America	2445.807	.25	1.01
AMX	Amax Inc.	1382.756	.16	1.72
AMB	American Brands Inc.	2528.080	.23	.52
ABC	American Broadcasting	1669.396	.16	.68

Ticker	Company	Market value (mil. $)	% of 500	*Beta
AC	American Can	574.151	.07	.70
ACY	American Cyanamid	1677.973	.19	1.00
AEP	American Elec. Pwr.	2985.248	.27	.38
AXP	American Express	6168.514	.75	.98
AGC	American General	1222.015	.13	1.11
AHP	American Home Products	6958.267	.57	.52
AHS	American Hospital	2949.555	.26	1.10
AIGR	American Int'l Group	4555.377	.45	.88
AMI	American Medical Int'l	1204.523	.12	1.84
AMO	American Motors Corp.	377.618	.05	1.11
ANR	American Natural Resources	795.223	.08	1.06
AST	American Standard	808.337	.08	1.01
ASC	American Stores	638.820	.07	.78
T	American Tel. & Tel.	52993.909	4.99	.19
ASR	Amstar Corp.	227.808	.02	1.02
AD	Amsted Inds.	254.270	.03	1.34
BUD	Anheuser-Busch	3113.415	.26	.64
AAPL	Apple Computer	1695.197	.28	N.A.
ADM	Archer-Daniels Midland	1640.687	.16	1.50
AS	Armco Inc.	1036.423	.10	1.34
ACK	Armstrong World	612.266	.06	1.07
DG	Assoc. Dry Goods	602.308	.06	.82
ARC	Atlantic Richfield	10263.264	.94	1.14
AUD	Automatic Data Processing Inc.	1262.477	.11	.82
AVP	Avon Products	1987.418	.20	.85
BKO	Baker International	1558.800	.11	1.74
BGE	Baltimore Gas & Elec.	1059.322	.10	.35
BAC	BankAmerica Corp	2970.732	.29	.57
BT	Bankers Trust N.Y.	1034.562	.11	.86
BCR	Bard (C. R.) Inc.	447.276	.05	1.21
BSET	Bassett Furniture	270.880	.03	1.05
BAX	Baxter Travenol Labs	3426.740	.32	.88
BRY	Beatrice Foods	2326.030	.23	.56
BDX	Becton, Dickinson	866.362	.08	1.04
BKI	Beker Inds.	70.986	.01	1.70
BMS	Bemis Company	122.710	.01	.78
BX	Bendix Corp.	1498.230	.15	.93
BNL	Beneficial Corp.	538.447	.05	.92
BS	Bethlehem Steel	846.339	.09	1.39
BDK	Black & Decker	763.208	.08	1.27
BBL	Blue Bell	397.248	.04	.62
BA	Boeing Company	3270.191	.32	1.66
BCC	Boise Cascade	1044.012	.10	1.80
BN	Borden, Inc.	1358.170	.13	.44

EXHIBIT 4-11   S & P 500 in alphabetical order (Standard & Poor's Corporation). (*Continued*)

Ticker	Company	Market value (mil. $)	% of 500	*Beta
BR	Borg-Warner	1569.692	.15	1.01
BGG	Briggs & Stratton	520.704	.04	.80
BMY	Bristol-Myers	4517.653	.45	.84
BU	Brooklyn Union Gas	248.022	.02	.45
BNS	Brown & Sharpe Co.	35.399	.00	1.10
BG	Brown Group	593.488	.07	.74
BFDB	Brown-Forman Distillers	903.010	.08	1.11
BFI	Browning-Ferris Ind.	1032.272	.12	1.57
BC	Brunswick Corp.	290.025	.04	1.06
BY	Bucyrus-Erie	298.569	.03	.98
BUR	Burlington Inds.	796.712	.08	.87
BNI	Burlington Northern	1966.794	.27	2.08
BGH	Burroughs Corp	1756.840	.19	1.07
CBS	CBS Inc.	1671.984	.16	.99
CI	Cigna Corp.	3329.635	.31	1.02
CAF	CNA Financial	847.327	.09	1.51
CPC	CPC Int'l.	2014.817	.16	.67
CSX	CSX Corp.	2148.579	.25	N.A.
CRK	Campbell Red Lake Mines	1343.832	.13	1.28
CPB	Campbell Soup	1561.206	.13	.35
CCB	Capital Cities Communications	1573.667	.16	1.02
CPH	Capital Holding	926.969	.08	.71
CMK	Carnation Co.	1615.214	.15	.75
CHH	Carter Hawley Hale	482.031	.06	.88
CAT	Caterpillar Tractor	3535.414	.37	1.10
CZ	Celanese Corp.	704.724	.08	.88
CNT	Centel Corp.	1009.798	.09	.40
CTX	Centex Corp.	565.513	.06	2.25
CSR	Central & So. West	1499.080	.13	.34
CHA	Champion International	1305.110	.12	1.54
CHM	Champion Spark Plug	407.362	.04	1.03
CMB	Chase Manhattan	1654.289	.16	.92
CHL	Chemical N.Y.	1021.491	.11	.72
CBM	Chesebrough-Pond's	1577.070	.12	.69
CGG	Chicago Pneumatic Tool	65.974	.01	.79
C	Chrysler Corp.	1410.362	.25	1.26
CHUB	Chubb Corp.	610.784	.06	.67
CHU	Church's Fried Chicken	449.998	.04	1.20
CMZ	Cincinnati Milacron	582.280	.06	1.78
FNC	Citicorp	4104.523	.43	1.03
CKL	Clark Equipment	337.626	.04	.90
CLX	Clorox Co.	593.159	.06	1.00
CLU	Cluett, Peabody & Co.	170.595	.02	.96
KO	Coca Cola Co.	7055.568	.60	.56
CLO	Coleco Industries	281.101	.05	2.15

Ticker	Company	Market value (mil. $)	% of 500	*Beta
CLN	Coleman Co.	195.556	.02	.94
CL	Colgate-Palmolive	1608.328	.16	.65
CK	Collins & Aikman	219.258	.03	1.00
CG	Columbia Gas System	1024.592	.09	.61
CSP	Combustion Engr'g.	1081..340	.10	1.51
CWE	Commonwealth Edison	3421.173	.36	.39
CSC	Computer Sciences Corp.	256.543	.02	1.21
COE	Cone Mills	184.938	.02	.80
ED	Consolidated Edison	2628.366	.24	.24
CFD	Consolidated Foods	1318.01	.10	.42
CNF	Consolidated Freightways	671.500	.06	1.27
CNG	Consolidated Natural Gas	947.386	.10	.90
CIC	Continental Corp.	1507.350	.04	.78
CCC	Continental Group	1108.944	.12	1.04
CIL	Continental Ill. Corp.	814.022	.08	.89
CTC	Continental Telecom	1064.394	.13	.50
CDA	Control Data	1379.157	.18	1.67
CBE	Cooper Inds.	1222.688	.11	1.28
ACCOB	Coors (Adolph)	428.897	.06	1.07
GLW	Corning Glass Works	1395.957	.15	1.13
COX	Cox Communications Corp.	1211.535	.12	.76
CR	Crane Company	240.623	.03	1.46
CTCO	Cross & Trecker	249.723	.03	N.A.
CCK	Crown Cork & Seal	412.764	.04	.85
ZB	Crown Zellerbach	788.836	.07	1.35
CUM	Cummins Engine Co., Inc.	411.450	.04	1.18
DCN	Dana Corp.	1263.684	.12	.68
DKI	Dart & Kraft Inc.	3746.539	.32	.51
DGN	Data General	430.811	.05	2.00
DPT	Datapoint	366.930	.04	2.21
DH	Dayton-Hudson	2644.895	.28	.87
DE	Deere & Co.	1996.383	.21	1.11
DAL	Delta Air Lines	1759.469	.14	.97
DEN	Denny's Inc.	477.169	.04	.79
DTE	Detroit Edison	1440.574	.15	.46
DEC	Digital Equipment	5522.700	.52	1.38
DIS	Disney (Walt) Prod.	2100.924	.22	1.13
DM	Dome Mines, Ltd.	1076.397	.13	1.57
DOW	Dow Chemical	5015.972	.54	1.22
DJ	Dow Jones & Co.	2096.965	.27	1.05
DOC	Dr. Pepper	287.383	.03	1.14
DI	Dresser Inds.	1546.921	.13	1.15
DD	DuPont (E. I.)	8478.195	.97	.99
DUK	Duke Power	2183.640	.19	.15
DNB	Dun & Bradstreet	2667.872	.29	.96

EXHIBIT 4-11   S & P 500 in alphabetical order (Standard & Poor's Corporation). (*Continued*)

Ticker	Company	Market value (mil. $)	% of 500	*Beta
ENS	ENSERCH Corp.	1018.381	.10	1.30
EFU	Eastern Gas & Fuel Assoc.	490.931	.04	1.64
EK	Eastman Kodak	13973.710	1.02	.78
ETN	Eaton Corp.	914.496	.10	.93
ECH	Echlin Incorporated	398.736	.03	.91
ECK	Eckerd (Jack) Corp.	919.128	.09	1.13
ELG	El Paso Co.	1127.080	.07	1.31
EDS	Electronic Data Systems	1345.320	.17	1.30
EMR	Emrerson Electric	4149.877	.34	.87
EAF	Emery Air Freight	247.281	.02	1.07
ESM	Esmark Inc.	844.363	.08	1.17
EVY	Evans Products	103.540	.01	1.20
XLO	Ex-Cell-O Corp.	376.324	.04	1.58
XON	Exxon Corp.	25754.464	2.49	.89
FMC	FMC Corp.	1044.481	.11	1.00
FBG	Faberge, Inc.	105.338	.01	1.50
FJQ	Fedders Corp.	41.606	.01	1.51
FDX	Federal Express	1617.388	.14	N.A.
FBO	Federal Paper Board	170.590	.02	1.33
FDS	Federated Dept. Store	2296.397	.23	.57
FIR	Firestone Tire & Rubber	964.072	.09	1.11
FCF	First Charter	532.836	.07	1.58
FNB	First Chicago Corp.	735.440	.09	1.13
I	First Interstate Bancorp	° 1266.891	.14	1.06
FRM	First Miss. Corp.	171.776	.02	1.65
FB	First National Boston	610.537	.06	.80
FPA	First Pennsylvania Corp.	80.535	.01	1.21
FLE	Fleetwood Enterpr.	453.713	.06	1.74
FPL	Florida Pwr. & Lt.	1783.210	.15	.34
FLR	Fluor Corp.	1527.143	.15	1.78
F	Ford Motor	4687.003	.48	.79
FWC	Foster Wheeler	442.771	.04	1.56
FTR	Fruehauf Corp.	346.966	I.04	.61
GTE	G T E Corp.	7166.428	.63	.64
GCI	Gannett Co.	3374.972	.29	.84
GAO	Gen. Amer. Oil Texas	1099.817	.11	1.36
GCN	General Cinema	269.930	.03	1.03
GD	General Dynamics	1785.861	.24	1.47
GE	General Electric	21556.549	1.99	.93
GF	General Foods	2052.258	.19	.62
GRL	General Instrument	1539.913	.13	1.89
GIS	General Mills	2457.487	.24	.32
GM	General Motors	⁻19178.005	1.74	.68
GSX	General Signal	1254.211	.11	.98

Ticker	Company	Market value (mil. $)	% of 500	*Beta
GCO	Genesco Inc.	66.272	.01	1.10
GPC	Genuine Parts	1609.678	.13	.80
GP	Georgia-Pacific	2660.070	.26	1.28
GEB	Gerber Products	329.212	.03	.63
GET	Getty Oil	3924.717	.46	1.28
GS	Gillette Co.	1368.720	.11	.74
GLM	Global Marine	286.334	.03	2.30
GR	Goodrich (B. F.)	567.617	.06	1.34
GT	Goodyear Tire & Rubber	2605.574	.21	.92
GLD	Gould Inc.	1619.625	.14	1.18
GRA	Grace (W. R.) & Co.	1847.756	.20	1.33
GWW	Grainger (W. W.) Inc.	764.248	.07	.93
GAP	Great A & P	308.575	.03	.90
GWF	Great Western Fin'l.	756.405	.06	1.76
GQ	Grumman Corp.	508.603	.06	1.25
GW	Gulf & Western Ind.	1239.617	.17	1.36
GO	Gulf Oil	5215.800	.53	1.05
HAL	Halliburton Co.	4176.868	.34	1.46
HDL	Handleman Co.	84.968	.01	1.20
HBJ	Harcourt Brace/Jov.	164.706	.02	1.18
HRS	Harris Corp.	1164.538	.12	1.34
HSM	Hart Schaffner & Marx	294.076	.03	1.23
GHB	Heileman (G.) Brewing	525.813	.06	.87
HNZ	Heinz (H. J.)	1907.921	.18	.70
HLR	Heller (Walt E.)	274.275	.03	1.43
HPC	Hercules, Inc.	1232.489	.14	1.22
HSY	Hershey Foods	883.340	.07	.43
HWP	Hewlett-Packard	9103.100	.88	1.52
HLT	Hilton Hotels	1193.214	.13	1.62
HIA	Holiday Inns	1380.176	.15	1.55
HM	Homestake Mining	943.258	.10	1.83
HON	Honeywell, Inc.	1901.935	.22	1.25
HCA	Hospital Corp. of America	3244.031	.33	1.25
HI	Household Int'l	1098.388	.11	.80
HD	Hudson Bay Mng./Smelt	135.114	.01	1.08
HT	Hughes Tool Co.	1221.167	.09	1.46
HUM	Humana Inc.	2684.430	.25	1.58
HYST	Hyster Co.	232.943	.03	1.01
ICX	IC Industries	459.515	.06	1.25
ISS	Interco, Inc.	860.954	.09	.77
IDL	Ideal Basic Inds.	257.606	.02	1.37
N	Inco, Ltd.	1059.345	.12	1.18
IR	Ingersoll-Rand	783.009	.08	.98
IAD	Inland Steel Co.	557.778	.06	.93
INTC	Intel Corp.	1722.399	.25	1.38

EXHIBIT 4-11 S & P 500 in alphabetical order (Standard & Poor's Corporation). (*Continued*)

Ticker	Company	Market value (mil. $)	% of 500	*Beta
IFC	Interfirst Co.	1673.579	.10	.89
IK	Interlake, Inc.	157.685	.02	.84
IBM	International Bus. Mach.	57458.362	5.64	.72
IFF	International Flavors/Frag.	1010.384	.09	.58
HR	International Harvester	137.241	.03	.97
IGL	International Minerals/Chem	855.335	.10	1.17
IP	International Paper	2382.952	.24	1.48
ITT	International Tel. & Tel.	4131.250	.44	1.22
INI	Internorth Inc.	1181.976	.12	1.31
JP	Jefferson-Pilot	632.686	.06	.68
JWL	Jewel Cos.	579.650	.05	.73
JWC	Jim Walter Corp.	607.808	.06	1.11
JNJ	Johnson & Johnson	9329.252	.79	.70
JOL	Jonathan Logan	104.019	.01	1.43
JOY	Joy Mfg.	465.975	.04	1.16
KM	K Mart	2785.486	.33	.72
KLU	Kaiser Aluminum & Chem.	657.229	.07	.95
KCC	Kaiser Cement	181.488	.02	1.53
KB	Kaufman & Broad	152.465	.02	2.08
K	Kellogg Co.	2035.002	.17	.60
KMB	Kimberly-Clark	1659.897	.16	.74
KRN	Knight-Ridder News	1601.276	.15	1.19
KR	Kroger Co.	1118.919	.15	.79
LTC	Leaseway Transportation	464.139	.04	.84
LVI	Levi Straus & Co.	1595.671	.17	1.01
LOF	Libby-Owens-Ford	332.820	.03	.78
LLY	Lilly (Eli) & Co.	4368.045	.42	.68
LNC	Lincoln National	938.676	.09	1.01
LIT	Litton Inds.	2064.198	.23	1.37
LCE	Lone Star Inds.	340.563	.03	1.28
LLX	Lousiana Land & Explo.	811.908	.09	1.16
LPX	Lousiana Pacific	921.084	.09	1.55
LST	Lowenstein (M) & Sons	122.671	.01	.83
LKS	Lucky Stores	878.810	.10	.75
MAI	M/A Com. Inc.	907.333	.10	2.28
MCA	MCA, Inc.	1689.944	.14	.84
MCIC	MCI Communications	3555.365	.47	2.02
MGM	MGM/UA Entertainment	329.614	.08	N.A.
MLL	Macmillan Inc.	226.255	.03	1.25
MZ	Macy (R. H.) & Co.	2018.856	.21	.90
MHC	Manufacturers Hanover	1445.178	.14	.63
MHS	Marriott Corp.	1549.841	.16	1.32
ML	Martin Marietta	1561.525	.09	1.75
MDC	Maryland Cup	304.882	.04	1.00

Ticker	Company	Market value (mil. $)	% of 500	*Beta
MAS	Masco Corp.	1487.758	.14	1.63
MNC	Masonite Corp.	196.539	.02	.62
MSE	Massey-Ferguson	162.330	.04	.86
MAT	Mattel, Inc.	277.464	.02	1.39
MA	May Dept. Stores	1370.254	.13	.95
MYG	Maytag Co.	520.053	.06	.64
MDE	McDermott, Inc.	754.790	.07	1.83
MCD	McDonald's Corp.	3622.319	.32	.58
MD	McDonnell Douglas	1609.398	.18	1.53
MGR	McGraw-Edison	661.676	.06	1.32
MHP	McGraw-Hill	1873.650	.19	.95
MEA	Mead Corp.	492.675	.07	1.34
MEL	Mellon National	745.304	.12	.80
MES	Melville Corp.	1836.599	.18	.60
MST	Mercantile Stores	682.462	.08	.61
MRK	Merck & Co.	6260.219	.59	.59
MDP	Meredith Corp.	269.577	.03	1.23
MER	Merrill Lynch	2330.520	.30	2.47
MSA	Mesa Petroleum	785.041	.08	1.72
MET	Metromedia Inc.	997.816	.12	1.01
MSU	Middle So. Util.	2011.059	.20	.35
MB	Milton Bradley	180.981	.02	1.68
MMM	Minn. Min. & Mfg.	8834.802	.86	.79
MOB	Mobil Corp.	10441.774	1.01	1.00
MOH	Mohasco Corp.	106.022	.01	1.08
MMO	Monarch Machine Tool	67.120	.01	1.38
MTC	Monsanto Company	3095.216	.29	1.04
JPM	Morgan (J. P.) & Co.	2637.765	.26	.58
MOT	Motorola Inc.	3321.834	.37	1.24
NCB	NCNB Corp.	413.719	.05	1.27
NCR	NCR Corp.	2271.432	.22	1.46
NL	NL Industries	1134.013	.09	1.56
NB	Nabisco Brands	2454.202	.22	.65
NAC	National Can	211.232	.02	1.32
DR	National Distill. & Chem.	798.219	.08	.95
NG	National Gypsum	432.648	.05	1.45
NME	National Medical Entpr.	1479.000	..16	1.79
NSM	National Semiconductor	514.492	.16	1.92
NS	National Steel	329.235	.04	.85
NES	New England El. Sys.	780.145	.07	.49
NEM	Newmont Mining	1488.025	.14	1.66
NMK	Niagara Mohawk Pwr.	1428.844	.13	.33
NSC	Norfolk Southern Corp.	3429.978	.32	1.24
NC	North American Coal	78.953	.01	1.12
NSP	Northern States Power	900.090	.08	.36

109

EXHIBIT 4-11   S & P 500 in alphabetical order (Standard & Poor's Corporation). (*Continued*)

Ticker	Company	Market value (mil. $)	% of 500	*Beta
NT	Northern Telecom	2466.450	.29	1.29
NWA	Northwest Airlines	1018.067	.09	1.14
NOB	Northwest Bancorp	660.319	.08	.91
NWT	Northwest Inds.	707.311	.07	1.05
NSI	Norton Simon	671.832	.05	.80
OKE	Oneok Inc.	315.240	.03	1.21
OXY	Occidental Petroleum	1881.662	.19	1.51
OEC	Ohio Edison	1310.918	.14	.49
OM	Outboard Marine	249.307	.03	1.34
OVT	Overnite Transportation	230.282	.03	1.26
OCF	Owens-Corning Fiberglas	1149.525	.10	1.23
OI	Owens-Illinois	758.180	.08	1.13
PCAR	Paccar Inc.	745.843	.07	1.35
PPG	PPG, Inc.	1791.482	.19	.96
PABT	Pabst Brewing	171.906	.01	1.25
PCG	Pacific Gas & Elec.	3948.638	.39	.18
PLT	Pacific Lighting	768.594	.08	.26
PN	Pan Amer. World Airways	297.123	.04	1.34
PEL	Panhandle Eastern	1075.200	.10	1.35
PBD	Peabody Int'l	89.160	.01	1.34
JCP	Penney (J. C.)	3529.488	.37	.52
PGL	Peoples Energy	300.239	.02	1.12
PEP	Pepsico, Inc.	3325.072	.28	.55
PKN	Perkin-Elmer	1214.535	.10	1.64
PFE	Pfizer, Inc.	5178.023	.51	.68
PD	Phelps Dodge	611.409	.06	1.93
PSB	Phibro Salomon Inc.	3309.570	.42	1.87
PE	Philadelphia Elec.	2083.978	.20	.41
MO	Philip Morris	7546.380	.62	.79
P	Phillips Petroleum	4995.507	.44	1.17
PSY	Pillsbury Co.	1085.300	.11	.75
PBI	Pitney-Bowes	741.836	.09	1.01
PCO	Pittston Company	521.001	.05	1.61
PRD	Polaroid Corp.	781.614	.08	1.13
PCH	Potlatch Corp.	562.790	.05	1.48
PG	Procter & Gamble	9779.630	.76	.60
PEG	Public Serv. Elec. & Gas	2181.594	.19	.46
PIN	Public Serv. Indiana	1180.592	.11	.30
OAT	Quaker Oats	842.579	.08	.68
RCA	RCA Corp.	1697.918	.19	1.04
RM	Rolm Corp.	891.373	.11	2.08
RAL	Ralston Purina	1775.900	.19	.71
RAM	Ramada Inns	139.497	.03	1.23
RTN	Raytheon Co.	3768.979	.37	1.37

Ticker	Company	Market value (mil. $)	% of 500	*Beta
RB	Reading & Bates	375.165	.04	2.41
RE	Redman Inds.	191.069	.02	1.77
RS	Republic Steel	252.859	.03	.82
RDS	Revco D. S. Inc.	830.250	.08	.89
REV	Revlon, Inc.	1042.566	.11	1.04
REX	Rexnord, Inc.	230.472	.03	1.01
RJR	Reynolds (R. J.) Inds.	5746.170	.48	.72
RLM	Reynolds Metals	502.653	.06	1.12
RAD	Rite Aid	649.304	.07	1.27
ROAD	Roadway Service	1136.813	.11	.88
ROK	Rockwell Int'l	3246.405	.36	1.16
ROH	Rohm & Haas	1007.994	.13	.97
ROP	Roper Corp.	66.882	.01	.98
RCC	Royal Crown Cos.	163.313	.02	.54
RD	Royal Dutch Petroleum	9280.816	.96	.86
RDR	Ryder System	1052.135	.10	1.62
SAFC	SAFECO Corp.	972.816	.09	.88
SED	Sedco	682.168	.07	1.75
SFN	SFN Co.	336.672	.03	1.01
SA	Safeway Stores	1194.899	.13	.61
SFF	Sante Fe Industries	1921.748	.20	1.62
SGP	Schering-Plough	2095.222	.20	.75
SLB	Schlumberger Ltd.	13597.707	1.20	1.09
SFA	Scientific-Atlanta	377.422	.04	1.52
SPP	Scott Paper	863.784	.08	1.07
VO	Seagram Co. Ltd.	2218.179	.24	1.30
SRI	Searle (G. D.)	2068.419	.20	1.14
S	Sears, Roebuck & Co.	10565.802	1.15	.95
SUO	Shell Oil	11431.298	1.12	1.39
SHW	Sherwin-Williams	452.452	.05	1.56
SGN	Signal Cos.	1800.150	.27	1.78
SMF	Singer Co.	315.628	.04	1.13
SKY	Skyline Corp.	269.208	.03	1.52
SKB	Smith Kline Beckman Corp.	5713.545	.46	.75
SNA	Snap-On Tools	546.480	.05	1.10
SNT	Sonat Inc.	1071.845	.10	1.03
SCE	Southern Calif. Edison	3241.105	.30	.40
SO	Southern Co.	3141.516	.27	.37
SX	Southern Pacific Co.	1014.753	.15	1.10
SY	Sperry Corp.	1477.478	.14	1.68
SMI	Springs Industries Inc.	345.636	.03	1.26
SQD	Square "D"	941.772	.09	1.10
SQB	Squibb Corp.	2211.748	.19	.74

EXHIBIT 4-11   S & P 500 in alphabetical order (Standard & Poor's Corporation). (Continued)

Ticker	Company	Market value (mil. $)	% of 500	*Beta
STPL	St. Paul Cos.	1304.713	.12	.90
SRT	St. Regis Paper	840.328	.10	1.25
SD	Standard Oil of Calif.	10947.488	1.07	1.25
SN	Standard Oil of Indiana	11630.254	1.14	1.26
SOH	Standard Oil of Ohio	8730.160	.97	1.43
SWK	Stanley Works	656.576	.06	1.26
STF	Stauffer Chemical	1023.605	.09	.96
STY	Sterling Drug	1365.480	.13	.60
STN	Stevens (JP) & Co.	310.954	.03	1.26
SVC	Stokely-Van Camp	129.880	.01	.55
STO	Stone Container	200.805	.02	1.68
STK	Storage Technology	719.270	.06	1.86
SUN	Sun Co., Inc.	3699.960	.40	1.62
SOC	Superior Oil	3661.686	.40	1.26
TRW	TRW Inc.	2294.990	.21	1.17
TFB	Taft Broadcasting	357.140	.04	1.11
TAN	Tandy Corp.	5270.692	.54	2.02
TEK	Tektronix, Inc.	1089.743	.12	1.17
TDY	Teledyne Inc.	2672.629	.26	1.94
TGT	Tenneco, Inc.	4245.755	.44	1.26
TX	Texaco Inc.	8068.773	.75	1.10
TET	Texas Eastern Corp.	1491.296	.12	1.35
TXG	Texas Gas Transmis.	539.396	.06	1.44
TXN	Texas Instruments	3181.054	.31	1.40
TXO	Texas Oil & Gas Corp.	3239.690	.37	1.55
TXU	Texas Utilities	2628.052	.24	.37
TXT	Textron, Inc.	806.360	.10	1.22
TNB	Thomas & Betts	406.718	.04	.95
TGR	Tiger Int'l	143.956	.01	1.31
TL	Time Inc.	2896.638	.31	1.31
TMC	Times Mirror	2130.293	.21	1.23
TKR	Timken Co.	570.531	.06	.89
TKA	Tonka Corp.	18.509	.00	1.22
TRA	Trane Company	302.522	.03	1.02
TA	Transamerica Corp.	1516.944	.17	1.21
TIC	Travelers Corp.	2029.757	.22	.69
TYM	Tymshare, Inc.	214.362	.02	1.69
FG	USF&G Corp	1302.580	.13	.68
UAL	UAL Inc.	983.768	.09	1.59
USH	USLife Corp	440.703	.04	1.23
UN	Unilever N.V.	2344.586	.19	.66
UCC	Union Camp	1465.641	.15	1.16
UK	Union Carbide	3690.041	.41	.90
UCL	Union Oil of Calif.	4623.138	.51	1.35
UNP	Union Pacific	5397.982	.59	1.56

Ticker	Company	Market value (mil. $)	% of 500	*Beta
R	Uniroyal Inc.	313.807	.03	1.18
USG	United States Gyupsum	832.947	.07	1.17
UH	United States Home	435.166	.05	2.53
X	United States Steel	2099.916	.23	1.09
UTX	United Technologies	3059.109	.31	1.31
UT	United Telecommun.	1673.862	.15	.79
UPJ	Upjohn Co.	1399.226	.15	1.02
VFC	V. F. Corporation	646.759	.10	1.04
VEL	Virginia Elec.	1678.641	.17	.28
WMT	Wal-Mart Stores	3342.124	.41	1.26
WAG	Walgreen	854.784	.08	1.24
HWR	Walker (H) Resources	1107.936	.12	1.29
WANB	Wang Labs	3624.783	.44	2.52
WCI	Warner Communications	2142.530	.16	1.37
WLA	Warner-Lambert	2251.412	.19	.93
WMX	Waste Management Inc.	2428.311	.20	1.62
WEN	Wendy's Int'l.	593.614	.06	1.76
WPM	West Point-Pepperell	389.621	.04	.73
WSN	Western Co. of North America	384.474	.03	1.78
WX	Westinghouse Electric	3403.662	.36	1.48
WMOR	Westmoreland Coal	98.890	.01	1.04
W	Westvaco Corp.	687.680	.07	1.20
WY	Weyerhaeuser Co.	4593.240	.41	1.37
WFI	Wheelabrator-Frye	829.593	.08	1.56
WHX	Wheeling-Pitts. Steel	60.228	.01	1.56
WHR	Whirlpool Corp.	1586.856	.15	.92
WSW	White Consolidated Indus.	479.772	.05	.78
WMB	Williams Cos.	506.124	.06	1.49
WIN	Winn-Dixie	1106.444	.11	.18
WPC	Wisconsin Elec. Pwr.	738.237	.06	.20
Z	Woolworth (FW)	785.487	.08	.74
WWY	Wrigley, (WM) Jr.	314.192	.03	.49
XRX	Xerox Corp.	3176.738	.37	1.03
YELL	Yellow Freight Systems	269.914	.03	.74
ZE	Zenith Radio	274.282	.04	1.20
ZRN	Zurn Industries	168.171	.02	1.16

Total Market Value $\qquad$ 1015134.827

*Five-year monthly beta based on total return including dividends as calculated by S&P Compustat.
N.A. = not available.

Most of the stock index contracts are very similar. Let's take a closer look at some of the indexes, their similarities, and their differences.

As one might guess, the S & P 100 and S & P 500 contracts are very similar. The S & P 500 cash index has been around for years and is familiar to most investors. The S & P 100 index has existed since 1982 but was recalculated back to January 2, 1976. This index was originated by the Chicago Board of Options Exchange (CBOE) as the CBOE 100. The name was changed in the middle of 1983 as part of an arrangement between Standard & Poor's, the Chicago Mercantile Exchange, and the CBOE. It is a broadly based industrial index that is a subset of the S & P 500. By necessity, the S & P 100 is not as broad as the S & P 500. The S & P 500 is composed of 400 industrials, 40 financials, 40 utilities, and 20 transportation stocks. There are an additional 86 industry groups. Each group has its own index, though no futures contracts are being traded on them. The S & P 100 is narrower and does not cover 40 industry groups.

Certain industries are more heavily weighted in the S & P 100 than in the S & P 500 because it is not as broadly based. There are several industry groups that have at least 150 percent more weighting in the S & P 100 than in the S & P 500. They are:

- Aerospace
- Automobiles
- Beverages (soft drinks)
- Chemicals
- Electrical equipment
- Electronics (instrumentation)
- Fertilizers
- Hospital supplies
- Miscellaneous
- Office and business equipment
- Oil well equipment and services

The S & P 100 has less representation than the S & P 500 in drugs, foods, and department stores. The biggest difference is that transportation, utilities, and financials are significantly more important to the S & P 500 than to the S & P 100. The following table illustrates this:

	S&P 100 percent of total	S&P 500 percent of total
Utilities	1.1	6.2
Financials	4.6	6.2
Transportation	1.9	2.7

EXHIBIT 4-12 Graph showing the deviations between the S & P 100 and the S & P 500. (Reprinted with permission of the Chicago Mercantile Exchange.)

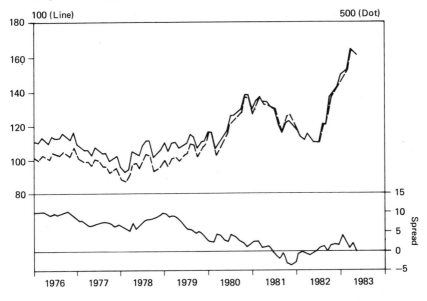

EXHIBIT 4-13 Graph showing the deviations between the S & P 100 and the S & P 500. (Reprinted with permission of the Chicago Mercantile Exchange.)

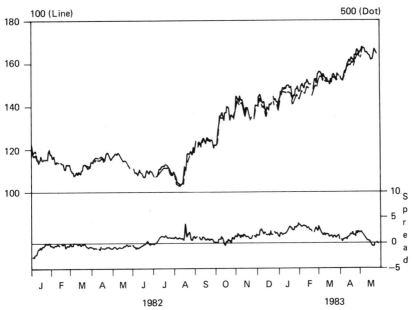

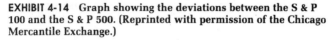

EXHIBIT 4-14 Graph showing the deviations between the S & P
100 and the S & P 500. (Reprinted with permission of the Chicago
Mercantile Exchange.)

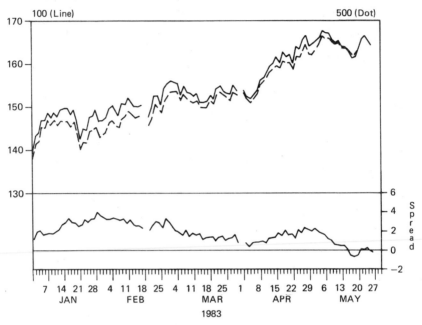

In spite of these differences, the two contracts are broad-based
enough to have similiar price behavior. Statistical studies show a correlation between the two indexes' price movements of over .97. A correlation of 1.00 would be perfect; a price movement in one index
would be matched exactly in the other index. The .97 correlation thus
shows an extremely close relationship.

This does not mean that there are no deviations. Exhibits 4-12
through 4-15 show the two indexes on several charts. Significant price
divergences can be seen. The differences are rarely in direction, but
mainly in magnitude. Price action differences between the two
indexes are related for a couple of reasons. First, the weighting of the
various stocks and industries is different. Thus, a large move in utilities will affect the S & P 500 more than it will affect the S & P 100
because it represents a larger share of the S & P 500. Second, the S &
P 100 is a subset of the S & P 500 and represents 100 of the largest
companies in the S & P 500. This additional group of smaller stocks in
the S & P 500 can move the market away from the level suggested by
the larger stocks.

EXHIBIT 4-15 DJIA versus S & P monthly cash average, 1963–1983
(Commodity Price Charts, 219 Parkade, Cedar Falls, Iowa 50613).

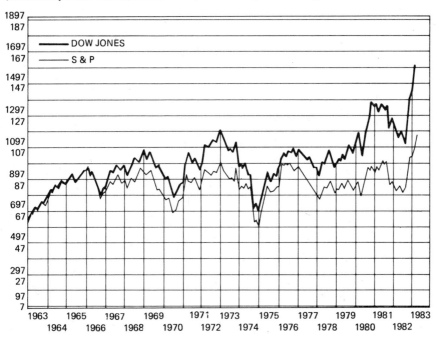

The S & P 100 moves slightly more slowly than the S & P 500 but is
more volatile. The S & P 100 moves more slowly than the S & P 500
because it contains, on average, larger-capitalized stocks than the S &
P 500. It takes more dollars to move the larger-capitalized stocks than
it does to move the smaller-capitalized stocks. An index composed of
larger-capitalized stocks will thus require more money to move than
will the index with smaller-capitalized stocks.

The S & P 100 is more volatile because it is less broadly based. The
broader the index, the more chance that there will be offsetting price
movements, thus the more chance of price stability.

There are other factors that differentiate the various stock indexes.
These factors can be used to provide rationales for spread trades. This
will be covered in more detail in Chapter 6.

chapter 5

Technical Price Analysis

Technical analysis uses the market itself as an analytical tool. It seeks to predict future price action based on past price behavior, volume, and open interest. It looks at the market itself rather than the supply and demand of the components of the market.

There are two major styles of analysis of stock index futures. The most common and popular is technical analysis. The other style is fundamental analysis, which will be covered in the next chapter. Fundamental analysis focuses on the supply and demand of stock index futures rather than on the market itself.

Technical analysis is popular largely because of the time necessary to become knowledgeable in the fundamentals of stocks. The principles of fundamental analysis typically require a much greater investment in time before a thorough understanding can be achieved. On the other hand, the basics of technical analysis can often be mastered in only a few hours. The principles outlined in this book provide the basis for virtually all technical analysis. Advanced topics not covered in this book are basically further delineations of these principles.

The commonly held belief in the futures industry is that fundamental analysis is a superior method of determining the long-term trend whereas technical analysis is better at defining shorter trends and timing entry and exit of positions. Virtually all fundamentalists rely at some time on the examination of technical factors to help to determine their entry into and exit from market positions. Fundamentalists may use their knowledge and analysis of economics and the supply and demand for stocks to determine which side of the market is most desirable. And yet many fundamental-

119

ists use technical analysis to determine the exact entry and exit points to achieve the most profit. Even commercial interests who are trying to hedge the exposure in the cash side of the market will use technical analysis. They are usually very familiar with the fundamentals and are in contact with them on a day-to-day basis. Fundamentalists can often become victims of their own knowledge. It becomes a case of seeing the trees and not the forest. Fundamentalists usually find that a periodic examination of technical factors aids them in keeping a better perspective on the market.

There are several types of technical analysis. The most popular form is bar chart analysis. This can be simple or advanced. Point and figure is another major form of analysis, though its popularity does not come close to that of bar chart analysis. Another style of technical analysis focuses on the character of the market itself by examining value, open interest, and momentum of the marketplace. Cycles and seasonals are becoming increasingly popular in the field of technical analysis. The final area of technical analysis is that of mechanical trading systems, which are used to generate trading signals on an automatic and often computerized basis.

Chart analysis is the analysis of price patterns formed on charts containing price information. It is a subjective art subject to many controversies. Even the physical layout of the charts themselves is a matter of some controversy. Many analysts suggest that the chart should have logarithmic scales instead of arithmetic scales for price, which would show percentage gains in a clearer fashion. Thus, as the markets moved to higher levels and became more volatile, price chart formations would appear similar to those at lower levels because of the logarithmic nature of the scale. Nonetheless, the vast majority of technical analysis takes place on simple arithmetic charts.

Price chart analysis focuses on patterns of price behavior that are believed to be predictive of future price behavior. Chartists believe that human nature follows certain repetitive patterns and that these behavior patterns are illustrated by the price patterns on a chart. These price chart patterns occur as human behavior patterns occur. Chartists believe that the early detection of these patterns can be used to find profitable trading opportunities. Chart analysis is therefore the study of price action or price chart action in an effort to discover the underlying behavior patterns of the market participants.

Chart analysts and all technical analysts believe that the price of a given object is the final arbiter of the supply and demand of that object. If one studies the market itself, all known or expected supply and demand factors can be determined. The market represents the current opinions of all market participants having an opinion on the market and the ability to back up their judgment with money. The technician therefore believes that it is unnecessary to know what the supply and demand are for stock index futures when the market will reveal that information through its own behavior.

The primary object of the technician and chart analyst is to discover price trends. A trend in prices is the direction that prices are moving. The trend will be defined in many ways and for many time periods. It is possible that the trend for the last 10 days is down, the trend for the last 10 weeks is up, and the trend for the last 10 months is down. The trend is therefore not a unitary concept but a concept that must be tempered and qualified by a time parameter. Traders should accustom themselves to saying that the short-term trend is up or the tendency trend is up rather than that the trend is up. No matter what the time horizon is, the major goal of the technical chart analyst is to determine the trend. The key to technical analysis is to determine the trend early enough to be able to initiate a position and ride it to a profitable point. Technicians will focus on the beginning and end of trends in an effort to optimize their entry and exit points from the market.

The most basic concept in chart analysis is support and resistance. Support and resistance are opposite sides of the same coin. Support and resistance are points on the chart that are difficult for the market to break on the downside or upside. Support is defined as a point below the current market price that is expected to support the market price and either slow or stop a decline. Resistance is the point above the market that is expected to slow or stop a price advance.

There are many theories on why support and resistance exist. A common one originated around the turn of the century in the stock market. It was theorized that the smart money and big money in the stock market would accumulate and distribute the stocks as a profit-making venture similar to the wholesaling or retailing of any other product. The big stock operators were assumed to accumulate stock at a low price level whenever prices approached it. This would, in effect, set a floor on the price and make it difficult for the price to drop any further. It was assumed that the price could drop further only if the operators determined that they could buy the inventory they desired at a lower level. The operators were then expected to allow the market to move higher on its own natural course or possibly through manipulation. When the public and institutions stepped in to buy the stock at a higher level the stock operators would distribute the stock at this high level, increasing the supply and making it difficult for the price to continue higher. The accumulation and distribution of the stock occurred at levels that became known as support and resistance levels.

In commodity futures there has been very little experience of the equivalent of the stock operators and their ability to manipulate stock. Nonetheless, the concepts of support, resistance, accumulation, and distribution still remain. The stock operators were assumed to be a small group of people or even a single person who overtly accumulated and distributed a particular stock. In commodities, the smart money is not considered as monolithic an entity. It is simply assumed that the most intelligent and best traders will tend to be on the same side of the market at the same time and will tend to accumulate and distribute their holdings of the futures contract at approximately the same time. These times should define the lows and highs of a given major price move.

Another theory of support and resistance is the idea that individuals who had purchased a contract at a specific level only to find it go against them will tend to liquidate that product when it approaches their purchase level. They supposedly do this because of their relief at being able to liquidate the position on a no-lose basis. Those traders that had sold it at that point tend to come in and buy the contract back as it approaches their entry level.

The theory that makes the most sense to me and that even can include those outlined above is that support and resistance largely define levels where the price has moved beyond that justified by the underlying fundamentals. Commercial users of commodities buy goods when economically useful and therefore "support" the market; they sell goods when the price level is economically attractive and therefore provide "resistance." In the final analysis, the price of any commodity is related to the supply and demand. Technical analysis hopes to achieve an analysis of the supply and demand through the shorthand of the market price itself. Each trade on a stock index futures contract is the market as a whole trying to determine the underlying value in that contract. The tendency of human beings is to go slightly too far in any direction past the underlying value of the commodity. This emotional bias has the net effect of causing the price to oscillate around the underlying value as it tracks and backtracks in an effort to determine that true value. Support therefore occurs when the market has gone too far below the underlying market value and must move higher. Resistance is the opposite; that is, it represents an area where more people are likely to sell the commodity because it has gone too far above the underlying value.

Whatever theory one subscribes to, the use of support and resistance is a central and vital issue in chart analysis. It is a quantification of the ebb and flow of human behavior and provides a useful tool in the initiation and liquidation of trading positions.

The starting point for many formations is the trendline. This common formation is used for determining the trend and support and resistance. The two types of trendlines are the uptrend line and the downtrend line. An uptrend is defined as a price pattern in which each low is higher than the previous low. The opposite of an uptrend is a downtrend, which has each high lower than the previous high. An uptrend line is a line drawn across the bottom of the lows in an uptrend while a downtrend line is the line drawn across the highs of a downtrend.

The easiest way to understand uptrend and downtrend lines is to look at an example. Exhibit 5-1* is of the cash New York Stock Exchange Index from April until December 1982. The first trendline in Exhibit 5-1 is a downtrend line. It connects the highs that occurred in May and July. Because the highs of rallies were occurring at lower and lower levels, we can say that the market was in a downtrend. The line drawn across these highs has a downward slope. This is an indication that the market should only be traded from the short side. The downtrend is considered valid until the downtrend line is broken. The breaking of the downtrend line finally occurred in August when prices traded up above 62.50, which is where the downtrend line crossed on that day. Notice that one attempt was made before that to break the downtrend line at the very beginning of August. As prices approached the downtrend line resistance entered the market and pushed the market back to new lows.

After the market had broken the downtrend line traders should have known that the market had entered into a new uptrend. At that point, they did not know where the new uptrend line would be as one major setback is required to delineate where to draw the uptrend line. Nonetheless, they did know to begin to trade the market only from the long side. One of the usual trading techniques is to have a buy stop order just above the downtrend line. This has the advantage of getting the trader into the market as soon as the trend has changed. The disadvantage is that there are occasional false breakouts that will create losses for traders buying just above the downtrend line. One variation of this tactic is to buy only when the market closes above the downtrend line. This eliminates intra-day breakouts and will tend

*Exhibits 5-1 to 5-9 and 5-14 are reprinted from CRB Futures Chart Service, a weekly publication of Commodity Research Bureau, Inc., 75 Montgomery St., Jersey City, N.J. 07302. Technical formations and enhancements were added by the author.

EXHIBIT 5-1 Graph showing the uptrend and downtrend of the cash New York Stock Exchange Index from April until December 1982 (Commodity Research Bureau, Inc.).

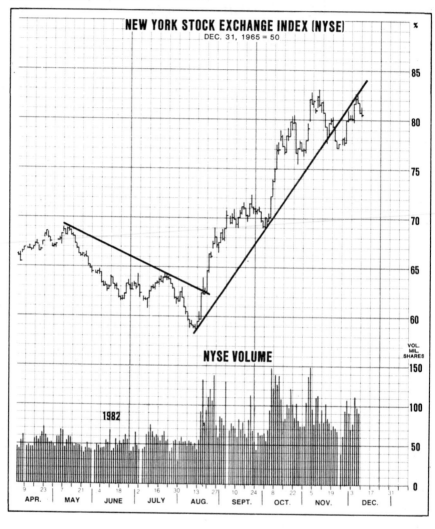

to keep the trader out of some of the false breakouts at the expense of not putting the trader into the trade as early in the trend. Long-term and intermediate-term traders will find this to be an insignificant disadvantage as their profit potential is considered to be much larger on any given trade. It is therefore quite possible that a trader using trendlines would have purchased the NYSE Index at approximately 62.50.

The first major setback in the market occurred in early October, when prices completed a rally up to 72.50 and set back to around 69.00. When prices rallied above that level, traders were able to draw in a new uptrend line. Technicians were then able to determine the angle of the advance expected as well as to define the trendline to be used for determining whether the market had moved from an uptrend to a downtrend. Notice that prices suffered another substantial decline in late October, but support from the uptrend line moved the market to a new high in the early part of November. A subsequent dip moved prices back to the uptrend line during the week of November 12, near 78.00. The uptrend line defined the exact bottom of that dip but prices only subsequently rallied a little over 2.00. The next dip broke the uptrend line, giving technical traders a signal that the trend had changed and that it was time to trade the market from the short side. This particular example shows an additional feature of trendlines that occurs fairly frequently. The market broke the trendline but then advanced back to the uptrend line before heading lower (not shown). This snap back to a broken trendline is a common occurrence. Conservative traders will often ignore the buy signal on the initial breakout of the trendline, preferring to wait until the snap back enabling them to make purchases or sales at a more advantageous price level.

A downtrend line is an obvious indication that the underlying supply and demand for commodities are dropping and that the bears are in control of the market. A bull trend shows that the buying power of the bulls is greater than the selling power of the bears. The breaking of the trendline shows that the forces that had moved the trend have changed and that consolidation or an opposite trend will occur.

A trendline gains in validity the more times it is touched. In Exhibit 5-1, the downtrend line was a less valid trendline than the uptrend line because it was touched only twice before being broken whereas the uptrend line was touched three times and almost four times.

Trendlines are also useful tools for the placing of stop loss orders for open positions. When a trade is made, traders can use the trendline as a trailing stop by placing their stop loss order just under the trendline in the case of an uptrend line or just above the trendline in the case of a downtrend line. The breaking of a trendline, remember, is an indication of a change in trend, and traders should not be trading against the trend. The trendline thus makes a perfect trailing stop loss point for conservative long-term traders.

A formation closely associated with the trendline is the channel. A channel is a set of parallel trendlines, one connecting the lows and one connecting the highs. An example of an up channel is found in

Exhibit 5-2. Both the highs and lows fell within a clearly defined channel formation. The lows of August and October defined the bottom of the up channel and the highs of September, October, and November defined the top of the up channel. There was a false breakout during the latter part of November on the downside, but with the exception of this small anomaly, the channel was a classic example. Channels may be up channels or down channels depending on their direction.

Channels are one of the most valuable chart formations as they help define both entry and exit points. In addition, short-term traders can use both sides of the channel as support and resistance for initiating and exiting trades. The long-term trader will prefer to buy as prices approach the bottom of the up channel and to continue to hold that position until that channel line is broken. Shorter-term traders may wish to exit their positions when they approach the upper boundary of the channel and reinitiate their positions when they approach the bottom of the channel. This can dramatically increase profits but it also has a couple of drawbacks. The first is that prices do not dip from the top of the channel but simply consolidate and move sideways until the bottom of the channel moves up to the sideways formation. This came very close to occurring in Exhibit 5-2 during September when prices essentially chopped sideways and there was little profit potential on the sale near the top of the up channel.

EXHIBIT 5-2 Example of an up channel (Commodity Research Bureau, Inc.).

It is also worth noting that the top of an up channel (and the top of the down channel) often have a relationship with previous formations. Notice that in Exhibit 5-2 the top of the up channel was actually an old support line from the early part of July.

Some traders like to use channels to combine both short-term and long-term trading strategies. They will initiate two units of a single trade, holding one for the long pull and exiting it when the trendline is broken and using the other unit as a trading unit. The trading unit is bought when prices approach the bottom of the channel and sold when prices approach the top of the channel. Some traders may think the best approach is to buy two units at the bottom of the channel and liquidate two at the top of the channel to double the profits on the short-term swings. The problem with this approach is that the market may accelerate when it approaches the top of the channel and break that resistance, moving into a new up channel at an accelerated pace. This would leave a trader in the unenviable position of being short in an accelerating bull market. The risks of using that tactic are simply too great. Traders utilizing that strategy must be extremely nimble to withstand the pressures as the market accelerates. Within the basic channel in Exhibit 5-2 we have drawn a small channel. The low in early November did not reach the bottom of the up channel and the highs that were made throughout October formed a parallel line with the new shorter uptrend line within the major up channel. This was very suggestive that prices might indeed break out of the up channel and accelerate at a new increased rate. This is also a good example of how channels can be used within other channels to define short-term entry and exit as well as additional support and resistance points.

Channels are extremely common in stock index futures, though there is the tendency for false breakouts to be more common than in other commodity futures. Traders should therefore filter their opinions and seek confirmation of the breakout from other indicators that will be discussed below. Nonetheless, channels are a powerful tool for achieving profits through trading stock index futures, and traders should be alert at all times for their formation. Note that in Exhibit 5-3 a whole series of channels and trendlines has been drawn in an effort to show the use and number of these chart formations. Notice that just about every day has a trendline or channel affecting it and providing support, resistance, and trend information.

The two channels we have described are the up channel and down channel. A channel that is essentially horizontal is called a trading range or, in stock market parlance, a line formation. This is simply a channel that has been laid on its side. The prices are chopping back and forth with no direction. The trading range was formed in Septem-

EXHIBIT 5-3   Example of a whole series of channels and trendlines in an effort to show the use and number of these chart formations (Commodity Research Bureau, Inc.).

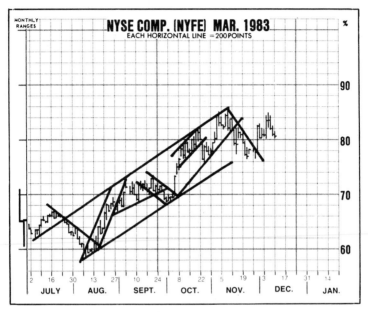

ber in Exhibits 5-2 and 5-3. Prices moved up and down, finding support near the lows and resistance near the highs, and were unable to move in any direction for any length of time. The same type of analysis that is applied to a channel formation can be applied to a trading range. The preferred trading strategy is therefore either to buy near the lows and sell near the highs or to use a breakout of the trading range to initiate a position.

The line formation occurs fairly frequently and can be used profitably by technically oriented traders. It often occurs, as it does in Exhibit 5-2, as a consolidation period in a trending market. It therefore represents a potential entry point for those who are unable to enter the trend when it first occurs or to initiate additional units on an existing position.

Another common formation is the triangle formation. The triangle formation comes in three varieties: the symmetrical, or pennant, triangle; the ascending triangle; and the descending triangle. The pennant formation, sometimes called a symmetrical triangle, has each successive high lower than the previous high and each successive low higher than the previous low. It therefore forms something that resembles a pennant. A pennant can be clearly seen in the far left-hand corner of Exhibit 5-4. The highs are getting progressively lower and the lows are getting progressively higher, causing the market to wind into a pennant formation. A pennant is a neutral formation as it is being formed but provides a tremendous spring to the market when prices break out of it.

This also shows how one uses the triangle as a trading tool. Note that the triangle is composed of two opposite slanting lines. The two lines that comprise a triangle pattern can be utilized as two trendlines rather than as a pennant formation. The same techniques used for trading trendlines are used with the pennant formation. For example, one would want to buy near the lows of the pennant formation near the uptrend line with a reversal stop underneath the bottom of the triangle that lies under the uptrend line. Conversely, one would consider selling near the highs of the triangle pattern when prices approach the downtrend line that forms the top of the pennant. A reversal stop would be placed above the downtrend line in an effort to get long should that trendline be broken. It is quite possible that there will be many trades within the triangle before it is broken. A long-standing pennant formation can have prices bounce from the top to the bottom several times before it is broken. Nonetheless, the most profitable trade is usually the one that breaks the pennant formation.

EXHIBIT 5-4   Example of a pennant formation (Commodity Research Bureau, Inc.).

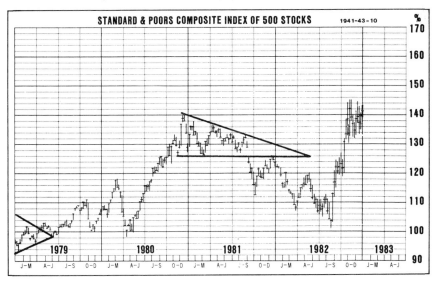

This is the one that usually has the most power behind it and the ability to move the farthest. The trades near the point of the pennant are typically very short-term trades with low profit but also low-risk. They are for nimble traders only, while the breakout of the pennant formation is more for position traders as it usually delineates a much stronger move. Notice how prices broke out of the top of the pennant formation and then set back to hit what used to be the top several months later. This is also similar to the techniques used in trading with trendlines. As we mentioned, the market will often set back to the broken trendlines before continuing higher. In this example, the prices set back to the broken pennant and the market then continued higher after giving slow-reacting traders a second chance to get into the market.

A particularly useful price pattern for short-term traders is the flag. A flag formation is a price formation in the shape of a flag. The pole of the flag is never vertical but is typified by a sharp upmove followed by a choppy downward pattern in a bull market or vice versa in a bear market. Exhibit 5-5 shows a perfect example of a flag formation. The trend is up, but prices chop in an irregular down channel, forming the flag formation. The flagpole is the price movement upward from the August lows to the mid-September highs. Flags are usually broken with an explosive price movement, as occurred in this case in early October. Flag formations are excellent formations as they provide an opportunity for the traders to enter the position with the trend but at an advantageous price level. For example, let us assume that traders were unable to enter the market when it first took off but still believe that the market is bullish. When the flag formation was established in late September traders would put buy stop orders just above the top of the flag, which is the mini-downtrend line. This buy stop would be lowered daily as the flag formation continued lower. A breakout of a flag formation is usually a highly reliable indicator of future price direction.

One of the most famous chart configurations is the head and shoulders formation. It is so named because the pattern of the highs or lows resembles a head with shoulders. A head and shoulders formation is shown in the soybean chart in Exhibit 5-6. Unfortunately, there have been no valid head and shoulders formations in the short history of stock index futures, although there have been a couple of invalid head and shoulders formations.

A head and shoulders formation can be a bearish signal, as in Exhibit 5-6, or it can be a bullish signal, as it would be if this head and shoulders had been a bottom. The head and shoulders is formed by a high in a move surrounded by two lesser highs. A neckline is

130

EXHIBIT 5-5 Example of a flag formation (Commodity Research Bureau, Inc.).

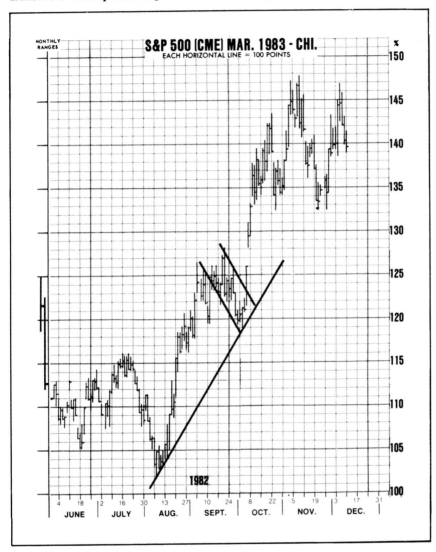

drawn across the lows that occurred between the two shoulders. A sell signal is given in the head and shoulders top when the neckline is broken. The head and shoulders formed in March, April, and May on the soybean chart is a classic head and shoulders that is almost textbook-perfect. The head and shoulders formed in September and October is the more usual form. Head and shoulders formations are

**EXHIBIT 5-6   Example of a head and shoulders formation
(Commodity Research Bureau, Inc.).**

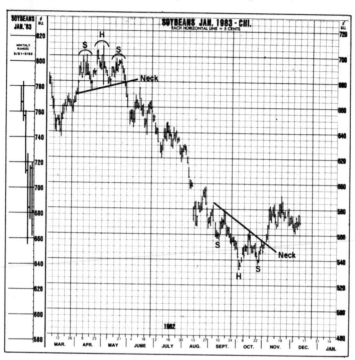

very complex in many instances, with multiple shoulders possible. Some analysts will use head and shoulders formations that contain two shoulders on each side of the head for a total of four shoulders. Some analysts believe that all top and bottom formations are head and shoulder formations if looked at with a discerning enough eye.

Gaps are another useful technical tool for determing support and resistance. Gaps come in three varieties: ordinary gaps, breakaway gaps, and exhaustion gaps. A gap is in the area on the chart in which the low from 1 day does not overlap the high from the following day or the high from 1 day does not overlap the low from the second day. The easiest way to understand this is to examine Exhibit 5-7, where six gaps have been pointed out. The first three gaps can all be considered ordinary gaps.

The way to use ordinary gaps is for support and resistance. The first gap on the chart provided very little support after it had occurred. The support points to watch are the top and bottom of the gap, and in this instance, neither one held up very well. The second gap in the middle of June is a more usual example, where prices gapped lower and were unable to surmount the gap for another 3 days on the upside.

The gap in early July is a similar example as it provided resistance for 2 days before finally being broken. The breaking of the gap is a powerful signal that prices are going to be headed in the direction of the breaking. This was the case in all three of these initial gaps.

EXHIBIT 5-7 Six gaps appear in this chart (Commodity Research Bureau, Inc.).

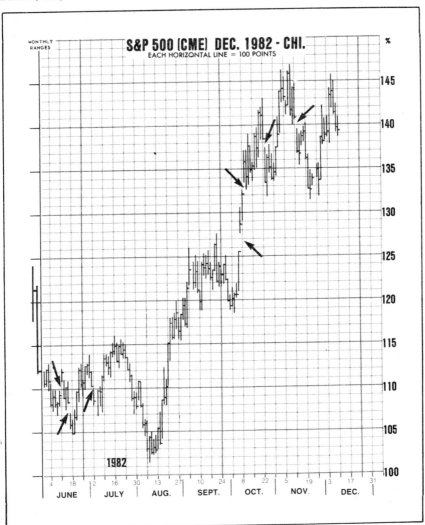

The major and most dramatic gap on the chart is the runaway gap in early October. A runaway gap is exactly what it sounds like: a time when prices run rapidly higher, leaving a gap that takes some time to be filled. A runaway gap is the strong indication of a continuation of the existing trend. It is often used to set price objectives, as runaway gaps often occur at the midpoint of a major move. This particular example shows a runaway gap that identified the price objective extremely well.

EXHIBIT 5-8 An excellent example of the recurring-angle method as it shows parallel lines in both uptrends and downtrends (Commodity Research Bureau, Inc.).

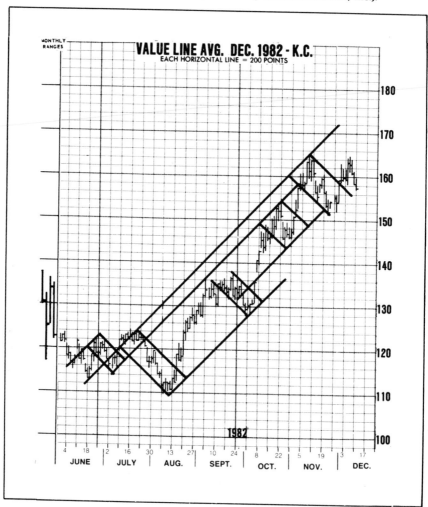

The final three gaps are all excellent examples of ordinary gaps. Prices gapped higher, set back into the gap to fill it, and then continued in the direction of the near-term trend. These gaps are excellent areas in which to initiate positions to go with the existing trend. One common trading strategy is to initiate the positions as the market moves into the gap and put a stop just on the opposite side of the gap.

The recurring-angle method is one of the best techniques for discovering support and resistance as well as indications of trend. A series of trendlines is drawn on the chart at major and minor support and resistance points. It is very common that these trendlines form angles that are the same with all of the lines. Exhibit 5-8 shows an excellent example of the recurring-angle method as it shows parallel lines in both uptrends and downtrends. It is a common property of the recurring-angle method that the lines drawn tend to be perpendicular; that is to say the downtrend lines and the uptrend lines are at equivalent angles, though perpendicular. This method can be utilized frequently to determine support and resistance breakouts of near-term trendlines and give indications of price direction. Another common attribute of the recurring-angle method is that the trendlines are often equidistant from each other. This is shown by the downtrend lines in October and November, which are essentially equidistant from each other. This technique can be used to suggest further resistance above the market where we have as yet no indication. The analyst would then extend another downward-sloping line above the uppermost line the distance between the top two downtrend lines.

Advanced Bar Chart Analysis

One of the advanced bar chart techniques is the use of Fibonacci numbers. These numbers are used in several different ways. Fibonacci numbers are the numbers in the sequence 1, 1, 2, 3, 5, 8, 13, 21, 34, 55, 89, and so on. The sequence is formed by the addition of the two numbers immediately preceding any given number. Thus the number 13 is derived by adding the two preceding numbers, 5 and 8, the number 21 comes from the addition of 8 and 13, and so on. This sequence of numbers has several interesting properties. As the numbers become larger, the ratio of one number to the number below it in the sequence approaches 1.618. The ratio of the number to the number immediately succeeding it approaches .618. The ratio .618 was called the golden ratio, or golden mean, by the Greeks, and Pythagoras suggested it may have contained the secret of the uni-

135

verse. Aficionados of Fibonacci numbers claim that these numbers have extra importance in the scheme of the universe. They point out the many occurrences of Fibonacci numbers and Fibonacci ratios. Elliott, of Elliott Wave fame, considered them to be the foundation of his Elliott Wave theories. Many other market analysts have also used Fibonacci numbers and ratios to derive important trading techniques. Let us examine a couple of these techniques.

The first technique is to derive points of support and resistance on setbacks in major trends. The technique is to measure the distance between the high and the low of the move and to find the Fibonacci ratio of that number. For example, from August until September prices rallied from 63.00 to just over 73.00 in the December NYSE Index, as can be seen in Exhibit 5-9. The total move of 10 points is multiplied by the Fibonacci ratio of .618. This yields the sum of 6.18 points. This sum of 6.18 is added to the low of the move and subtracted from the high of the move to give us 2 Fibonacci points. These 2 points have been circled just under the actual low of the move. The theory says that a very strong move will approach the first downside Fibonacci point and then continue higher. A normal bull market will reach halfway between the 2 points before continuing the rally, and a very weak market will make it all the way down to the bottom of the 2 Fibonacci points before rallying. The theory also states that if the second Fibonacci point is broken then the market is in a new downtrend and should be traded from the short side. We have also taken a couple of instances where Fibonacci points could have been used and marked the relevant levels. It is also uncanny how often 1 of the 2 points will become a major support and resistance level.

Fibonacci ratios can also be used to project possible objectives on a move. The procedure is to take a setback in the marketplace and multiply the distance represented by the setback times the golden ratio of 1.618 or its square 2.617 to project an objective. In Exhibit 5-9 the setback from July to August was 9 points. Nine points times the golden ratio of 1.618 projects a subsequent high of 14.6 (rounded off). This is essentially where the market ran into trouble on its subsequent rally. The next dip in the market occurred during the latter part of September and the first couple days of October. This 5-point drop projects to an initial objective of just over an 8-point rally, which would move the market to 76.00. The astute analyst knew that this objective was not the final objective when prices gapped over the level in the early part of the week of October 8. This was the signal that the analyst should use the square of the Fibonacci ratio of 2.617 as the factor to multiply to achieve the next objective. In actual fact, this objective came very close to the high of the next rally.

EXHIBIT 5-9   December NYSE Index (Commodity Research Bureau, Inc.).

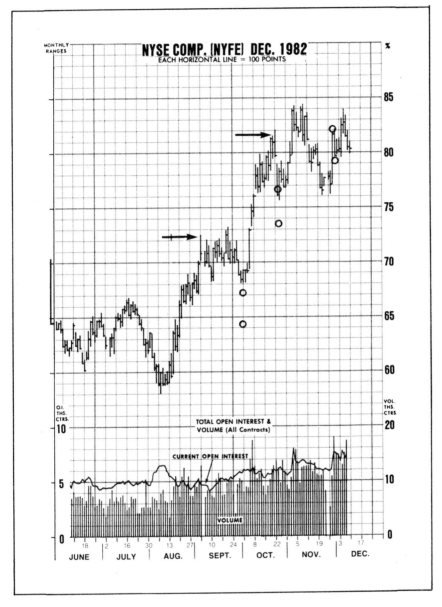

It should be noted that Fibonacci ratios do not give exact points. The support and resistance and objective points given by Fibonacci numbers tend to be approximate and do not have the rigidity that most uptrends or other chart patterns have. Nonetheless, they are powerful indicators that should be utilized by all techniques.

Point and Figure Charting

Point and figure charting represents a different slant to charting. Many analysts believe that point and figure charts can lead to greater trading profits than the regular bar charts that were discussed above.

Point and figure charts are a way of simplifying the examination of price action to allow a clearer picture of price trends. Bar charts graph prices on the side axis and time across the bottom. Point and figure charts do not have a time axis because time is ignored. Point and figure charts only graph price. An example would make this clear.

A bar chart is constructed by drawing a bar on a line representing a single day. The top of the bar lies on the price level representing the high of the day, and the bottom of the bar lies on the price level representing the low of the day. A horizontal tick is drawn on the right side of the bar to represent the closing or settlement price. Each bar corresponds to 1 day's price action. Exhibit 5-10 shows a typical price chart of a stock index futures contract.

Point and figure charts contain price information only. Charting is done in the squares, not on the lines. Each square represents one price unit. Stock index futures often use a box size representing 50 points. This means that any price movement less than 50 points will not show on the chart. Exhibit 5-11 shows a point and figure chart of the same price action as in Exhibit 5-10. Notice that price movement is reduced to blocks of 50 points each.

All upward price action is represented by a column of X's. Downward price action shows as a column of O's. A move from 150.00 to 151.30 in a given day will be shown by two X's. If, on the next day prices move to 152.50 then chartists will draw an additional three boxes directly above the previous two boxes. X's are stacked upon X's as long as prices remain in an uptrend. Unlike the bar chart, the point and figure chart does not move one column to the right at the beginning of each day. A new column is used only when prices reverse direction.

A price reversal occurs whenever prices retrace a price move equivalent to three boxes. For example, suppose prices moved

EXHIBIT 5-10   A typical price chart of a stock index futures contract
(Commodity Price Charts, 219 Parkade, Cedar Falls, Iowa 50613).

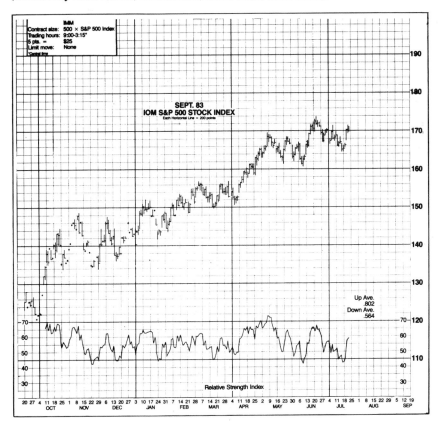

straight up from 150.00 to 160.00. Prices then run into resistance at
160.00 and retrace to 159.00. This 100-point retracement will not show
on the chart because it did not retrace to 150, which is the distance
represented by three boxes. Another X would be added to the column
if prices subsequently moved to 160.50. On the other hand, if prices
continued lower to 150.50, chartists would move over to the right one
column, drop down one box, and draw three O's straight down. The
column of O's continues as long as prices do not rally three boxes.

The point and figure chart is therefore a chart of price action with
no reference to time. The price action has been smoothed by eliminating price movements less than one box size of 50 points and by
eliminating price reactions less than 150 points. This smoothing helps

139

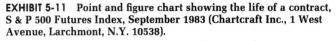

EXHIBIT 5-11 Point and figure chart showing the life of a contract,
S & P 500 Futures Index, September 1983 (Chartcraft Inc., 1 West
Avenue, Larchmont, N.Y. 10538).

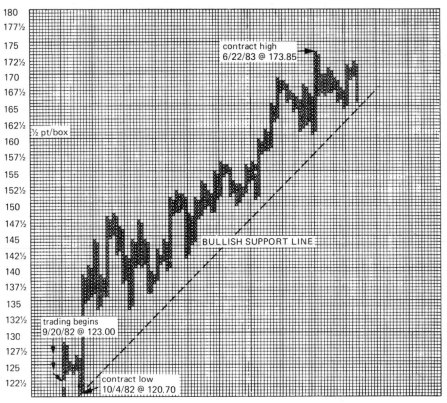

keep traders focused on the important trends in the market instead of
every little wiggle.

The technique of trading with point and figure charts is similar to
that employed with bar charts; trade recommendations and support
and resistance can be derived from both styles of charts. The major
difference is that bar chart analysis is largely subjective, but point and
figure analysis can be entirely mechanical.

Basic point and figure trade recommendations follow very simple
rules. In fact, there is really only one entry rule, and all other entry
rules are compounded from the first rule. Traders should buy stock
index futures whenever prices break above a previous column of X's
and sell whenever prices break below a previous column of O's.

Exhibit 5-12 illustrates a buy signal. Prices had rallied from 150.50

to 153.00 and set back to 151.50. Prices then turned bullish and surmounted the previous high at 153.50. Traders would probably have gotten long by having a buy stop order at 153.50. The stop loss order is placed one box below the previous column of O's. In fact, the simplest versions of point and figure analysis suggest that traders initiate short positions at the stop loss point. This means that traders would sell two contracts at 151.00 stop. The basic rule is therefore to buy a contract whenever prices move one box higher than the previous column of X's and to sell a contract whenever prices move one box lower than the previous column of O's.

Basic point and figure trading keeps traders always in the market. Traders will be either long or short at all times. Whenever a long position is stopped out, a short position is initiated. Whenever a short position is stopped out, a long position is initiated.

There are many other price patterns that can trigger the initiation of trades. Exhibit 5-13 and Exhibit 5-14 show more complicated patterns to enter trades. Note that each one of them is triggered by the basic rule of breaking the previous high or low.

A significant advantage of point and figure charting is that it is easy to construct and maintain. Bar charts must be updated daily. Point and figure charts are updated only when price action dictates.

Another advantage of point and figure trading is that it forces traders to trade with the trend. Traders must trade with the trend of the market because point and figure signals require a breaking of a previous high or low. Many traders lose money trading commodity futures because they try to fight the trend. Point and figure analysis helps traders keep the self-discipline necessary to stick with the trend. This one feature can improve most traders' track records.

The critical issue in point and figure analysis is the box size. A small box size will produce more reversals, create more whipsaws, provide more trades, and get into trend changes sooner. A large box size will reduce trades and whipsaws and keep traders in the major

EXHIBIT 5-12 Illustration of a buy signal.

153.5			X	buy
153.0	X		X	
152.5	X	O	X	
152.0	X	O	X	
151.5	X	O		
151.0	X			stop
150.5	X			

EXHIBIT 5-13   Complicated price patterns to enter trades (P. J. Kaufman, *Commodity Trading Systems and Methods,* John Wiley & Sons, New York, 1978).

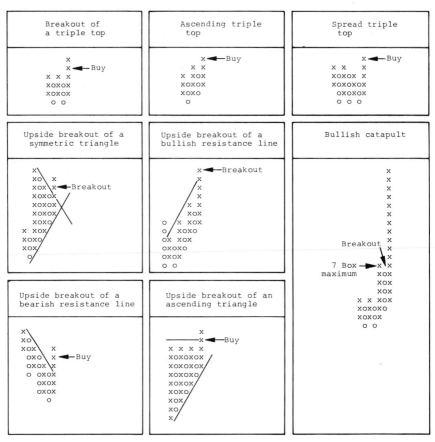

trends better. A related question is how many boxes prices should retrace before a reversal is graphed.

One of the interesting features of point and figure analysis is that it can be used as a mechanical trading system. A purchase is made whenever a previous high is broken and a sale is made whenever a previous low is broken. Point and figure analysis can therefore be optimized on computers. Analysts can test the profitability of various box and reversal sizes. Point and figure charting is the only style of charting that can be optimized.

In general, it is not necessary to computer-optimize the box and reversal sizes. Most traders find that the basic three-box reversal

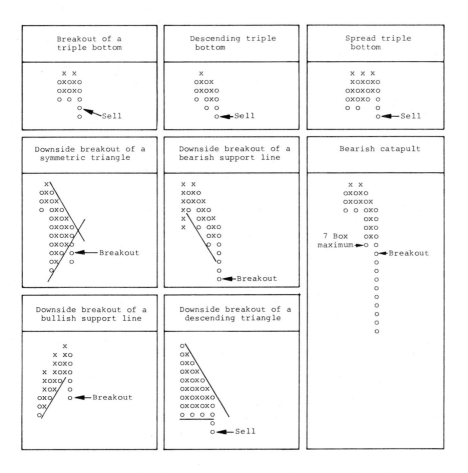

works very well. The box size is often a function of the investors' trading style rather than the optimization of profits. Most studies that have attempted to optimize point and figure box and reversal sizes have found that large box sizes and a three-box reversal have been the most profitable. This means that traders must risk very large amounts and trade infrequently. Many traders will not want this style of trading or have the funds needed to support the wide stops that come with large box sizes. These traders may want to sacrifice the higher profits of the optimized box and reversal sizes for a point and figure chart that achieves other objectives.

It is often best to establish box and reversal sizes as conditions

EXHIBIT 5-14 Complicated price patterns to enter trades (*Guide to Commodity Price Forecasting*, Commodity Research Bureau, New York, 1965).

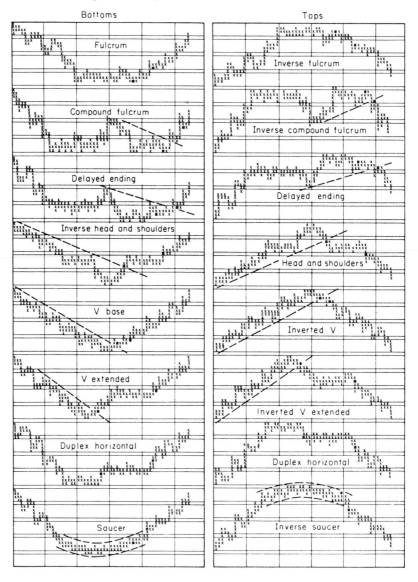

change rather than accept "optimized" parameters. "Optimized" box and reversal sizes are usually tested over 5 to 10 years. The optimized parameters are therefore the best for most circumstances over the long run, but not necessarily the best in the current year. It would be absurd to suggest that the same box and reversal sizes that produce big profits during major trending markets with wild swinging moves will be the best sizes in a low-priced market with low volume and prices in a tight trading range.

The alternative to using the optimized parameters is to adjust the box and reversal sizes as conditions change. This means that traders change the parameters if, say, the market suddenly breaks out of a tight trading range into a major trending market. As a practical matter, it is suggested that only the box size be changed and the reversal size left at three boxes. The three-box reversal size has been found to be very servicable in most circumstances. In addition, traders can concentrate on finding the best box size. Adding reversal size to the investigation generally creates unnecessary complication and wastes the trader's time.

Empirical evidence suggests that the following box sizes work well with a three-box reversal for traders wishing to take position trades:

Contract	Box size (points)
Standard & Poor's 500	80
Standard & Poor's 100	80
Value Line Index (maxi- and mini-)	80
New York Stock Exchange Index	50

Traders wishing to day-trade should stick to the S & P 500 contract. Its large size means that intraday price swings are worth enough to allow the trader to cover commissions and show a profit. The smaller contracts, the NYSE Index, the S & P 100, and the mini-Value Line have equivalent price swings but they are worth less in dollars because of the smaller contract size. The original Value Line contract is even larger than the S & P 500 contract but the liquidity in the pit is not as good. The more liquid the market, the smaller the spread between the bid and ask prices. Day-trading usually aims for relatively small profits. Thus, a wide bid/ask spread can decrease the profit potential of the day trader. It is therefore recommended that traders use a 5-point box size with a 25-point reversal for day-trading the S & P 500.

Market Character Analysis

Market character analysis aims to discover the underlying strength of the marketplace through volume, open interest, and momentum of price. Traders usually use market character analysis as a way of confirming buy and sell recommendations derived from other sources. There are very few systems that rely entirely on market character analysis to enter and exit positions. The major exception is oscillators, which we will cover later.

Open interest and volume are often used in conjunction with price charts to understand further why price movements occur.

Open interest is perhaps the most interesting of the two factors for gaining insights into the underlying strength or weakness of a price move. When open interest rises, new positions are being initiated. If prices are rising, buyers are the dominant force in the market. Their buying is more aggressive than the selling of the new shorts coming into the market. As prices move higher, the recent sellers may have to become buyers to cut their losses. This means that the bull move can fuel itself as the shorts bail out of their short positions. This is a very bullish circumstance as it shows that the bulls are in control. Conversely, rising open interest combined with weakening prices is an indication that the shorts are in control of the market and that prices will continue lower. Rising open interest should be interpreted as a supportive factor for whatever chart formations are being created.

The shorts are the dominant force in the marketplace if open interest is falling and prices are rallying. The main impetus to increasing prices is shorts covering their own positions. This implies that bullish chart formations will not last long because when the shorts finally stop covering their positions, prices will dip. This means that bullish chart patterns should be given a skeptical eye as they will probably be short-lived. Obviously, the converse holds for bearish chart patterns.

Volume gives additional insight into the underlying market character. Increasing volume tends to add credence to a chart pattern whereas light volume should make traders wary of developing chart patterns. Volume can be viewed as an urgency indicator. Higher volume is an indication that the market participants who are moving the market are feeling more urgency than if volume is lower. This can be combined with open interest to gain further insights. For example, if prices are moving strongly upward , volume is strong, and open interest is moving higher, traders can assume that the bulls are urgently buying the market and are in control. If prices are higher, volume is

146

higher, but open interest is down, then we can say that the shorts are urgently trying to escape their losing positions.

In brief, the following table can be used as an overview of the use of volume and open interest in analyzing price action.

Price up	Price up	Price up
Open interest up	Open interest up	Open interest down
Volume up	Volume Down	Volume up
Very bullish	Bullish	Trend change likely
Price up	Price down	Price down
Open interest down	Open interest out	Open interest down
Volume down	Volume down	Volume up
Underlying weakness	Underlying strength	Trend change likely
Price down	Price down	Price down
Open interest down	Open interest up	Open interest up
Volume up	Volume down	Volume up
Trend change likely	Bearish	Very bearish

One of the major characters of market indicators is the price oscillator. The oscillator looks at the rate of price change rather than the absolute price level. The simplest oscillator would compare today's price with a price at some set time in the past. If the price is higher than, say, 10 days ago, then the oscillator will be above zero. If the oscillator is negative, it means prices have dipped during the last 10 days. The most common oscillators are usually the difference between two moving averages. One classic oscillator is the 3-day moving average of the closing prices minus the 10-day moving average of the closing prices. When the 3-day moving average is above the 10-day moving average, the market is in a bull trend; and when the oscillator moves below zero, a bear trend is in force.

The oscillator is used not so much to determine trend as to determine when the trend is running out of momentum. An examination of an oscillator chart, as seen in Exibit 5-15, shows that the short moving average can move to a certain level above the longer-term but that when it does, it runs out of momentum and begins to contract. These levels are called overbought on the upside and are called oversold on the downside. This simply means that the market has gone too far too fast in one direction. The oscillator monitors excessive rates of price change that show too much emotion in the market and therefore possible turns in the price level.

Another use of oscillators is to show possible near-term tops or bot-

EXHIBIT 5-15   S & P 500 Futures Index (CME) (Golden State Commodity Publications).

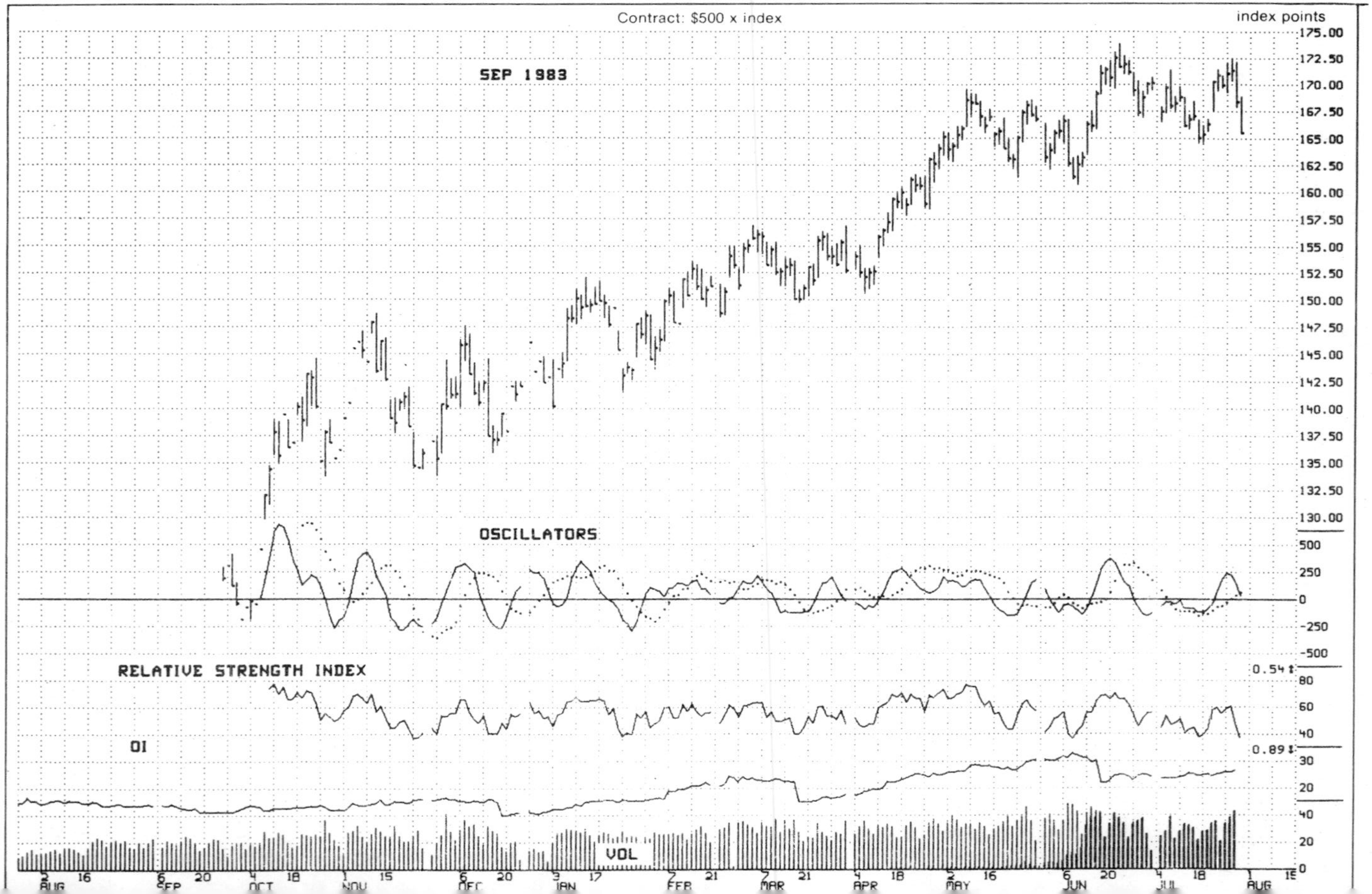

toms in the marketplace. When the 3-day moving average is gaining on a 10-day moving average, the trend is up. On the first day that the 3-day moving average is gaining less than the 10-day moving average, the oscillator will move downward. This is often an indication of a near-term top in the market that will last for 3 or 4 days. If the oscillator continues lower, it may signal an even more substantial top. The same concepts can be flipped over to indicate near-term bottoms. This can be a particularly useful tool in a trendless or trading market. Traders can, for example, sell the first sign of weakness after the market moves into an overbought situation. This will usually occur during the following day. This position may be a day trade or held for only a short time because of the trendless nature of the market.

A momentum divergence occurs when prices move to new highs on the move but the momentum oscillator does not move to new highs. This is a very strong indication that prices do not have great strength behind them and that a major turnaround is expected.

The advantage of the overbought or oversold oscillator is that it provides a check on the emotions of traders who are extremely bullish or extremely bearish. Traders who are very bullish on a market after a sharp rally will find that the oscillator will be flashing that the market is overbought. The overbought/overload oscillator thus can prevent traders from buying highs or selling lows before the trend actually turns. The problem with trading strictly from an oscillator is that it is trading against the trend and thus leaves the traders open to major losses. Nonetheless, it can provide an excellent opportunity for timing of entry or reentry into a market with the trend by waiting after the overbought or oversold condition is eliminated.

Mechanical Trading Systems

Mechanical trading systems are technically oriented systems for obtaining buy and sell signals without human intervention. These are often referred to as computer systems because computers are often used to do the math necessary to generate the signals. They are becoming increasingly important in the commodity futures industry; most commodity pools and managed accounts use mechanical trading systems for trading. The importance of these systems is bound to increase as managed accounts become a more vital part of the commodity industry.

The major advantage of mechanical trading systems is that they have no human emotion or input after the initial design of the system.

One criticism of humans as traders is that they tend to get overly bullish after a price rise and overly bearish after a price dip. This has the effect of getting traders long on the highs and short on the lows. A mechanical trading system, on the other hand, will not become overly bullish as it has no emotions to be manipulated by market action. A second major advantage of mechanical trading systems is that they often save traders many hours of work. Instead of poring over charts or fundamental information, traders input recent price information into their computers and come back after the computer has manipulated the data and generated the buy and sell signals.

Mechanical trading systems come in many styles. They can be trend-following, as is the usual case, or they can be contratrend systems. A trend-following system tries to identify what the underlying trend of the market is and to trade with that trend. A contratrend system, which is far more rare, will try to identify periods where the market has gone too far in a single direction and capitalize on the retreat of the price toward a more reasonable level. In addition, contratrend systems are often used in trendless trading markets.

The moving average crossover system is one of the all-time-classic mechanical systems. It has been around for at least 20 years in one form or another and is the usual starting point for many trading systems. It is easy to compute and use.

A moving average is the average price of the sum of a certain number of days of settlement prices. For example, a 10-day moving average is constructed by adding together the previous 10 price closes and dividing by 10. Exhibit 5-16 shows a 10-day moving average computed over a 20-day period.

Notice how the 10-day moving average lags behind the price movement. This lagging effect also smooths the data so that traders can see the underlying trend rather than the irregular noise that occurs on a day-to-day basis. A moving average crossover system utilizes this feature to make trading decisions. The moving average crossover system uses two moving averages of different lengths to define two different trend lengths. One popular moving average crossover system is the 3-by-20 moving average crossover. This means that a 3-day and a 10-day moving average are computed for the commodity in question. By definition this is an effort to establish a short-term 3-day trend and a long-term 10-day trend. If both the short-term and the long-term trends are up, traders should be long the stock index futures; if the short-term and long-term moving averages are both down, then traders should be short the stock index futures. Because the 3-day moving average is shorter than the 10-day moving average, it will be more sensitive to recent price movements. Traders are initiated or liqui-

EXHIBIT 5-16 Ten-day moving average
computed over a 20-day period.

Day	Close	10-day moving average
1	132.80	
2	131.90	
3	131.20	
4	132.00	
5	130.30	
6	129.10	
7	129.30	
8	129.40	
9	129.20	
10	130.80	130.60
11	133.50	130.67
12	135.90	131.07
13	134.90	131.44
14	134.80	131.72
15	135.30	132.22
16	137.90	133.10
17	139.10	134.08
18	140.40	135.18
19	141.10	136.37
20	140.10	137.30

dated when the 3-day average crosses the 10-day moving average. The procedure for using this system is very simple.

Traders first compute the 3-day moving average by summing the last 3 closes and dividing by 3. The 10-day average is found by adding the previous 10 closing prices and dividing the result by 10. If the 3-day moving average is above the 10-day moving average, traders should be long; and if the 3-day moving average is below the 10-day moving average, traders should be short. Day after day, traders should recompute the averages. If, for example, the 3-day moving average is above the 10-day moving average, the trader should stay long until the 3-day moving average moves under the 10-day moving average. Traders should then reverse their trades by covering the long and going short on the open of the next day's price action. These short positions should be carried until the 3-day moving average moves back above the 10-day moving average.

This simple trading system accomplishes all the goals of a mechanical trading system. There are no human emotions involved, and the time required to generate the signals is very little. Further refinements of the system are possible, and moving averages of different lengths can be generated. One of the more popular versions of this is the 5-by-20 moving average popularized by Richard Donchian. Many traders have exponentially weighted the moving averages and placed filters around the moving averages in efforts to improve trading performance. Traders wishing to go further into mechanical trading systems should read the superlative *Commodity Trading Systems and Methods* by P. J. Kaufman (John Wiley & Sons, 1978).

Relative Strength Index

One of the most interesting technical indicators is the Relative Strength Index (RSI). This was first published by Welles Wilder, who correctly pointed out several possible problems with oscillators and proposed the RSI as a way of retaining the positive aspects of oscillators while eliminating some of the negative aspects. The problems with the oscillator are outlined very well by Wilder as follows:*

> The first problem is erratic movement within the general oscillate configuration. As example of this, using a ten-day oscillator, suppose that ten days ago the price moved limit down from the previous day. Now, suppose that today the price closed the same as yesterday. When we subtract the price ten days ago from the price today, we will get an erroneously high value for the oscillator today. To overcome this problem, there must be some way to dampen or smooth out the extreme points used to calculate the oscillator.
>
> The second problem characteristic of oscillators is the scale to use for the "Y" axis. In other words, how high is high and how low is low? The scale will also change with each commodity being charted. To overcome this problem there must be some common denominator to apply to all commodities so that the amplitude of the oscillator is relative and meaningful.
>
> The third problem is the necessity of having to keep up with the enormous amounts of data. This is the least of the three problems; however, it can become burdensome to the trader who is following several commodities with an oscillator technique.

Wilder proposed the RSI as a way of dealing with these three problems. The RSI basically takes the average of the recent up movements, based on the close, and divides this by the average down movements of the recent past. This basic math is then converted into an index

*W. Wilder, *New Concepts in Technical Trading Systems*, Trend Research, Box 450, Greensboro, N.C. 27402.

form so that all commodities at all times have an index somewhere between 1 and 100.

To calculate the RSI traders must first collect the settlement prices of the last 14 days. Step two is to find the average up movement from close to close on those days that the market closed up. For example, if the September Value Line Index closes up 100 points on 1 day and 50 points on another day, and these are the only 2 up days in the 14 days, then the average up close is +.75. Traders then do the same procedure on the down closes. At this point, the traders have two numbers, one representing the average up movement on up days from close to close and the second number giving the average down movement on down days from close to close.

The third step is to divide the average up movement by the average down movement. This number is called the relative strength by Wilder.

The next step is to convert the relative strength into an index from 0 to 100. This is accomplished by adding 1.00 to the relative strength and dividing the result into 100 and subtracting the result of this from 100.

In other words, the RSI is 100 divided by 1 plus the relative strength. The relative strength is simply the average up movement over the last 14 days divided by the average down movement over the last 14 days. This has given us the initial RSI. Each day the trader must store the average up movement and the average down movement as this will be necessary to calculate the RSI for subsequent days.

To keep up the RSI on a daily basis, it is necessary to use the previous average up movement and the previous average down movement. By using these previous averages, a smoothing factor is brought to the calculation to eliminate one of the three errors in oscillators outlined above.

Each day it is necessary to compute the new average up movement and new average down movement. To do this, multiply the previous average up movement by 13, add today's up close, if any, and divide the total by 14. The same procedure is used to compute the new average down movement. If the current day is an up day, then add zero to the day's down movement. If the day is a down day, add zero to the up movement. Divide the average up movement by the average down movement to find the relative strength. Add 1.00 to the relative strength, divide the result into 100 and subtract this result from 100. This is the new RSI.

Let's look at an example of calculating and updating the Relative

EXHIBIT 5-17 Twenty days of
hypothetical closing prices.

Day	Closing price	Change
0	151.00	
1	152.00	+100
2	153.85	+185
3	153.70	−15
4	155.30	+160
5	156.15	+85
6	158.95	+280
7	157.10	−185
8	157.20	+10
9	157.05	−15
10	158.45	+140
11	159.60	+115
12	160.25	+65
13	159.10	−115
14	160.20	+110
15	161.10	+90
16	159.35	−175
17	158.80	−55
18	158.40	−40
19	158.80	+40
20	157.90	−90

Strength Index. Exhibit 5-17 shows 20 days of hypothetical closing prices.

During the first 14 days, prices rallied 10 days at an average of the up days of 125 points. Prices dropped 4 days at an average of 82 points. The next step is to divide the average up movement of 125 by the average down movement of 82. This product is 1.52 and is called the relative strength by Wilder. We now want to convert the relative strength into an index. This is done by:

Adding 1.00 to the relative strength = 2.52.

Dividing 2.52 into 1.00 = 40.

Subtracting 40 from 100 = 60 = the RSI.

To update the RSI for the close of Day 15:
Multiply the previous day's up average of 125 by 13 = 1625.

Add the current day's up movement, +90 to the up total, 1625 = 1715.

Divide the new up total, 1715, by 14 = 122 = the new up average.

Multiply the previous day's down average of 82 by 13 = 1066.

Because the current day was an up day, add zero to the down total, 1066 = 1066.

Divide the new down total, 1066, by 14 = 76 = the new down average.

Divide the new up average, 122, by the new down average, 76 = 1.61 = the new relative strength.

Add 1.00 to the new relative strength, 1.61 = 2.61.

Divide 100 by the new relative strength, 2.61 = 38.

Subtract this result, 38, from 100 = 62 = the new RSI.

This process is repeated each day after the close of trading. The only tricky part is to add zero to the down total if the close is lower than the previous close.

Exhibit 5-18 is a repeat of the previous table, but with additional columns filled in.

The best way to use the RSI is to graph it on the price chart. The relationship between the RSI and prices can easily be seen.

The first way to use the RSI is the way you would use the oscillator.

EXHIBIT 5-18 Twenty days of hypothetical closing prices with additional data.

Day	Closing price	Change	Up average	Down average	Relative strength	Relative strength Index
0	151.00	0				
1	152.00	+100				
2	153.85	+185				
3	153.73	−15				
4	155.30	+160				
5	156.15	+85				
6	158.95	+280				
7	157.10	−185				
8	157.20	+10				
9	157.05	−15				
10	158.45	+140				
11	159.60	+115				
12	160.25	+65				
13	159.10	−115				
14	160.20	+110	125	82	1.52	60
15	161.10	+90	122	76	1.61	62
16	159.35	−175	113	83	1.36	58
17	158.80	−55	105	81	1.30	56
18	158.40	−40	98	78	1.26	56
19	158.80	+40	94	72	1.31	57
20	157.90	−90	87	73	1.19	54

It can be used as an indication of an overbought or oversold market. Exhibit 5-19 shows the September 1983 contract of the S & P 500 with the RSI below it. Trends have difficulty continuing when the RSI goes above 70 to below 30. Occasionally, the RSI will move into a range. Overbought (O/B) and oversold (O/S) conditions will then occur when the RSI moves to the limits of the range rather than at 70 or 30. In Exhibit 5-19 the market became oversold when the RSI approached 45. Bull markets tend to get oversold before reaching 30; bear markets tend to get overbought before reaching 70.

These are strong indications of overbought or oversold markets.

Secondly, the index can be analyzed using classical chart analysis

---

EXHIBIT 5-19   The September 1983 contract of the S & P 500 with the RSI below it (Commodity Price Charts, 219 Parkade, Cedar Falls, Iowa 50613).

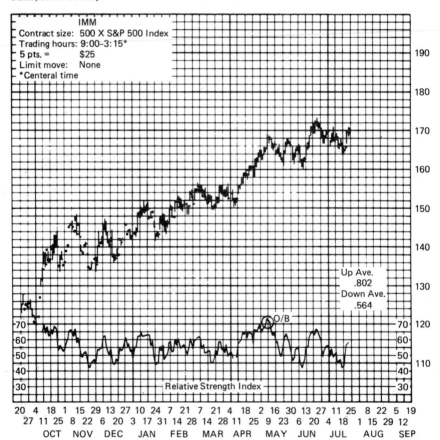

EXHIBIT 5-20   Examples of support points (Commodity Price Charts, 219 Parkade, Cedar Falls, Iowa 50613).

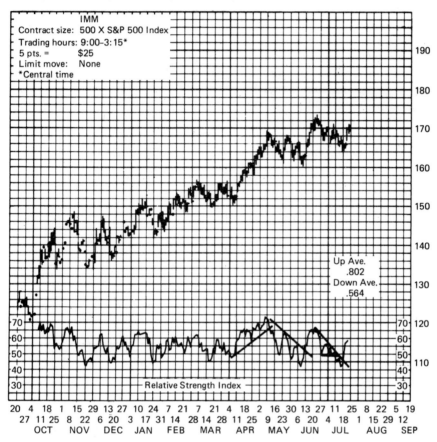

outlined above. Trendlines, flags, pennants, and other chart formations can be seen on the charts of the RSI. For example, a trendline drawn on the RSI can be used to define support and resistance for the price chart. When the RSI comes back to a previous point after moving higher this point will define a support point on the price chart. Exhibit 5-20 shows some examples of this. An examination of this figure will show many uses of chart formations in RSI.

Divergence between the price chart and the RSI is an important guide to major market reversals. If prices are making new highs but the RSI is not, this is an indication that the market is running out of upside momentum and will soon have a correction or even a major reversal. The converse is true for defining reversals that will be bottoms in the market. Exhibit 5-21 shows several examples of momentum divergence. Not all retracements are preceded by momentum divergences, but momentum divergences nearly always lead to retracements.

A final indication is the failure swing. A strong indication that the market will have a major reversal is when the RSI moves to above 70, drops down, moves up, but then fails to make a new high. Once again, the converse is true; if the RSI moves below 30, bounces higher, and then dips toward 30 but does not exceed the previous low in the RSI, then this is a good indication that the market will move higher near term.

It can be seen that the RSI solves several of the problems associated

EXHIBIT 5-21 Examples of momentum divergence (Commodity Price Charts, 219 Parkade, Cedar Falls, Iowa 50613).

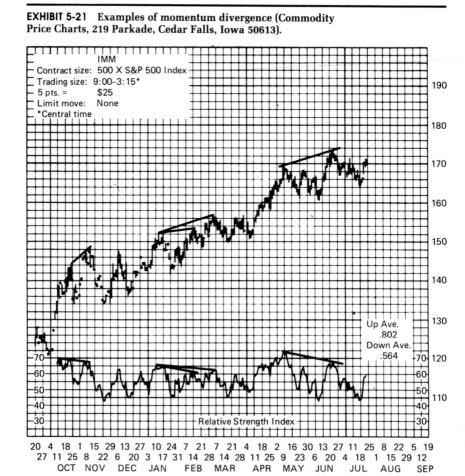

with oscillators and provides new insights into the character of the market. Traders are urged to read Wilder's book as it contains other useful insights into the use of the RSI.

Stock Market Technical Analysis

We have focused here on techniques of commodity futures analysis rather than examining classic stock market technical analysis. Stock market technical analysis uses the same chart patterns outlined above but also has some unique indicators such as the advance decline line, short interest ratio, and odd lot sales. These are extremely useful tools in analyzing the underlying stock market. The drawback is that the futures and underlying cash index may move in opposite directions on some days and may form different patterns. Traders wishing to gain the maximum profit should utilize both techniques in conjunction with each other. Confirmation or divergence from major patterns can be an important clue for technically oriented traders. Many excellent books and articles have been written about stock market technical analysis, so we will refer the reader to the last section of this volume rather than cover the techniques here.

chapter 6

Fundamental Factors and Spreads

The fundamental factors affecting stock index futures are simple but subtle. We will examine the factors that affect stock index futures evaluation in detail. We will not discuss analysis of cash market fundamentals but will focus on those aspects that differentiate the stock index futures from the cash stock indexes. A discussion of fundamentals such as a stock's earnings and the economic climate is beyond the scope of this book. The reader is referred to the list of excellent publications at the end of this book.

An understanding of the fundamental factors differentiating the cash stock market from the futures market will help traders profit and allow readers to expand into more advanced areas. This chapter should not be considered a how-to-do-it or practically oriented chapter. We will cover theory and leave the practical aspects to other chapters, particularly Chapter 7.

This chapter will focus on the flip side of the previous chapter on technical analysis. Technical analysis seeks to examine the behavior of the price, volume, and open interest as it relates to predicting future price trends. This chapter will focus on the underlying factors that allow us to evaluate a stock index futures contract as it relates to the cash indexes and to other contracts. The same methods that allow us to evaluate the futures contract will allow us to evaluate the fundamentals that affect the spreads between various contracts and options of the same index futures.

The differences between the contract specifications were outlined in Chapter 4. We will show additional factors that traders should examine when determining whether to enter long, short, or spread positions. We will occupy ourselves with factors that rule the relative values of the major stock index futures contracts. In addition to considering those factors that create the differences between the various contracts we will also consider what factors drive the differences between the months in a given futures contract.

In a nutshell, we will examine these basic aspects of stock index futures analysis:

- What is a stock index futures contract?
- How does it relate to a cash index?
- How does a stock index futures contract relate to convertible securities?
- How does it relate to interest rates?

These are basic questions that well-rounded traders must consider to help maximize profits. The same analysis that goes into determining the differences between months and contracts will be applied to examining the relationship between the price of the futures contract and that of the cash contract.

Much of the discussion in this chapter will be theoretical but of great help to investors. The theory can be used as the basis for the concepts outlined in the next chapter. The individual strategies in the next chapter are based on the discussions and theories presented in this chapter. In addition, the theories outlined in this chapter can be used by readers to develop new strategies. The subject of stock index futures is brand new and has had very little research. Strategies for trading stock index futures have barely begun to be developed, and much new work will be done over the coming years, reaching beyond the beginnings outlined in this book.

Stock Index Futures

The first and most basic question is: What is a stock index futures contract? There are two answers. The first is that it is a hypothetical portfolio of stocks. The second is that it is a commitment to make or take delivery of cash at a price determined by an index. Let us look at both of these more thoroughly.

A stock index represents a hypothetical portfolio of stocks. Each stock index contract represents a different portfolio and different weighting of the stocks. The methods of weighting and the stock portfolios were outlined in Chapter 4. The portfolios and weightings are combined into an index that is the foundation of the stock index futures contract.

Analysts must analyze each of the different portfolios and weightings to be able to trade the various stock index futures contracts profitably. The fundamentals of the various indexes will always be at least slightly different. Astute traders will examine the differences and be alert to the changes in the supply and demand for the different contracts. One contract may be poised for a greater move than another contract. For example, the Value Line contract tends to gain on the New York Stock Exchange Index during bull markets. This is particularly pronounced during the later stages of a bull market. This is because of the heavier weighting of secondary stocks in the Value Line contract versus the New York Stock Exchange Index. Alert traders could capitalize on this observation in two ways. They could buy the Value Line contract instead of the New York Stock Exchange contract if they are bullish on the market. If the basic trade is correct, traders will make more money being long the Value Line instead of being long the New York Stock Exchange Index.

Spreads

The second way to profit by the differences in portfolio composition and weighting is to spread the two contracts. For example, in a bull market, the trader could buy the Value Line Index and simultaneously sell the S & P 500 Index. A major advantage is that the margin requirement is much less. A typical margin charge for a contract of the Value Line would be $6500, while the margin for the Value Line/S & P 500 spread would be about $1100. This means that traders could initiate approximately six spreads for each outright position of the Value Line or S & P 500. The profit potential on six spreads is likely to be greater than the potential on the single outright. The disadvantages of the substitution of multiple spreads for a single outright are that the liquidity is generally lower for a spread than for outrights and that the commission cost is much greater. Traders will have to pay commission on both sides of the spread for each spread. In this example, traders would have to pay 12 commissions instead of 1. This strategy has the disadvantage of less profit potential for each position initiated. But less reward means less risk. Traders have different thresholds of risk. The lower risk associated with spreads may be adequate compensation to many traders willing to forego the higher reward.

Hypothetical Index

Stock index futures were not the first commodity to be based on a hypothetical index. The Eurodollar contract at the International Monetary Market of the Chicago Mercantile Exchange is based on an index of Eurodollar quotes from several large international banks. The Eurodollar futures contract was also the first to use a cash settlement delivery. The cash settlement was necessary because the contract is an artificial index of Eurodollar rates and there is nothing to deliver. The Eurodollar contract uses the index to make the contract more homogeneous. Each bank selling Eurodollars has a different price. The reduction of the various prices into a single index makes the contract more representative of the current Eurodollar market. Theoretically, a market based on an index is harder to manipulate. It would be possible to manipulate the contract value on the last day of trading by manipulating the Eurodollar quotes of just one of the banks selected for delivery. The index method would require manipulation of the positions of all the banks, which is virtually impossible.

Cash Settlement

The Eurodollar contract was the pioneer of a cash settlement based on a hypothetical index. It preceded the stock index futures contract by about a year. Nonetheless, stock index futures have brought these concepts to their highest level of development and popularity.

The analysis of the stock index futures and the underlying index is made easier because the futures contract is a hypothetical portfolio of stocks. This helps keep the analysis of the cash and that of the futures similar. Stock market analysis can be used with only slight modification on stock index futures. The areas of significant difference are the trading of inter-index and intra-index spreads, basis trading, and hedging.

In the final analysis, a stock index futures contract is a commitment to make or take delivery of an amount at a price determined by an index. This highlights the fact that the futures contract has to be equal to the cash index only on the last day of trading. This is generally true of all futures contracts. The futures and the cash converge as the contract expires.

Traders often complain that futures markets do not behave rationally. Usually, it is traders who are reacting irrationally. Traders expect the futures to respond to the fundamentals of the underlying stock index. They expect this even though the cash market is a different commodity. The futures contract has its own supply and demand and is related to the underlying cash index, but not on a tick-by-tick basis. The crux of the point is that the supply and demand of the futures contract, which represent the future value of the cash index, do not have to be worth the same as the cash stocks, which, by definition, represent the value of stocks here and now.

Nonetheless, the analysis of the underlying stock index will be useful in projecting prices of the stock index futures. It will undoubtedly be very profitable and useful because the two will not stray far apart. But it is necessary to take the analysis of the cash stock market one step further and examine not only the supply and demand of the underlying stock index but also the futures contract.

Theoretical Price Framework

Basically, the futures contract will represent future expectations within a theoretical price framework. In other words, the stock index futures price will have a theoretical price but will oscillate around that theoretical price because of expectations of future market direction. These two statements are another way of saying that the supply and demand of future stocks will determine the price of the futures contract. We will discuss at some length what the theoretical price of a futures contract is as well as what factors move the market away from that theoretical price.

The theoretical price is analogous to the "fair" price of an option. Much research has gone into determining what is the fair value of the option. A similar type of analysis can be applied to the futures contract. Both have the equivalent of an intrinsic value and a time value.

The theoretical price of a stock index future can be described by a theory called the capital asset pricing model. Its application to stock index futures is direct and simple. Readers are urged to read the references in the final section, which detail the capital asset pricing model.

The theoretical value of a futures contract is the same as the value of the underlying cash index on the last trading day of the futures contract. For example, if today is March 1 and traders wish to know what the value of the December stock index futures contract will be on the last trading day, they can apply the concepts of the capital asset pricing model as it relates to the value of what the stock market will be in December.

The main focus of the model is the risk that investors must acquire when they invest in stocks. Risk in stock market investing is the probability of monetary loss due to changes in dividends and price. There tends to be a direct relationship between risk and return. The higher the risk, the higher the return tends to be. Therefore, the identification of risk can be of use in determining the potential return. More important, the identification of risk can lead to opportunities where the risk is proportionately lower than the expected return and leads to increased profits in the market. However, the main point of the model for stock index futures is its outline of the relationship of any given stock or portfolio to the market and its implication for the evaluation of stock index futures.

The total risk of any investment can be identified by the construction of a probability distribution showing past rates of return. A probability distribution is a graph showing the rates of return during set times in the past. For example, the probability distribution could show rates of return for each month for the last 10 years. The bottom axis of the graph would show the return on the investment and the

EXHIBIT 6-1   Three possible probability distributions, one normal, two skewed.

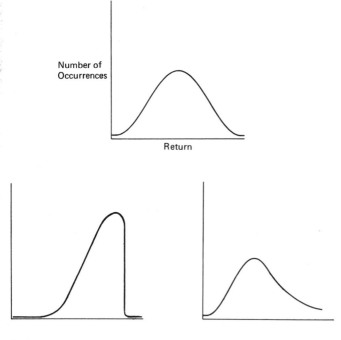

left axis would show the number of occurrences of that return. Exhibit 6-1 shows three possible probability distributions. The top distribution is called a normal distribution because it is symmetrical with the high point in the center. The other two graphs are skewed; that is, they are not symmetrical and the high point is to the side of the center of the graph. The returns from owning an investment can fall into any of the three types of probability distribution shown. In general, it is easier to use a normal distribution than a skewed distribution. It would be very difficult for average investors to be able to chart the returns from an investment, particularly if the distribution was skewed. Empirical studies show that this asymmetry is reduced by shortening the unit of time used in the study. As a practical matter, all public studies of rates of return and risk assume a normal distribution. For average investors this assumption will be more than adequate. Managers of large portfolios should be alert to the possibility of hedging errors arising from a skewness in returns that was not accounted for.

Return

The return is the point in the middle of the normal probability distribution. It is the point where the most occurrences are graphed and is therefore the highest point of the graph. This represents the return on the investment during the time span studied. It is the rate of return that would have been received from a particular investment carried for a long time. It is assumed that investors can expect to receive this rate of return over the long run. However, traders should recognize that this isn't necessarily so. A company that goes bankrupt will not yield a return as high as suggested by the probability distribution. A company that invents the cure for cancer will likely have a return significantly higher than the return suggested by the probability distribution.

Risk

Risk is the possibility of loss while waiting for the expected returns to materialize. Risk is defined as the total variability of returns. The probability distribution represents many rates of return. Any individual investor may receive any one of the rates of return that make up the curve. Investors know what is the most probable return but cannot guarantee it.

One investment that is considered riskless is buying and holding treasury bills. The return at the end of the holding period is known at the time of purchase. In addition, there is no chance of default because T-bills are guaranteed by the U.S. government. The risk of holding T-bills is nil. There is no possibility of receiving anything other than the expected return.

There are two types of risk: systematic and unsystematic. We will discuss each in turn.

Systematic Risk

Systematic risk is that portion of the total risk that comes from the market as a whole. Systematic risk is caused by events that simultaneously affect all the securities that make up the market. These events include economic and political changes.

Systematic risk is a large component of the risk of holding an individual stock. Stock and groups of stocks tend to move in the same direction as the market. There is a high correlation between the prices of the most actively traded stocks and the broad stock indexes. Stocks listed on the New York Stock Exchange have an average of 30 percent of their price variation explained by changes in the price of a broad market index. This allows hedgers to use stock index futures as hedging instruments. If there were no correlation between individual stocks and portfolios there would be no possibility of using stock index futures to hedge. Each stock has a unique relationship to the market. We will show that relationship later in this chapter and use it to construct hedging strategies.

Unsystematic Risk

Unsystematic risk is the risk that is unique to that particular stock or industry group. Changes in products, competition, the labor situation, and government regulation cause unsystematic risk. These are factors that affect individual stocks but not the whole market. Unsystematic risk is usually analyzed by securities analysts who are examining individual stocks.

Stocks that have a high degree of systematic risk are those stocks whose profitability is highly dependent on the economy. Railroads and steel companies are examples of companies with high systematic risk. Unsystematic risk is highest in companies that are not dependent on the economy for their profits. This usually means companies producing consumer nondurables such as food and basic clothing. People still buy food and clothes in the middle of a recession but are less likely to buy large-ticket items, such as automobiles, which use a lot of steel.

It is important for hedgers to be able to identify the proportion of systematic to unsystematic risk in their portfolios. Without this knowledge they will be unable to construct meaningful hedges; in other words, they will not be able to quantify the amount of systematic and unsystematic risk in each stock and portfolio.

Regression Analysis

The technique for quantifying the amount of systematic and unsystematic risk in each stock and portfolio is regression analysis. Regression analysis is a simple statistical technique for determining the relationship of several factors. Readers who are not familiar with regression analysis will not find this chapter difficult. We will not be using advanced math or Greek symbols. The basics of regression analysis are simple and will be easily understood by even the most unmathematical of readers.

Scatter Diagrams

The first step in using regression analysis is constructing the scatter diagram. The scatter diagram has many other uses for investors or hedgers in stock index futures, so let us examine it before returning to the discussion of systematic and unsystematic risk.

A scatter diagram is a graph of a series of points representing two numbers. To construct a scatter diagram, analysts place one set of numbers on the left side of the graph and the other set on the bottom of the graph. Exhibit 6-2 is an example of a scatter diagram.

The scatter diagram has a greater importance the less it is dispersed. For example, Exhibit 6-3 is a more important scatter diagram and is more useful than the scatter diagram in Exhibit 6-4. This is because a narrow dispersion shows a stronger relationship between two factors. Exhibit 6-4 has dots scattered in a wider pattern than Exhibit 6-3 and therefore shows a loose relationship between the two factors being graphed. A tight relationship is more important because it means that investors can have a greater confidence that if one of the

EXHIBIT 6-2   Example of a scatter diagram.

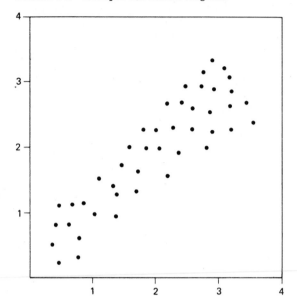

EXHIBIT 6-3   Example of a scatter diagram.

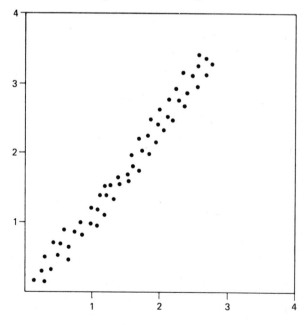

EXHIBIT 6-4 Example of a scatter diagram.

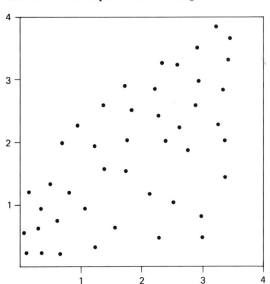

factors is at a certain level the other factor can be predicted with little chance of error.

The ideal scatter diagram is one that has no dispersion. In other words, it is a straight line. This would mean that a given value of one factor always leads to a given value of the other factor. The worst scatter diagram is one where the points are scattered randomly on the graph. This shows that there is no relationship between the two factors. Most scatter diagrams drawn by analysts and investors fall somewhere between the two extremes.

Regression analysis is the technique that determines a line through the middle of the points on the scatter diagram. Most traders can draw a line by sight through the middle of the points. This can be an adequate technique in many cases where absolute accuracy is not needed. It is better to use regression analysis because it gives an exact mathematical description of the line and gives the correlation between the two lines. Investors who are not familiar with regression analysis should be assured that they do not need it to understand the concepts in this chapter. Nonetheless, it is a useful technique for every investor to know.

The method of determining the systematic, unsystematic, and total risk is to draw a scatter diagram of the return on a stock versus the return on the market for given time intervals and draw a regression line through the resulting points. The regression line will be examined for several clues as to the characteristics of that particular stock. In fact, the regression line drawn through the scatter diagram for an individual stock is called the characteristic line.

Exhibit 6-5 is a scatter diagram showing the relationship between Kaiser Aluminum and the S & P 500 Index. The S & P index is used as a proxy for the market. A characteristic line has been drawn through the points on the graph showing a mathematical relationship between Kaiser and the market. The graph is constructed by plotting the intersection of the returns for Kaiser and the market. Kaiser is plotted from top to bottom and the market is plotted from left to right. The return on an investment in Kaiser is positive if the dot is above the center line and negative if below the line. The return on an invest-

EXHIBIT 6-5   A scatter diagram showing the relationship between Kaiser Aluminum and the S & P 500 Index (Jack Clark Francis, *Investments—Analysis and Management,* McGraw-Hill, New York, 1972).

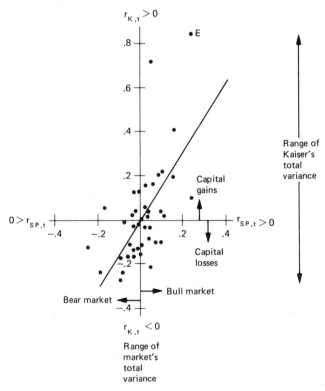

EXHIBIT 6-6   Explanation of Exhibit 6-5.

Kaiser:	Positive	Kaiser:	Positive
Market:	Negative	Market:	Positive
Kaiser:	Negative	Kaiser:	Negative
Market:	Negative	Market:	Positive

ment in the market is positive if the dot is on the right of the center and negative if the dot lies to the left of the center line. The meaning of the four quadrants of the chart is outlined in Exhibit 6-6.

The line obtained through regression analysis of this scatter diagram can yield tremendous insights into the characteristics of Kaiser Aluminum. A regression line has various components. We are mainly concerned with the beta, but first let us touch on the alpha. Alpha and beta are standard terms for parts of the regression or characteristic line. The alpha is the point on the graph where the characteristic line crosses the axis drawn vertically through the middle of the graph. In this example, it is the point where the market has a zero return. This allows analysts to determine what the return on an investment in Kaiser Aluminum would be if the market remains unchanged. Readers can see that the characteristic line crosses the vertical axis at essentially the zero point of the horizontal axis. This means that the return from investing in Kaiser Aluminum is essentially zero if the return from investing in the market is zero. This shows that the return from investing in Kaiser is highly dependent on the return from investing in the market.

Beta

Beta is the statistic (mathematically called the coefficient) that is the index of systematic risk. It describes the amount of systematic risk involved in carrying a particular investment. It can be used to rank various investments by their systematic risk. It cannot be compared to show the amount of risk. In other words, the beta coefficient can show relative amounts of risk between two investments but not the absolute amount of risk. It allows analysts to identify which investment has the greater systematic risk and what portion of the total risk is systematic for a given investment.

A beta of 1.00 means that the stock has a volatility equivalent to the stock market. A beta greater than 1.00 shows a stock that is more vol-

173

atile than the stock market, called an aggressive asset. A beta less than 1.00 shows a stock that is less volatile than the market and is often called a defensive asset. Most stocks have beta between .50 and 1.50.

Kaiser has a beta of 1.56. This shows that Kaiser is more volatile than the market. A beta of 1.56 means that the return on this stock tends to increase 56 percent more than the return on the market during bull markets. In bear markets, the return from holding Kaiser Aluminum will decrease 56 percent more than the returns from holding the market. Thus, bullish investors should prefer to hold Kaiser Aluminum stock instead of the market in bull markets.

The returns from holding a stock are composed of price appreciation and dividends. In general, the majority of the return on an investment comes from the price appreciation or depreciation. Dividends tend to be a small and stable component of total returns on holding a stock or portfolio. The beta is often referred to as an index of the volatility of an individual stock versus the market. This is not strictly true. Dividends play a part in the returns of a stock, and therefore we cannot say that the beta measures the difference in volatility. Nonetheless, the concept of beta as a measure of volatility is a useful rule of thumb because the return to a stock is largely composed of price appreciation or depreciation rather than dividends. Thus, though it is not strictly true, it is useful to think of the beta as an index of volatility versus the market.

The beta can also be used to indicate the relative volatility between two stocks. Remember, beta includes dividends in its estimation of the return to the stock versus the return to the market. We said that, as a rule of thumb, beta measures volatility. The beta of two stocks gives a quick estimate of which stock will outperform or underperform the market more. This can be useful when trying to examine a large number of stocks to find one that fits a criterion of volatility. Nonetheless, serious traders must remember that the beta measures the total return to investors from owning that stock compared to that from owning the market portfolio. A stock with a dividend yield of 15 percent can appreciate less in price than the market and still have the same return if the market portfolio has a dividend of less than 15 percent. To use beta as a more accurate indicator of volatility in relationship to the market requires that the investor know the dividend yield of the stock compared to the dividend yield of the market.

Portfolio Beta

Beta can also be applied to portfolios of stocks. Any given portfolio will most likely have a different beta than any other portfolio. The principles of comparisons between betas of stocks apply to comparisons of portfolios. In general, the greater the diversification, the closer the beta will move to 1.00. On the other hand, investors could assemble a portfolio consisting of only stocks with beta over 1.50, under .73, or whatever.

Mathematically, the best way to calculate the portfolio beta is to use regression analysis of the portfolio versus the broad stock market index. I recommend using the regression method if you have the time and resources. However, a relatively accurate rule of thumb can be applied quickly and easily. Most readers will find the following quick and dirty method, outlined below, to be adequate.

Construction of the beta of a portfolio is easy. The beta of each stock in the portfolio is weighted by the dollar value of the stock. Exhibit 6-7 gives an example of a simple portfolio and the calculation of its beta. Add the dollar values of the individual stocks together to find the total unweighted dollar value of the portfolio. Multiply the dollar value of the stock by its beta to find the beta-weighted dollar value. Add the beta-weighted dollar values and divide by the total unweighted dollar value to find the portfolio's beta. Notice that the stocks with high betas have their value accentuated and the portfolio is weighted toward them.

It is important to understand the math of constructing the beta of a portfolio. Most hedging strategies require an ability to ascertain the beta of a portfolio.

The beta represents an average relationship between the total returns of an individual stock or portfolio, and those of the market. Betas are usually constructed by examining monthly price and dividend behavior over a 5- to 10-year period. As with any average, there is a lot of variation. This variation can be very wide. It can create problems with trying to evaluate the stock index futures. One of the problems with the published beta numbers is that they are based on historical data that may not be applicable. For example, if a stock has

---

EXHIBIT 6-7 Example of a simple portfolio and the calculation of its beta.

Stock	Shares	Price	Dollar value	Times beta	Beta-weighted dollar value
ABC	100	150	15,000	.83	12,450
BCD	200	83	16,600	1.26	20,916
CDS	300	96	28,800	1.89	54,432
			60.400	1.45	87,798

been at $100 for 9 out of 10 years and all of a sudden plunges in value to $10, the beta will be very different for this stock. The beta studies, however, would have considered the 9 years at $100 to be more applicable and important than the most recent year at $10. Also, betas typically change with the price level of the stock. In general, the higher the value of the stock, the lower the beta. This is because a high-price stock requires a much larger dollar investment to move the price of the stock a given percentage. For example, it would take far more dollars to move a $100 stock up 1 percent than it does to take a $10 stock up the same percentage. Lower-priced stocks are known for their greater volatility because of the reduced dollars necessary to cause price changes. Thus, this increased volatility will represent itself as an increase in beta compared to the same stock at a higher level. If at all possible, investors should develop their own betas by using recent price data, and taking into account recent changes. The data could be collected from brokerage houses or exchanges or from private advisory firms. This would yield the greatest results but would also require the greatest investment of time and energy by the investor. Small investors will probably not find the investment worthwhile, but investors with millions of dollars in their portfolios will find it almost mandatory.

A stock split is one of the less common ways that price changes occur quickly and force betas to different levels. A stock that splits from $80 to $40 a share will increase the volatility of the market. This can have a major effect on hedging plans.

An additional factor that can affect the beta is a time period dominated by news that is specific to that particular stock or portfolio. This would be a time period when investors are focusing on the prospects for that individual stock and ignoring the general marketplace. This would mean that the unsystematic factors would temporarily outweigh the systematic factors. Unsystematic factors would include strikes, new product announcements, and government actions. A situation in which the unsystematic factors suddenly direct the market's total focus on an individual stock can take place suddenly. The effect can last as little as 1 day but may preoccupy the market for over a year. Factors such as this will not show up in beta studies until they have been extended for many months. This should underline the importance of a continual reevaluation of stock betas, as well as the use of recent data. Investors may consider weighting recent data more heavily than previous data.

It is also possible that betas will change for a stock as it changes its product mix. For example, there has recently been a major resource-oriented company that has expanded more aggressively into financial services. This will have a major impact on the beta of the firm. The change in beta will be relatively gradual, however, not showing up in beta studies for many months.

Sophisticated investors who wish to derive their own betas can add a time component to the beta in the regression equation. This will simulate the fact that betas change with time. All stocks' betas change, but most change slowly and slightly. The regression equations for these stocks will not gain by adding the time component subscript to the beta. There is, however, a large minority of stocks that have betas that change yearly or even more frequently. These stocks' betas would be significantly more valid if time were added to the equation. Average investors will find the extra work necessary to include time to be of little value. Investors controlling large amounts of money will probably find it worthwhile.

The back data showing the returns of the stock versus the returns of the market can be examined to estimate the tracking ability of the beta. The tracking ability is the correlation between the two factors. The higher the correlation between the stock returns and the market returns, the greater the confidence we can have in our analysis and/or hedge.

There is a mathematical way to estimate the variation of the beta from its average. We have noted that the average figure is the one given by most services and in published studies. We have also noted that it is important to know what the variation is around that average. The variation away from the average is estimated by a statistic number called the correlation coefficient. This is a number that is derived from the regression analysis of the relationship between the returns of the stock and the market. It measures the variation around the average. A correlation coefficient of 1.00 means that there is a 100 percent correlation between the two factors. A correlation coefficient of .00 means that there is absolutely no correlation between the two factors. The Kaiser Aluminum correlation coefficient is .60. This shows that Kaiser follows its regression line at about an average level. It is not a strongly or weakly correlated stock. The correlation coefficient can be used to estimate the strength of the relationship between the market returns and the stock returns. As the beta of a stock changes, the correlation coefficient will change. One suggestion is to analyze that time frame over the past to determine the beta that has the highest correlation coefficient. This will provide greater confidence in hedging or trading. Remember, the closer the correlation coefficient is to 1.00, the stronger the relationship.

We have so far been talking about systematic risk. The question often comes up as to how much the total risk of any given stock is systematic and how much is unsystematic. There is a way of determining this. The regression equation to determine the regression line and correlation coefficient can be taken one step further. By simply squaring the correlation coefficient, we can obtain the coefficient of determination. Thus, in the case of Kaiser Aluminum, the coefficient of determination is .36, which is the correlation coefficient of .60 multiplied by itself. The coefficient of determination tells us what percentage of the total risk is systematic risk. Thus, 36 percent of the risk of holding Kaiser Aluminum comes from the market as a whole. The remaining 64 percent of the total risk of holding Kaiser is unsystematic risk.

The average correlation coefficient of the stocks listed on the New York Stock Exchange is .50. This means that roughly 25 percent of the total risk inherent in the stocks comprising the market is explained by movements in the whole market. The remaining 75 percent comes from the risk in holding the individual stock.

Diversification

Systematic risk is also called undiversifiable risk, and unsystematic risk is also called diversifiable risk. One of the important features of unsystematic risk is that it can be virtually eliminated. The technique to use is diversification. The wider the diversification across industries and across many stocks, the lower the unsystematic risk will be. The diversification must be across the lines of industries that are unrelated. A group of 10 stocks all in the trucking industry will be highly correlated with each other; this is not diversification. The inclusion of one trucking company, one computer company, one soft drink company, and so on will provide the necessary diversification to eliminate unsystematic risk.

Diversification works because a well-diversified portfolio will have stocks that are are not correlated with each other. (Correlation analysis can be done on the price action of various stocks to discover which stocks are correlated and uncorrelated.) Diversification thus increases the chances that when one stock is moving lower in price, another stock will be increasing in price. A completely diversified portfolio will be a mimic of market action. The ultimate diversified portfolio is an investment in each stock comprising the market. An obvious alternative to investing in each and every stock is to invest in an index fund or a stock index futures contract.

Stock market analysts have for years recommended diversification to investors as a method of reducing risk. We have shown that approximately 75 percent of the risk of a given stock comes from activity that is particular to that stock—not from the market. A well-diversified portfolio can therefore eliminate 75 percent of the risk associated with holding any individual stock. Those stocks that may be plunging in value because of poor earnings or government action will be offset by those stocks whose price is skyrocketing due to bullish news such as introduction of new products or increases in earnings.

The ability to diversify and eliminate unsystematic risk is a powerful concept when used in conjunction with stock index futures. A well-diversified portfolio can eliminate unsystematic risk, leaving just the systematic risk. The systematic risk can be eliminated through the use of stock index futures so that the position becomes essentially a risk-free portfolio.

It should be noted that a risk-free portfolio is most likely a portfolio that will have exceptionally small returns to investors. Hedging is a tool to use when investors wish to go from a risky situation to an essentially riskless situation. This may occur when investors believe their portfolios are about to decline in value temporarily but do not wish to liquidate the whole portfolio because of a minor correction. Hedging with stock index futures to create a riskless investment becomes a powerful tool to those individuals.

It is important that serious investors and hedgers understand this discussion of beta and systematic and unsystematic risk. The analysis of the relationship between an individual stock or portfolio and the market as a whole is essential if hedging is to be done. Nonetheless, these topics are but a part of the realm of topics that tie the market in with stock index futures and define the relationship between the two factors.

Carrying Charges

The two most important factors for evaluating the futures contract relative to the underlying index are the expectations of future price value and the dividend yield on the investment. The value of that stock portfolio in 1 year will be the equivalent of the change in price plus the yield in dividends. The two components of future value, dividends and price changes, have significantly different attributes. We know the value of dividends with a fair degree of confidence during the coming year because dividends change relatively slowly for the major companies represented by the various stock indexes. Price changes are the dominant factor because of their volatility. It is difficult to estimate the total return of the portfolio because of the difficulty of estimating what the price of the portfolio will be in 1 year.

Although individuals may not have market opinions, market participants as a group do have an opinion on the market price in 1 year. Each person may have a unique perception of the future direction of the market, but these unique perceptions combine into the outlook of the market itself. Future expectations were difficult to estimate for the stock market before the advent of stock index futures. Stock index futures now give us an opportunity to estimate the market's future expectation. It is possible to estimate future expectations by examining the way the cash index, the futures index, and the carrying charges are related. We'll come back to this point after outlining the carrying charges.

Let us assume that there are traders who have enough money to duplicate the S & P 500 portfolio. If they were to invest in the cash stock market, the S & P 500 in this example, they would receive a return on their investment equal to the yield from the dividends plus the appreciation or depreciation of the underlying portfolio. Instead of buying cash stocks, they could buy stock index futures and hold the margin money in T-bills. These two investments should have identical returns. If one of the two investment alternatives appears to be underpriced relative to the other, investors will tend to sell the overpriced alternative and buy the underpriced one. This constant reevaluation of investment alternatives and readjusting of investment portfolios keeps the value of the two alternatives very close. Theoretically, the return on these two investments should be equal over the long run. This means the price of the futures contract must be related to the spot index through some mechanics. The relationship centers on the components of the total return on the investment, that is, the dividend yield and price change.

Let us simplify the example temporarily and presume there will be no price appreciation or depreciation for the next year and that the market does not believe there will be an appreciation or depreciation for the coming year. This means the relationship between the spot and the future is reduced to only the yield on the investment. In the case of the spot cash index, this is the dividend yield. For the futures market there is an additional step.

Commission houses allow investors to post T-bills for position margins. The brokerage houses allow this only for accounts with significant amounts of money, because they will typically require $5000 in cash over the amount in T-bills. For example, brokers may require that a $28,000 account keep roughly $8000 in cash to go with approximately $20,000 in bills. Some brokers will allow an account of

$31,000 to own only two T-bills because they want the extra $10,000 cushion before having to liquidate another T-bill.

Investors in stock index futures will maximize their return by putting their money posted for margin in T-bills. For example, let us assume that the full value of a contract is $65,000. This currently requires $6500 in margin. It can be assumed that investors will post at least 90 percent of the full value of $65,000 in T-bills. Thus, they will receive the T-bill yield for their investment in stock index futures. Because T-bills are sold in units worth just under $10,000, investors will be able to buy six Treasury bills. The yield on the T-bills has to be reduced slightly as most commission houses will only pay T-bill yields on 90 percent of the face value of the T-bills. This is, however, a subject open to negotiation between the commission house and the investor.

The preceding paragraph outlines most of the practical aspects for average market participants. The largest participants, who may be professional dealers, will be able to earn T-bill yields on their full investment. It is for this reason that the following analysis and, indeed, nearly all analysis assume that the full investment in stock index futures is receiving the full T-bill yield on the investment.

When discussing carrying charges, it is best to assume the situation closest to that of the large institutions. For example, if institutions earn full T-bill rates on their total investments (most individuals receive only 90 percent of T-bill yields), then we will assume that "the market" will receive full rates. This is because, theoretically, the market must take into account the most extreme case and, practically, the largest market participants are often the only participants who utilize the more advanced trading and hedging techniques that rely on this level of information.

The price for the futures contract 1 year in the future should therefore trade at the difference between the dividend yield and the T-bill yield, assuming no change in the underlying value or expectations of a change in the underlying value of the stock index.

This is much simpler to understand than options. Stock index futures have a very simple valuation model, while options have valuation models that require computers to calculate.

Rational investors have a choice of buying stocks and receiving dividends or investing an equivalent amount of money in T-bills and buying stock index futures. To repeat, this means that the value of the stock index contract is equal to the price of the cash index today, plus a premium equal to the difference between the dividend rate and the T-bill rate. The futures contract will sell at a discount to the cash index if the T-bill rate is below the dividend rate. Remember, this assumes that expectations of price fluctuations are ignored. We'll discuss that complexity later.

This outline of the valuation of stock index futures is the same for all commodity futures that are storable and redeliverable. Gold is a classic commodity that follows the same basic valuation formula as stock index futures. The difference in price between the cash and a futures contract, or between any two futures contracts, is the interest cost of carrying the commodity between the two time frames. For example, if cash gold is selling for $500 and the interest rate for a 1-year time frame is 11 percent, then a futures contract one year distant will sell for about $555. The investment result of buying gold and holding it for a year should be identical to that of buying T-bills and a 1-year gold futures contract. Notice that the gold ignores market expectations as a pricing factor.

Rational investors are confronted with two possible investment paths at every minute that the markets are open. They can buy either cash stocks or stock index futures. Rational investors should buy whichever investment medium provides the greatest return.

If investors choose to purchase a portfolio of stocks representing the cash stock index, their return (CR) is equal to the dividend yield (D*C0) plus the price appreciation or depreciation (C1 − C0). If they instead decide to invest the money in T-bills and buy stock index futures, their return (FR) is equal to the T-bill yield (TY) plus the price appreciation or depreciation of the stock index futures (F1 − F0). On the final day of trading, the futures contract price (F1) will be equal to the cash stock index price (C1) because of the contract specifications of the stock index contract. This means that we can also say that the stock index futures contract will have a return (FR) equal to the T-bill yield (T*F0) plus the price change of the stock index future (F1 − F0), which is the same as the eventual value of the cash stock index minus the current stock index price (C1 − F0). The two possible investments must have the same return to investors. The relationship between the two investments will be easier to see if we outline it in algebraic form

$$CR = (D*C0) + (C1 - C0)$$

(The cash investment return is equal to the dividend yield times the initial cash index price plus the difference between the price of the cash index on the final futures settlement day and the initial cash index price.)

$$FR = (T*F0) + (F1 - F0)$$

(The futures investment return is equal to the T-bill yield times the initial cash investment plus the difference between the final settlement futures price and the current futures price.)

However, on the final settlement day for the futures contract, the futures price will equal the cash price (F1 = C1). This means that:

$$FR = (T*F0) + (C1 - F0)$$

In general, dividend yields are relatively stable over a long period of time. This means that investors can essentially ignore dividends as a source of risk. The risk of the T-bill yield is nil as investors can buy 1-year T-bills and lock in the yield. Thus, for all practical purposes, investors can ignore both dividend and T-bill yields as sources of risk and uncertainty. This means that:

$$CR = FR$$

By algebraic substitution, we replace that equation with this one:

$$(D*C0) + (C1 - C0) = (T*C0) + (C1 - F0)$$

By further algebraic manipulation we find:

$$(D*C0) - C0 = (T*C0) - F0$$

$$(D*C0) + F0 - C0 = (T*C0) - F0$$

$$\frac{(D*C0) + F0 - C0}{C0} = \frac{(T*C0) - F0)}{C0}$$

$$\frac{F0 - C0}{C0} = T - D$$

This final equation means that when the difference between the current futures price (F0) and the current cash index price (C0) is divided by the current cash index price (C0), the result is equal to the T-bill yield minus the dividend yield. In plain English, this means that the percentage difference between the current cash index price and the current futures contract price is equal to the percentage difference between the T-bill yield and the dividend yield.

This same model can be used to evaluate intra-index spreads such as March/June Value Line. To find the value of a futures spread, calculate the value of each of the two contracts using the final equation given above. The theoretical value of the spread is calculated by subtracting the value of one contract from the value of the other contract.

The above equation can be taken a couple of steps further to obtain an equation that gives the current value of a futures contract.

$$\frac{F0 - C0}{C0} = T - D$$

$$F0 - C0 = (T - D)*C0$$

$$F0 = ((T - D)*C0) + C0$$

Let's look at an example of evaluating the cash index/futures index relationship.

September 15, 1994

Cash Standard & Poor's 100 index: 200.00
Dividend yield on cash index: 7%
1-year treasury bill yield: 12%

Current value of September 1995 stock index futures equals the T-bill yield minus the dividend yield times the current cash index price added to the current cash index price. In other symbols:

$$F0 = ((T - D)*C0) + C0$$

$$F0 = ((.12 - .07)*200) + 200 \quad F0 = 210.00$$

If the futures contract is for a period other than a year, then the calculations should be adjusted. For example, if the futures contract expires 6 months from the present, then the T-bill yield and dividend yield should be cut in half. Also, investors should use a 6-month instead of a 1-year T-bill yield. Even though investors use the 6-month T-bill yield, this yield must also be adjusted because all T-bill yields are quoted on an annualized basis. For example, a 6-month T-

EXHIBIT 6-8   **Yield adjustment table.**

Months	Adjustment factors	Months	Adjustment factors
1	.0833	13	1.0833
2	.1667	14	1.1667
3	.2500	15	1.2500
4	.3333	16	1.3333
5	.4167	17	1.4167
6	.5000	18	1.5000
7	.5833	19	1.5833
8	.6667	20	1.6667
9	.7500	21	1.7500
10	.8333	22	1.8333
11	.9167	23	1.9167
12	1.0000	24	2.0000

bill may be quoted to yield 10 percent but the actual return to an investor will be half the quoted rate. This is because the 6-month term is one-half the 12 months in a year. To find the actual yield over a given term, multiply the stated annualized yield times the adjustment factor listed next to the number of months until the futures expires. For example, if traders were quoted a yield of 11.89 percent for a T-bill that matures in 2 months, the actual yield would be 1.98 percent over the 2 months. The same adjustment should be made on the dividend yield. For example, a dividend yield of 5.20 percent for a year is only .87 percent over 2 months.

Let's take another look at an example of a futures contract that expires 7 months in the future. Notice that the yield adjustment factor is multiplied by the Treasury bill yield *and* the dividend yield.

November 15, 1994

Cash Standard & Poor's 100 Index: 200.00
Dividend yield on cash index: 7%
7-month treasury bill yield: 12%
Yield adjustment factor: .5833

$F0 = (((T - D)*.5833)*C0) + C0$
$F0 = (((.12 - .07)*.5833)*200) + 200$
$F0 = 205.83$

The yield adjustment factors are a necessity for calculating spread values. For example, let's examine a June/September S&P 100 spread. Remember, the basic technique is to calculate the difference between the theoretical values of the two contracts.

September 15, 1994

Cash Standard & Poor's 100 Index: 200.00
Dividend yield on cash index: 7%
1-year treasury bill yield: 12%
Yield adjustment on June contract: .7500
Yield adjustment on September contract: 1.000

June contract:
$F0 = (((T - D)*.75)*C0 = C0$
$F0 = (((.12 - .07)*.75)*200.00) + 200.00$
$F0 = 207.50$

September contract:
$F0 = (((T - D)*1.00)*200.00) + 200.00$
$F0 = (((.12 - .07)*1.00)*200.00) + 200.00$
$F0 = 210.00$

Thus, the June/September spread is evaluated at 207.50 — 210.00 or 250 points premium the September.

The 250 points that the September was over the June is called the carrying charges. In the previous example, the September contract was worth 205.83 while the cash was worth 200.00. Thus, the carrying charges between the cash index and the September contract were 5.83.

Carrying charges represent the maximum that the far contract can go over the near contract or cash index. If the September 1994 contract went beyond the carrying charges over the June contract, investors would be able to buy the June, sell the September, and deliver the equivalent of the June contract against the September contract. This would be a risk-free trade, and the market does not allow risk-free trades. The mechanism of keeping the two legs of these spreads in line is called arbitrage. We'll discuss this later in this chapter.

Let's repeat the major point about carrying charges. The value of a contract in the future is equivalent to the carrying charges between any two contracts or between the cash index and any futures contract. The carrying charge, simplified, is the difference between the T-bill rate and the dividend yield. This gives a fairly accurate estimate of the carrying charge, though there will be slight discrepancies from time to time. Nonetheless, this basic statement provides the key to the relationship between the various futures contracts and that between the futures contracts and the cash index.

The carrying charge must be appropriate for the time span under examination. We have been using a simplified example with the futures contract 1 year in the future compared to the cash stock index. A 6-month spread or a spread between the cash index and a futures contract 6 months distant would obviously have carrying charges half those of a 12-month time period. It is important to remember this simple point as it is easy to overlook and could have disastrous consequences. It is also important to understand the difference between an index futures contract's value and its price. The value of the contract is the price of the nearby contract or the cash index plus the carrying charges. The price is decided by buyers and sellers in an open auction on a commodity exchange. The price will nearly always be different from the value. Nonetheless, the price and value of an index futures contract affect each other.

There are several factors that have not been included in this very simplified model. The reason we have not included them is that they represent a very minor change to the basic scenario. We do not need to have an extremely accurate estimate of carrying charges because there are other factors that will affect the futures price more than the minor changes to the simple model. The simple model will be within about five ticks of the most accurate model. Sophisticated arbitrageurs, those who trade the cash versus the futures, will need to know more sophisticated valuation techniques. These techniques are discussed in books listed in the last section of this volume. Some of the points that are being left out of this particular discussion are transaction costs, margin variations, and the differences in borrowing rates. These have an impact on the carrying charges, though the impact varies at different times.

It should also be noted that carrying charges continually change. It is very possible to calculate carrying charges at any given moment to the penny. However, as the market T-bill rates, margin rates, dividend yields, and just about every factor involved move, then the carrying charges also move. Once again, the level of sophistication needed for 98 percent of all traders is such that the room for error is so great because of changing conditions that a rule-of-thumb measurement is better than a highly accurate one.

The theoretical futures price that is represented in the carrying charges will rarely occur. It will not occur largely because of changes in market expectations. Remember, we stated that the price of a futures contract is composed of carrying charges and market expectations. If the market is bearish on the future value of stocks, then the price will trade for less than full carry. If the market is very bullish on future stocks, then it will trade up to full carry but not beyond. In addition, market inefficiencies and the difficulty of arbitrage will tend to keep the market away from a perfectly theoretical price level. The uncertainty surrounding the moment-by-moment changes in carrying charges will make it extremely difficult for the market to evaluate and calculate a new theoretical trading value on a tick-by-tick basis.

Dividend Flows

A major factor that affects carrying charges is the timing of the dividend flows. Exhibit 6-9 shows the dividend flows for the Dow Jones's 30 industrials throughout the year. There is a basic seasonality of dividend payouts. During times of high dividend flows, it is reasonable that the futures contracts sell for less than the cash index because the yield on dividends for that short time period will be greater than that on the T-bill for the same period. Remember, the theoretical price difference between the nearby and far contracts or between the cash index and the futures contract is the T-bill yield minus the dividend

EXHIBIT 6-9 Dividend distribution for the 30 stocks making up
the Dow Jones Industrial Index (ACLI International).

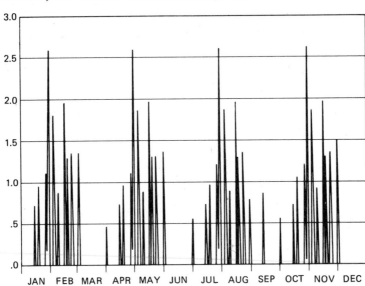

yield. The far contract was always priced higher than the near contract because our examples always had the T-bill yields higher than
the dividend yield. If the dividend yield is higher than the T-bill
yield, then there are negative carrying charges. This means that the
nearby contract will sell for more than the far contract.

The seasonality of dividend flows is a major determinant of the
value of the basis and the various spreads between indexes and contract months. Dividend flows are measured by the ex–dividend date,
which is also called the ex-date, or date of record. This is the last date
that ownership of stocks entitles the owners to the current dividend
payout. Purchases of the stock the day after the ex-date do not entitle
the owner to the current dividend. For example, let's say XYZ Company declares a dividend on March 31 for shareholders of record on
March 10. Purchasers of the stock after March 10 will not receive the
dividend. The stock's value will drop by the value of the dividend on
the opening of trading on March 11. This is because the share price
includes a premium representing the value of the dividend until the
ex-date. The date of the actual payment is irrelevant because the
prices of the stock no longer are directly related to the dividend after
the ex-date. Therefore, when we discuss dividend flows, we are dis-

cussing the ex-dividend dates and their effect on prices, not on the actual dividend payout.

Investors should have a list of the stocks on the New York Stock Exchange Composite list, showing the ex–dividend dates for a recent year. Analysts who need to fine-tune their index futures valuation models should keep this list up to date. Ex-dates can change from year to year and companies may add or delete dividends at any time. *Barron's*, a weekly publication, lists the ex-dates and the amounts. This is the easiest way to keep the list up to date.

Our basic model suggests that an investment in stock index futures and an investment in T-bills or cash stocks are equivalent at full carry. We further pointed out that the key factor was the T-bill rate minus the dividend yield. It is essential that the time spans represented by the two investments be the same. Dividend payments from ex–dividend dates falling after the expiration of the futures contract should be ignored. Only on the last day of trading do the futures and cash prices have to be equal. This means that the two equivalent investments should be considered as having a fixed holding period.

When most people talk about dividend yield, they are typically talking about the yield received if the stock or market basket is held for a constant and continuous time. For example, if I say the dividend yield on the S & P 500 index is 5.5 percent, then I am assuming that I owned the index at the beginning of the year and continued to own it at the end of the year. When we evaluate stock index futures versus the underlying cash index, we assume instead that there is a fixed holding period. This means that every day changes the return on the investment because the stocks are being purchased at different prices and the dollar amount of dividends can change each day. For example, let's assume that investors initiate a position in the cash index that will be liquidated at a set time several months from now. If no dividends are paid to the investor on the first day, then an investment made on the second day will have a higher yield than the same investment made the day before. Investors will be receiving the same dollar amount but over a shorter time frame. Each day, the decision is made to buy, sell, or stand aside either of the two equivalent investments, stocks or futures/T-bills. Each day the dividend yield must be recomputed because the index price has changed, the holding period has been reduced by 1 day, and ex–dividend dates may have occurred. Let's look at an example to illustrate this point.

January 1

Price of investment: $10.00

Dividends due on January 3: $.20

Annual return on investment: 365 percent. (The dividend $.20 divided by $10.00. This result is multiplied by 365 days in a year divided by the 2 days the position is open.)

January 2

Price of investment: $10.00
Dividends due on January 3: $.20
Annual return on investment: 730 percent. (The dividend $.20 divided by $10.00. This result is multiplied by 365 days in a year divided by the 1 day the position is open.)

This absurd example dramatizes the changes in dividend yield due to the progression of time. It is imperative that analysts take this into account in evaluation of the basis and spreads.

ACLI International Commodity Services, Inc. (717 Westchester Avenue, White Plains, New York 10604) did an interesting graphical presentation on the changes in dividend yield over different time spans. In Exhibit 6-9, notice the sharp seasonality and that there are no dividends during large parts of the year. Most of the ex–dividend dates are in February, May, August, and November. Most ex–dividend dates are roughly 1 month before the actual dividend payment date. Most dividends are paid on the last day of March, June, September, and December. This means that the ex–dividend dates are roughly 1 month prior to the payment dates. This is borne out by the chart showing the ex–dividend dates.

Exhibit 6-10 shows the declining balance of the dividends that the portfolio earned if held until the end of the year. Investors would receive $73.52 if they held the portfolio for the entire year. They would have received just under $20 had they bought the portfolio in the middle of September and held it until the end of the year. Notice that there are periods that investors would receive the same balance of dividends no matter when they initiated the trade. The dividend balance was $37.53 on every day between June 1 and June 29. In addition, there was no dividend payout after December 1. This means that those buying the Dow Jones portfolio after December 1 would have no dividend yield.

We discussed above how there will often be significant differences between the return on an investment if considered on a constant holding period and the return on an investment if considered on a fixed holding period. Exhibit 6-11 shows the return from the constant and fixed holding periods during 1981. Notice how the volatility of return increases in the fixed holding mode as it approaches the end of the holding period. This is another illustration of what we have in

EXHIBIT 6-10 Declining balance of dividends that the portfolio earned if helped until the end of the year (ACLI International).

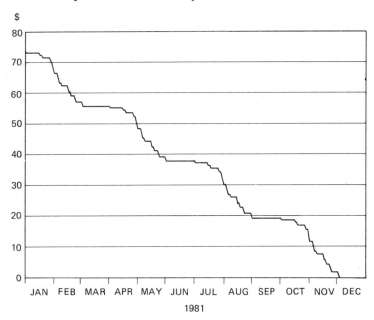

EXHIBIT 6-11 Return from the constant and fixed holding periods during 1981 (ACLI International).

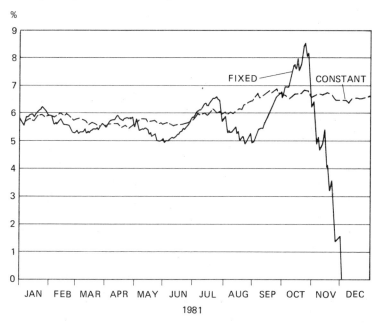

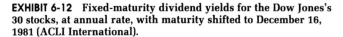

EXHIBIT 6-12   Fixed-maturity dividend yields for the Dow Jones's
30 stocks, at annual rate, with maturity shifted to December 16,
1981 (ACLI International).

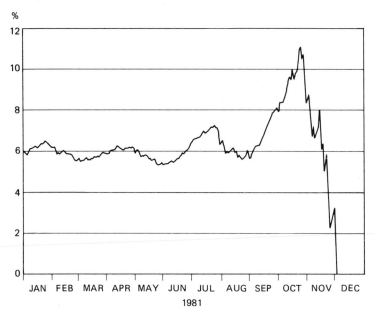

our absurd example above. As we approach the end of a fixed holding
period, a set amount of dividends will cause greater fluctuations in
yield because they are being compressed into a shorter and shorter
time span.

This effect is accentuated when we adjust the fixed holding period
to coincide with the last trading day of the S & P 500 contract, for
example. Now the yield fluctuations become even greater because of
the compression of time. Exhibit 6-12 shows the fixed holding period
dividend yield with the ending or maturity date shifted from December 31 until December 16, the last trading day of the S & P 500 futures
contract. The yield shows significantly more volatility even though
the ending date is moved just 2 weeks. For example, the yield peaks
at 8.5 percent in Exhibit 6-11 but peaks at over 11.0 percent in Exhibit
6-12. Notice that the values change but the timing doesn't.

ACLI took this interesting study a step further and applied the same
principles to the S & P 500 and the quarterly expirations of the futures
contract. Notice that the yields display a similar curve to that of the
Dow Jones dividends, with increasing volatility as expiration nears.

The curves all start with an assumed yearly yield of 6.0 percent and then oscillate as dividends are paid and time ticks away.

Dividends and Spreads

One of the most noticeable features of Exhibit 6-13 is that each expiring contract month has a sharp increase in yield starting about 6 weeks before the end of the contract. This increase peaks a couple of weeks before the end of trading and then collapses to a low level by contract expiration.

This large swing in the yield can have a big impact on the basis and spreads. This is because of the basic equation that says that the value of a contract is worth the spot index plus a premium equal to the T-bill rate minus the dividend yield for the given time frame. If T-bills yield more than the dividends, then the futures will be worth more than the cash index. If the dividend yield shoots over the T-bill yield, then the futures will be worth less than the cash index. Based on the dividend yield curve shown above, we would expect the cash to gain on the futures during the time period when the dividend yield is mov-

EXHIBIT 6-13 Fixed-maturity dividend yield for S & P 500 at annual rates (ACLI International).

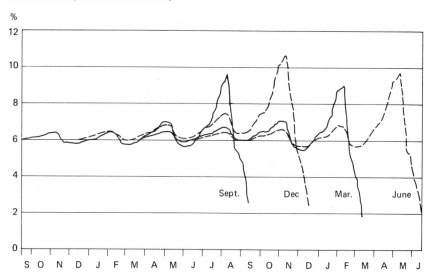

ing higher and the cash to lose sharply to the futures when the dividend yield collapses. This effect will be most pronounced in the relationship between the cash index and the nearest futures contract.

The same situation will affect the intra-index spreads. The value of the spreads will change as the values of the various contract months change due to the change in dividend flows. Exhibit 6-13 shows the relative dividend yields. Notice that the December contract has a peak yield 3.0 pecent higher than the March contract. The dividend yield for the March contract remains relatively stable while the December contract moves sharply up and down. We can state a general rule: If the dividend yield for one contract month is gaining on the dividend yield for a second contract month, then the first contract price will lose to the price of the second contract. If the dividend yield for one contract is dropping relative to another contract's yield, then the first contract's price will gain on the price of the second contract.

Based on the evidence in Exhibit 6-13, we would want to be long the March contract and short the December contract from about September 1 to about the third week in October. After dividend yields peak in the latter half of October, it would be better to be long the December and short the March.

The same dividend flow concept can be applied to inter-index spreads. Most investors simplify their inter-index trades by keeping them in the same months. In other words, when they want to spread Value Line versus S & P 500, they will select identical contract months, say, December Value Line versus December S & P 500. However, the spread might be more profitable if different contract months are used, say, December Value Line versus March S & P 500.

The profitability of the trade could be enhanced if different contract months are selected on the basis of dividend flows. We have just seen how dividend flows will change the intra-index spreads. For example, let us presume it is the beginning of September and we expect the far contracts to gain on the near because of dividend flows. Investors who are bullish the Value Line contract versus the S & P 500 may want to buy the March Value Line and sell the December S & P 500 to help maximize profits. These investors will be adding the effect of the change in dividend flows to whatever results from the underlying trade. Investors may want to adjust the contract months in the trade when the dividend flow effect changes bias. After the peak in dividend flow, investors will likely want to reverse the contract months in the inter-index spread.

In addition to the effect of dividend flows on basis levels, there is a slight bias toward greater volatility in the basis on far contracts whenever the far contracts are at a premium to the cash. The opposite is also true—basis volatility declines when the far contracts are at a discount to the cash. This effect occurs because an equivalent percentage change in the cash and futures indexes will cause the higher-priced index to move more in price than the lower-priced index. If far contracts are at progressively higher prices, then the relationship between the cash index and the furthest contract will be the most volatile. If the furthest contract is at a discount to the nearby contracts and the cash index, then the volatility in the basis between the cash and furthest contract will be less than the basis between the cash index and the nearby contract.

In general, this volatility effect will be minor. Differences in volatility should amount to only a few points. Nonetheless, hedgers should keep this effect in mind when determining which contract to hedge and what the hedge ratio of futures contracts to cash portfolio should be.

Compounding

Most discussions of stock index futures evaluation do not take into account the compounding of some of the returns in a given investment. Dividend and T-bill yields are the most important forms of return that could be compouded. For example, investors may invest in a futures contract due to expire in 6 months and buy a series of two 90-day T-bills rather than one 180-day T-bill. The interest earned on the expiration of the first 90-day T-bill could be used to purchase the second 90-day T-bill. Alternately, investors in cash stocks could use their dividends to buy more stock. Both of these actions can incrementally increase the return to investors.

However, it is recommended that investors ignore the effects of compounding except in rare circumstances. In evaluating stock index futures contracts, it is best to use the T-bill yield that corresponds to the futures contract holding period rather than assume a series of short-term T-bills. The problem with the shorter-term T-bills is that investors do not know what their yield will be on any of the investments except the first one. This means that investors are speculating on the price of T-bills. They can never know the final yield on their T-bill purchases until after the total investment is complete. These investors will not be able to compare adequately the relative merits of investing in stocks or stock index futures/T-bills.

The effects of compounding dividends should be ignored because the use of dividend payments to purchase additional stock is really another transaction. The dividend payment could be used to purchase a myriad of other investments or products and should therefore be considered a separate transaction with its own characteristics.

Some hedgers may want to consider adding a compounding effect if they feel confident of their ability to make the necessary forecasts, judgments, and adjustments. This may be an important consideration for hedgers who have a limited repertoire of investment possibilities. Thus, trustees of some pension funds may have to reinvest the proceeds from dividend payouts into the stock that paid the dividend or a similar investment. Note that transaction costs must be accounted for in any addition of compounding to the model.

Predicting Dividends

The worth of the valuation model can be increased by the ability to predict the dividend yield. The basic model assumes that the most recent dividend payments will be the same as those in the coming quarter. This dividend payout is compared with the current cash index price to identify a dividend yield for the time horizon of the trade. However, it is extremely unlikely that dividend payments for all stocks in an index will be static. This means that the dividend yield component of the valuation model will be wrong. First, it is likely that dividend yields in models will always be slightly wrong because no one can predict all dividend payouts with total accuracy. Second, accurately predicting the dividend payouts will increase the accuracy of the model. Thus, analysts should look to estimate the dividends of the major stocks as a means of increasing the efficacy of the model.

Dividends generally change in response to broad economic changes. As the economy expands and corporate profits increase, dividends are boosted. As the economy contracts and business profits contract, dividends are often cut or eliminated. This broad change in the economy can be considered when forecasting dividends.

Another possible way to forecast dividends is to use a regression line of recent dividend payouts to project the next payout.

Probably the best way would be to use the services of a major research company, such as PaineWebber or Value Line. These large research firms often forecast changes in dividends as part of their service. These forecasts can be plugged into the model as a way of attempting to increase accuracy. The research firms don't always predict dividend changes for every stock. Analysts may want to use research dividend projections whenever possible and adjust the remaining dividends en masse based on their reading of the economy and corporate profits.

Dividends, Treasury Bills, and Taxes

All estimates of yields must take into account taxes. The returns from both T-bills and dividends are subject to taxes. T-bill interest and dividend yields are taxed at the same rates for individuals. Corporations do not have to pay taxes on 85 percent of the dividends they receive from other corporations. They may have to pay up to 46 percent on the remaining 15 percent of dividends. This means their effective tax rate on dividends is only 6.9 percent versus 46.0 percent for T-bills. In other words, dividends become far more valuable than T-bills. For corporations, in general, investing in cash stocks would be far more profitable than investing in stock index futures/T-bills. Investors who do not receive the dividend exclusion will find dividends and T-bills to be of equivalent value, assuming that the yield is equivalent.

The majority of market participants do not receive the dividend exclusion. Private investors, pension funds, and mutual funds all will likely view T-bills and dividends similarly. However, private trading firms such as Salomon Brothers and other private corporations will find that the dividend exclusion rule will significantly increase their profitability of buying stocks and will significantly affect their analysis of the underlying value of stock index futures.

We have stated that the value of the cash index is related to the value of the stock index futures basically by market expectations and the yield on the two investments. Most individuals will be able to disregard the tax implications of the dividend exclusion rule. However, our model should assume the 85 percent dividend exclusion rule because extremely large and important traders can take it into account in their trading. Their economic power is such that they may have the ability through their trading to move the market to its value based on exclusion of dividends rather than equivalent taxation. In addition, commodity traders usually figure carrying charges on the assumption of the most advantageous situation that is generally available. For example, it is typically assumed that commodities can be financed for the prime rate plus 1 percent, whereas individual investors will not be able to borrow money at a rate that inexpensive.

Most analysts have constructed their models of stock index futures assuming that investors receive the full amount of their yield. That is to say that they receive a 5 percent dividend yield if it is stated that they receive $5.00 in dividends for every $100.00 that they invest.

However the reality is that investors must pay taxes on those dividends and their actual yield is often significantly less.

In addition, the effect of being in a 50 percent tax bracket is to reduce by one-half the difference in effective yield between the T-bills and dividends. For example, if T-bill yields are 10 percent and dividend yields are 5 percent, then there should be a 5 percent difference in price between 1-year futures and the spot index. If we assume a 50 percent tax rate, though, then the dividend yield is 2½ percent and the T-bill yield is 5 percent, thus reducing the differential to 2½ percent from 5 percent. This is a significant change in the value of the far contract in relation to the spot.

A company with 85 percent dividend exclusion will have an even more dramatic change in the relationship between the T-bills and the dividends. The corporation will pay 46 percent in taxes, meaning that the 10 percent yield on the T-bill will go down to 5.4 percent. The 5 percent dividend yield will be 85 percent excluded and the dividend yield will only be taxed at a rate of 6.9 percent for an after-tax yield of 4.66 percent. The difference in yield is now less than 1 percent instead of the 5 percent before taxes. The basic theory behind the model, as explained earlier in this chapter, is that every individual at every given moment will be deciding whether it is better to invest in stock index futures and T-bills or in the cash market. Over the long run, these two possible investments should come out even.

Market inefficiencies do exist, and the return on one investment may be higher than the return on the other investment. Nonetheless, in the long run, the return will be equal as market participants become more sophisticated in their use of the new futures contracts. In addition, there will be no free rides given to any market participants as the market becomes more efficient.

The market appears not to be taking into account after-tax yields on T-bills and dividends in basis movements. However, this may stem from an unsophisticated, inefficient market rather than from a fundamental flaw in the model.

The basic model of prices is simple and straightforward, because it does not take into account the fact that different market participants have different after-tax yields on alternative investments. The introduction of taxes makes the model fuzzier and less precise. However, there is probably a gain in accuracy by assuming the 85 percent dividend exclusion rule. This will tend to increase the value of cash stocks to a stock index futures/T-bill investment compared to current market participants' expectations.

A major effect of the dividend exclusion is that the dividend yield movements that are so dramatic in the last 2 months of trading will be accentuated on an after-tax basis for the major trading houses. In addition, these traders will have opportunities to profit from the market's different methods of dividend accounting. In other words, we have shown that the dividend yield can double during a several-week period before contract expiration. Basis levels generally take this into account near contract expiration.

Companies who have 85 percent of their dividend yield excluded from taxes will find the after-tax value of the dividends more than double relative to the T-bill yield. The market will be undervaluing the cash stocks relative to the futures if they do not take into account the dividend exclusion. Therefore, traders who do have the income tax inclusion will be in a position to be able to buy cash stocks and sell futures contracts against them as a potentially profitable strategy. Conversely, during that time period that the dividend yield contacts sharply just prior to contract expiration, this effect will also be accentuated for those corporations with dividend exclusion. During this time period, the market will be understating this value, and these corporations will be able to buy futures and cash and capture this differential in evaluation.

For example, let's assume a company pays 46 percent of its income in taxes but can exclude 85 percent of its dividend income. The strategy is to buy stocks and sell futures. Exhibit 6-14 assumes that there

EXHIBIT 6-14 Effect of price appreciation and depreciation on a hedge strategy.

July 1984	Buy stock	Sell June 1985
		S&P 500 Futures
	85,000 (170.00)	89,250 (178.50)
Situation 1		
June 1985	90,000 (180.00)	90,000 (180.00)
Situation 2		
June 1985	80,000 (160.00)	80,000 (160.00)

	Situation 1: prices rise profit/loss		Situation 2: prices fall profit/loss	
	before tax	after tax	before tax	after tax
Stock	+5000	+2700	−5000	−2700
Futures	−750	−405	+9250	+4995
Interest	−8500	−4590	−8500	−4590
Dividends	+4250	+3957	+4250	+3957
Total	0	+1662	0	+1662

is a holding period of 1 year, the purchase of cash stocks is financed at 10 percent, the dividend yield is 5 percent, and T-bill yield 10 percent.

This example shows clearly the profit available to a trading corporation buying stocks and selling futures if the market values the futures contract at simply the difference between before-tax dividend and T-bill yields. Corporations in this situation will buy stocks and sell futures to capture this arbitrage profit consistently. This anomaly will disappear as the market becomes more efficient and corporations use this strategy. The market will evaluate the futures contract at a value that takes taxes into account.

Taxes

There are other tax considerations in evaluating stock index futures. Sixty percent of the gains on noncash delivery futures contracts are considered to be long-term gains and 40 percent of the gains are considered short-term gains. This has been established in law very clearly. However, the tax treatment of cash settlement futures contracts such as stock index futures and Eurodollar futures has not been settled and may affect the evaluation of the futures contracts. At this point, it is suggested that analysts treat stock index futures as any other noncash delivery futures contract. It appears as though the market is working on this assumption. Traders should nonetheless be alert to changes in the tax interpretation of the gains and losses from stock index futures and these effects on the valuation model.

A more important factor is the timing option that is inherent in buying cash stocks but is not available in futures contracts. When individuals purchase stocks, they have the opportunity to defer taxes if the investment is profitable. Futures contracts, on the other hand, do not have this feature. Instead, futures contracts have their tax liability occur at the end of the transaction, or at the end of the calendar year, whichever comes first. If taxes are owed by the investor, then the payment is due April 15 even if the trade is closed out at a loss.

Owners of cash stocks have the opportunity to liquidate losing transactions before the end of the year and take a tax refund. Alternately, they can carry profitable investments into the coming year, thus deferring their tax liability. This has the tendency to increase the value of an investment in a portfolio of stocks relative to an investment in a futures/T-bill combination.

We have shown that the long-term return from holding a well-diversified portfolio of stocks and that from holding a futures/T-bill combination will be identical. The cash flow from the competing investments will be identical over the long run. However, the timing option that investors in cash stocks have will depress the value of the futures contract relative to the cash index.

It is useful to view the investment in stocks or a futures contract as two separate assets. The first asset is the return on the investment from price appreciation and either dividend or T-bill yield. The second asset is an option to defer taxes that is inherent in the investment in cash stocks but not in the investment in futures. Futures have a finite life span. Even those futures contracts that are initiated in 1 calendar year and carried into another calendar year are considered offset, or "marked to the market" on the last calendar day in the year the position is initiated.

This option has value only when there has been a capital gain. If the prices of stocks and futures have dropped, then there is no tax advantage to be gained in owing the cash stock relative to the futures contract. On the other hand, should the value of the stocks and the futures increase, then the deferment option has a value. The futures contract is marked to the market on the last day in the year and taxes must be paid on that gain in value. The investment in cash stocks, though, does not have to be offset, and the profits can be carried into succeeding years.

In general, one would therefore expect that futures contracts would be reduced in value relative to cash stocks in bull markets but that bear markets would see futures prices move more toward their theoretical value when taxes are not considered.

The timing option will also gain in value the more volatile the market is. The more volatile the market, the greater the potential of the timing option without a corresponding increase in risk. Thus, increasing volatility will reduce the value of the futures contract relative to the cash index, and vice versa.

The timing option also has a time value. The longer the time horizon to the end of the calendar year until the expiration of the futures contract, the greater the value of the timing option. The greater the time that prices may gain in value, the greater the value of the timing option. In other words, the greater the uncertainty concerning futures prices, the greater will be the value of the timing option. Once again, an increase in maturity will create the potential for an increase in the value of the timing option without a corresponding increase in the risk of the timing option.

An important implication of this concept is that tax-exempt investors will be able to increase their return without a commensurate increase in risk. The timing option is worthless to tax-exempt investors as they have no need for deferring taxes. For these investors, which include pension and mutual funds, the basic model outlined above is more accurate. However, a huge proportion of trading is done by investors who are not tax-exempt, including individuals and corporations.

The net effect is that the timing option will bias futures contract prices downward relative to the value of the underlying stock. Thus, tax-exempt investors who wish to carry a portfolio of stocks that is generally indexed to the market may increase their return without increasing their risk by buying a futures/T-bill combination rather than the stocks.

Market Expectations

We have shown that the value of a stock index futures contract versus the cash index comes from the carrying charges that are basically the difference between the dividend and T-bill yields and market expectations of future price direction. We have explained that the theoretical value of the stock index futures is exclusive of market expectations. By taking the actual basis and subtracting the theoretical value of the futures, we arrive at the expectations of the marketplace. For example, if full carry on the basis is 1000 points but the futures contract is only 100 points higher than the cash index, then we can say that the market is very bearish. The closer the basis comes to reaching full carry, the more bullish the market is. The oscillations of the value of the basis around its theoretical value give an important insight into the sentiment of the market toward future price action.

This information can be used in several ways. One potential use is as an indicator of an overbought or oversold condition. This simply means that when the market has gone too far too fast in one direction the market will retrace against the underlying trend. For example, if the market becomes overbought, a near-term correction downward should be expected. We can graphically see when the market sentiment has become overdone through the comparison of the basis with its theoretical value. Exhibit 6-15, reprinted courtesy of ACLI, shows the spread of the S & P 500 nearby futures minus the theoretical price. As the nearby futures move higher, market sentiment is said to be increasingly bullish, and vice versa. It can also be seen that market sentiment does not appear to stray too far from the theoretical value, but that when it does, it does not stray for very long.

EXHIBIT 6-15 Spread of the S & P 500 nearby futures minus the theoretical price (ACLI International).

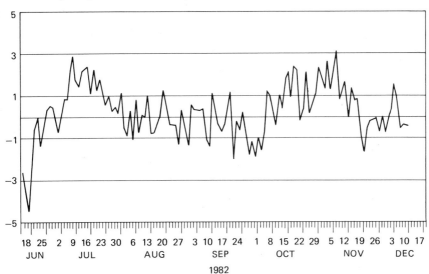

Traders could use a chart similar to this one to get an idea when the market has become overly bullish or bearish. For example, when the spread approaches 3 points over the theoretical value, the market could be said to be overbought, and long positions should be eliminated and/or short positions initiated.

Many academics have been searching for years for a way to measure market sentiment directly. They will no longer have to estimate market sentiment indirectly through put/call ratios and odd-lot sales. Stock index futures and valuation models provide the tools to measure market expectations of future prices directly.

Market expectations are often the dominant force in basis movements. Exhibits 6-16 and 6-17, reprinted courtesy of ACLI, show this clearly. Exhibit 6-16 shows the spot Value Line index as well as the June contract during the first few months of trading of the Value Line contract. Exhibit 6-17 shows a graph of the basis as well as the spread between the June and September futures contracts. It is interesting to note that the basis declined in value during late February and early march as the market moved lower. When the market bottomed in the middle of March, the basis bottomed as well, and they both moved higher until the peak in late April. This shows that the futures market tended to be more volatile and move more in any given direction than the spot contract.

Notice that the June/September spread had a slightly different pattern. The spread dropped in value longer than the basis did and bottomed late in March rather than in the middle of March. This suggests that market expectations remained more bearish into the June-to-September quarter than expectations of price action from the current date to the expiration of the June contract. This condition continued to occur as the spread remained flat into the middle of April while the general price level was increasing. This once again shows the potential difference in expectations of future market behavior between the current quarter and the June/September quarter. However, bearish expectations became evident in both quarters during May when both the spread and the basis retreated in value.

The major reason that there is a relationship between cash and futures is that on the last day of trading the futures must equal the cash price. This convergence will always create a profound effect on futures price evaluation. This effect becomes more and more pronounced the closer it is to the last trading day.

EXHIBIT 6-16 **VLA spot index versus VLA June contract (closes) (ACLI International).**

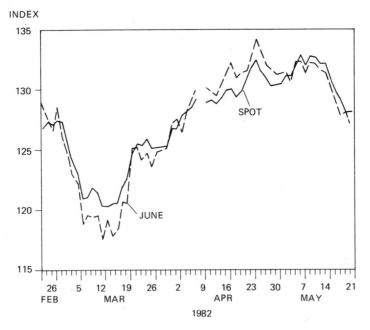

EXHIBIT 6-17   VLA contract—June basis* versus June/September spread** (ACLI International).

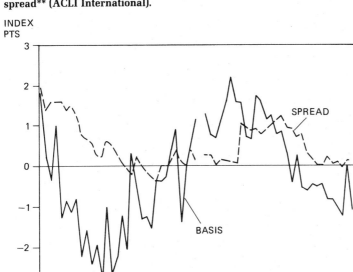

INDEX
PTS

*JUNE CONTRACT MINUS INDEX
**SEPTEMBER CONTRACT MINUS JUNE CONTRACT

Arbitrage

Another major factor affecting the relationship of cash and futures is arbitrage. Arbitrage is the spreading of cash stocks versus the index futures. It is possible to be long cash and short futures or short cash and long futures. It is also possible that a portfolio of options or convertible securities can be substituted for the investment in the cash stocks.

Most individuals find it difficult to arbitrage because of the large transaction and investment costs. A portfolio to simulate the stock market will cost hundreds of thousands of dollars to be reasonably accurate. Arbitrageurs rely on moving in and out quickly for their profits. Transaction costs for individuals make it prohibitively expensive to arbitrage. The transaction cost problem is the main reason that arbitrageurs are typically in a position of owning a seat on both the cash market and the futures market. Nonetheless, the market as a whole will simulate an arbitrage function. Those who think that the futures contract is proceeding too low in comparison to the cash index will tend to sell the cash and buy the futures, while those who believe that the futures are too high-priced compared to the cash will buy the cash and sell the futures. The sum total of all market participants will simulate an arbitrage function.

There are, however, portfolios of stocks or convertible securities that can be arbitraged against the futures. We will discuss this in greater detail in Chapter 7 when we go through a specific example of a portfolio and how it can be evaluated in relation to the stock index futures.

In most commodities there is a very simple arbitrage relationship. Gold is a classic arbitrage market because it is virtually identical on all markets in all cash and futures. It therefore becomes very easy to see the relationship between the price of gold and the gold futures contract. A futures index based on a whole basket of stocks is a much more difficult proposition. Tracking errors may creep in. This simply means that the arbitrage is not a very pure arbitrage and that errors are always going to occur because no one can duplicate the S & P 500 identically and be able to move quickly in and out of the market. This means that a pure arbitrage is not possible as transaction costs would eat up any profit potential. It is for these reasons that arbitrage and stock index futures must usually be considered a longer-term proposition to give the observed aberation time to be eliminated. In the gold market, arbitrageurs will usually try to make profits by initiating and exiting a position and carrying the position no more than 1 or 2 days. Stock index futures arbitrageurs will probably have to carry positions much longer before they are able to get the prices that they want. It is likely that a minimum length of time a stock arbitrageur will be able to carry a position will be 2 days before the price difference between the futures and the cash moves to a profitable level.

The related function to arbitrage is hedging. It is related to arbitrage not in its action but in its effect on market prices. Both arbitrageurs and hedgers look closely at the basis to determine the applicability of their trades. The basis is the difference between the futures price and the underlying stock index price. In the paragraphs above we simply referred to this as a "difference" but "basis" is the accurate term for it.

Hedgers are the most keenly aware of the cash/futures relationship and the basis. Let us quickly point out a few reasons for hedging and how the hedger will be relating the cash and futures prices.

Basis

The basis is the cash price minus the futures price. The basis should be related to the theoretical futures price discussion above. The value of the futures contract should be related to the cash price according to the theoretical price outlined above and expectations of future market direction.

The basis is the key point for hedgers to watch. It provides the clues to both long and short hedgers as to the desirability of their hedges. At some basis level it will induce long hedgers and at another basis level it will induce short hedgers. A long hedger is one who goes long the futures and short the cash and a short hedger is one who goes short the futures and long the cash. The basis will move back and forth within a range as it clears the market of hedging. As the market becomes more efficient, the oscillations may narrow. The narrowing of the oscillations is unlikely as market expectations and speculators will still play a big role in setting the price of the futures. In addition, the lag time between the onset of major commission house buying and the subsequent hedge selling can be considerable though the lags will shorten as the market becomes more efficient.

Hedging

The two basic styles of hedging are long hedging and short hedging. The typical hedger is a short hedger. Short hedgers usually own a portfolio of stocks and wish to hedge themselves against the decline in the value of those stocks. Short hedgers could include private individuals as well as the largest pension funds. Long hedgers would typically be short the cash stocks. This would usually be someone who was perhaps long a portfolio of puts or had written some calls. Another possibility might be someone who expected to be taking delivery of a relatively large quantity of stocks in the near future. A pension fund that is about to receive a payment would be an example of a possible long hedger. The pension fund may wish to ensure that the price of the stocks does not rise while it is waiting for the payment and may go out and buy futures as a hedge against rising prices. There will be many examples and strategies for both long and short hedgers given in the following chapter.

The basis level for hedging and the differences between the stock index futures contracts all have a heavy relationship to the carrying charges in stock index futures. We have a simplified discussion of that above when we mentioned that the carrying charge is, in its simplest but most usable form, the dividend yield minus the T-bill yield. Hedgers should note these carrying charges on a daily basis as an evaluation technique to determine whether the basis is out of line. If the basis is very close to full carrying charges then short hedges should be considered more strongly than at times when the basis is further away from carrying charges. The further the futures is from full carrying, the more attractive the long hedges will be. For example, let us suppose that full carry is 200 points between the cash index and the stock index futures. If the futures contract is priced at 190 points over the cash index, short hedges are likely be the most profitable. If the futures contract is only 10 points over the cash, then long hedgers will be more likely to initiate long hedges. This is not to say that long hedges should not be placed at a 190-point premium or that short hedges should never be initiated at only 10 points' premium; it merely means that a basis profit may accrue to hedgers.

A basis profit occurs when hedgers initiate a position and make a profit on the hedge due to a change in the basis level. Conversely, a basis loss would be a loss due to movements in the basis. Most discussions of hedging assume that the hedge nullifies all risk. The truth is that hedgers substitute basis risk for price risk. The changes in the basis level are much smaller than the changes in the absolute price level. The basis risk is considered a manageable risk by hedgers, whereas the outright price risk is much too high. Sophisticated hedgers will go so far as to hire basis traders to aid them in deciding when to initiate or liquidate their hedges in an effort to increase basis profits.

The factors that make the basis move are simply the factors that we outlined above—carrying charges and price expectations. The carrying charges vary due to changes in the price level of the stock index, dividend yields, and T-bill yields. Price expectations change in relation to many factors. These factors can include the state of the economy, interest rates, and so on. Let us now look at some of the factors that affect only stock index futures.

Future Stocks

Stock index futures represent the supply and demand for future stocks. This is the part of the theoretical price that deals with the expected price appreciation or depreciation, not the carrying charges. This is much the way it works with any commodity futures. For example, the December corn contract will be affected by both the carrying charges and the supply and demand of corn in December. The future supply and demand of stocks are affected by a number of considerations.

New issues are a factor as they will increase the supply of future stocks. This will tend to pressure the futures contract on an absolute level and in relation to the cash. By depressing the futures contract in relation to the cash, basis levels will tend to be narrower. This effect will be dampened if there is some prebuying hedging that is induced by current low basis levels. Traders must examine the new issues calendar in an effort to determine the effect of new issues on coming price levels. The higher the new issues the lower will be the value of the futures contract and the lower the level of the basis will be.

New Issues

Traders should also monitor those factors that lead to large new issues in an effort to predict when new issues will be increased or decreased. High interest rates will tend to lead to new issues as debt financing becomes prohibitively expensive and corporate treasurers are induced to raise capital through issuing new stocks rather than borrowing. A strong stock market makes this route doubly attractive to corporate treasurers, as it is easier to sell the stocks in the open market. These two factors, high interest rates and a strong market, tend to run contrary to each other and therefore must be weighed carefully before investors conclude what the new issue calendar will be.

Short Interest

Short interest is another source of supply or demand in the future for stocks. A high short interest has the effect of showing latent demand for stocks and vice versa. However, this demand may show up at lower price levels if there continues to be new selling or short selling. Thus, this factor is bullish for stock index futures if all other things are equal. A higher short interest will tend to move stock index futures toward full carry on the basis and spread levels.

Interest Rates and Stock Index Futures

Interest rates are another major indicator of the supply and demand for future stocks. Interest rates measure the preferences of investors and consumers for consuming goods now or at some time in the future. Suppose interest rates for a 1-year time period are 10 percent. This means that investors are saying they would rather have $1.10 one year from now than $1.00 right now. Because $1.00 is simply the most liquid form of wealth, we can say that interest rates measure the time preferences of consumers. At any given moment, everybody in the world can make a decision as to whether to consume his or her wealth now or save it until any time period in the foreseeable future. Even very poor people can decide whether they want to buy extra food now or wait until tomorrow. People who reduce their consumption today so that they may consume tomorrow are shifting their time preference for consumption into the future.

Interest rates simply measure the time preferences for the consumption of goods by the whole economy. When individuals buy stocks, they are buying shares in a company that represent productive capacity over a fairly lengthy time period. In addition, different stocks relate to different time preferences. If individuals purchase stocks of companies that make machine tools, they are buying stocks in companies with very long time preferences. This is because the purchase of machine tools is far removed from the consumption of consumer goods. If a company is making machine tools, those machine tools must be manufactured, then put into a factory where they then can make other machine tools or machinery to manufacture consumer goods. A machine tool also tends to last many years and therefore represents a long-term investment in the future. On the other hand, an investment in a company that makes movies would be considered a more short-term investment as the stock will rise and fall largely in response to the current popularity of the company's movies.

In general, stocks are considered to be a fairly lengthy investment and are considered a shift in time preference from nearby consumption into the future. In other words, individuals may either buy Big Macs now or invest in McDonald's stock, which is an investment in productive capacity over a number of years. Thus, a rise or fall in interest rates, which is linked to the rise and fall in time preferences of consumption of individuals, will show the supply and demand of productive capacity in the future.

High interest rates mean that investors are demanding a high price to lock up their money and to limit their consumption now. The lower the interest rate, the higher the demand for future goods, including stocks. A high interest rate level implies that investors are seeking to consume now rather than in the future and that stock prices will be low. Eventually interest rates will become so high and stock prices so low that investors will be induced to change their time preferences more toward the future and away from the present and purchase stocks and bonds, thus reducing interest rates and boosting stock prices.

A second effect of interest rates is their direct relationship to corporate profits. In general, higher interest rates mean a higher debt servicing load by corporations, and thus lower profitability. There is thus a direct relationship between interest rates and corporate profitability and, hence, stock prices.

Investors will find it very useful to examine the levels of interest rates in relation to each other. The yield curve can provide useful insights into the behavior of stock prices. A positive yield curve occurs when short-term interest rates have lower yields than long-term interest rates. A negative yield curve occurs when short-term interest rates have higher yields than long-term interest rates. Remember, we have stated that interest rates measure the time preferences of the individuals making up the economy.

A positive yield curve shows that the supply of near-term goods is higher relative to the demand than the long-term supply is relative to the long-term demand. The market is increasing the price of distant goods to try to induce an increase in supply of those goods and also to reduce consumption of future goods to bring it more in line with the supply. Thus, a positive yield curve is an inducement to reduce the supply of near-term goods and increase the supply of future goods.

An investment in stocks is a sensible response to this market inducement. It reduces consumption now by taking money out of the pockets of consumers and investors and investing it in capital goods, which produce goods for the future. It therefore reduces the supply of goods now and presumably increases it in the future.

A negative yield curve has the opposite effect of the positive yield curve. It therefore makes sense that the more the market moves toward a positive yield curve, the more bullish the stock market will be. The more the yield curve turns negative, the more negative the stock market will be. This effect will be most pronounced in stock index futures, as they represent stocks in the future rather than now.

Thus, the relationship between overnight money and relative short-term interest rates, which represent the price of near-term time preferences, will be a good indication of the supply and demand of current versus near-term stocks. This relationship will therefore have an effect on the stock index futures basis.

Call Option Premiums

The premiums on call options can be used to confirm a high or low basis as the premiums are also indicators of demand for future stocks. There are two drawbacks to this method, however. One is that the investor must be continually evaluating whether the premium on the option is "fair" or not. A second drawback is that premiums are often used as an overbought/oversold indicator. Options premiums will be contrary indicators at the most extreme levels, whereas at more moderate levels they may be more usable to provide insight into the supply and demand of future stocks.

Liquidity

Another factor that increases the demand for future stocks versus cash stocks is an increase in the liquidity of the economy. When corporate, personal, and government balance sheets become more liquid, much of the liquidity goes into purchases of stocks. A major increase in the money supply will lead to a major increase in the stock market. Thus, changes in the acceleration and deceleration of money supply, particularly M-2, can be used as a proxy for the supply and demand of liquidity. The liquidity is first injected into the economy through the banks, who use it mainly to buy government or corporate debt instruments. There is a lag time before this money works its way into stocks. Eventually, the liquidity reaches throughout the whole economy. Stocks are one of the first beneficiaries of changes in liquidity because they are a highly liquid investment compared with, say, opening a dry cleaning store, or building a new plant.

Cash

Many investors look at the amount of cash that portfolio managers are holding as a sign of a latent demand for stocks. The higher the cash level the more possible demand there will be for stocks in the future.

Intra-index Spreads

The points just outlined will affect both basis levels and intra-index spreads. Intra-index spreads are those spreads between different option months in the same index futures. June versus September S & P 100 would be an example of an intra-index spread. The same factors that affect the basis affect intra-index spreads. The spreads are moved by changes in carrying charges and expectations of future price changes. The expectations are heavily influenced by the factors just outlined.

Inter-index Spreads

Inter-index spreads are affected by three major factors. Different weightings, different stocks, and different sizes of contracts will be the dominant conditions affecting the price of the inter-index spread.

Weightings

Different weightings affect the spread relationships between the various stock index contracts such as S & P 500 versus Value Line.

The weighting of the Value Line accentuates the price action of smaller, less capitalized stocks. It is a truism that lower-price stocks have bigger percentage price swings. It is more common to see a $10 stock gain 10 to 20 percent in a day than it is to see a stock selling for $100 have the same percentage gain. It takes a far greater amount of money or buying power to move a $100 stock $1 than it takes to move a $10 stock $1. There is a tendency for smaller companies to have lower stock prices than larger companies. This means that the Value Line is more heavily weighted toward the smaller companies than the NYSE or S & P indexes. The S & P and NYSE indexes are weighted by capitalization. The larger the company, the more weight it has in the index. The S & P 100 is composed of essentially the 100 largest stocks. The S & P 500 index is an index of basically the 500 largest companies traded on the New York Stock Exchange. The NYSE Index is the index of all stocks on the New York Stock Exchange. The S & P 100 is a subset of the S & P 500. The S & P 500 is the subset of the NYSE Index.

This sets up a continuum of weighting. The S & P 100 is weighted the most toward the largest-capitalized industrialized stocks. The Value Line is weighted the most on the other end of the spectrum. The lesser-capitalized smaller companies are the dominant factor in the Value Line Index. The NYSE Index is somewhere in between. It

213

has a broader list of stocks in the S & P but does not use the weighting factors that the Value Line uses. The S & P 500 is between the NYSE Index and the S & P 100 in characteristics.

Thus, traders who believe that the secondary stocks will outperform the big-capitalization issues will buy the Value Line and sell the S & P 100. Traders who feel the other way around will tend to buy the S & P 100 and sell the Value Line.

Directional Bias

Another factor is that there is a tendency for the Value Line to gain on the S & P and NYSE indexes during bull markets and lose during bear markets. This is because the larger percentage gains of the small stocks will tend to accentuate the up movements in a bull market and the down movements in a bear market. For example, Exhibit 6-18 shows the cash Value Line index, the S & P 500, and the NYSE Index along with spreads formed by the three indexes. Notice that the Value Line generally gains on the other two indexes during bull markets and tends to lose to the other indexes during bear movements. This effect occurs because of the weightings and the size. The weightings were just discussed in the previous section.

The price level is the other major reason that this effect occurs. An index at 170.00 will climb more points in an up movement than an index at 160.00. If both climb 10 percent, then the absolute number of points by the first index will be greater than that by the second index. Similar percentage movements produce dissimilar point movements.

On the other hand, it doesn't necessarily have to occur every time. Other factors can override this, such as a change in interest rates affecting the large-capitalization stocks more than the smaller stocks, or it is possible that the major institutions are buying the "Nifty Fifty" and are ignoring the secondary stocks. Analysts can use this basic truism of buying Value Line and selling S & P 500 during the bull market and vice versa in a bear market, but there are other factors that over the short run can override this factor.

Index Composition

There are also major differences in that there are different stocks within each of the three major indexes. An excellent play here is the

EXHIBIT 6-18 Cash Value Line Index, S & P 500, and NYSE Index along with spreads formed by the three indexes (Spread Scope, Inc.)

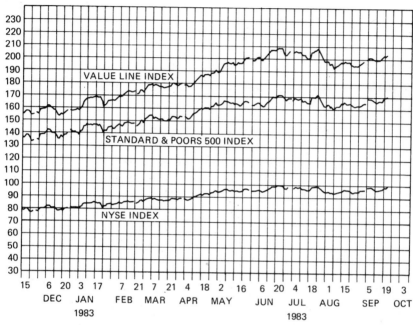

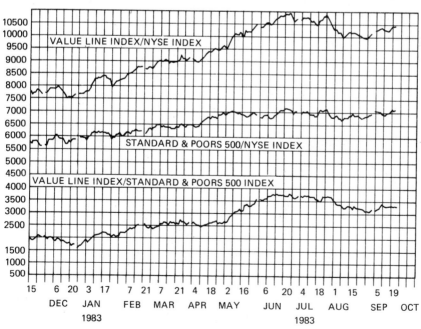

S & P 500 versus the NYSE Index. The S & P 500 is a subset of the NYSE. It is composed of 500 of the largest companies in the country (400 industrials, 40 utilities, 20 transportation companies, and 40 financial institutions) while the NYSE Index is composed of all stocks on the New York Stock Exchange. The relevant question is what will change the relative values of the NYSE Index and its subset, the S & P 500. The main factors are the relative strength of the secondary stocks in relation to the primary big-capitalization stocks. Either technical or fundamental analysis can be used to make this decision.

One fundamental example is the movement of interest rates. Higher interest rates affect the S & P 500 more than the NYSE Index because larger-capitalized firms are, by definition, more capital-intensive. Higher interest rates will be negative to the S & P 500 versus the NYSE Index and lower interest rates will tend to bull the S & P 500 up more than the NYSE Index.

The Value Line could be substituted for the NYSE Index in this trade. However, traders must take into account the different weighting features outlined above. These weighting factors may help or hurt the trader. In the case of the S & P 500 and NYSE, the weighting factors are identical so traders merely examine the difference between the secondary and the big-capitalization stocks. When you add the different weighting factors of the Value Line, a new variable is introduced into the equation. These weighting factors may help or hurt the trader. For example, we have said that a bull market will tend to help out the smaller stocks so we might see a situation where we have a bull market accompanied by higher interest rates. This would tend to help out the Value Line more than the NYSE Index and certainly more than the S & P 500. In this case the additional weighting factors of the Value Line would be helpful to the trader because they would accentuate the percentage gains of the smaller stocks. Lower interest rates but declining stock market would be a different matter, however. The weighting would tend to drive the Value Line down against the S & P 500 even though the higher interest rates would also be driving down the S & P 500 versus the Value Line. Traders might end up with a trade that goes nowhere because they have offset their trading advantage by adding in the weighting factors.

A simple way in which all the contracts are different is in size of the contracts. The contracts all have different values. The Value Line and S & P 500 are generally worth about the same value, although the Value Line has been worth slightly more during the last several years. The NYSE Index is worth about half the value of the other two contracts. For example, a recent day saw the Value Line at 177.40 × 500 = $88,700, the S & P at 151.60 × 500 = $75,800, and the NYSE Index at 87.45 × 500 = $43,725. Thus the NYSE was worth half the Value Line and slightly more than half the S & P 500. The S & P 100 is worth slightly less than the NYSE Index.

Traders wishing to spread between the various contracts should consider two major points. The first is that a contract worth more than another contract must move in price more to have the same percentage increase. If the Value Line is at 150.00 and the S & P 500 is at 140.00, then a 10 percent rise in "the market" will mean the Value Line index will move 15 points and the S & P 500 14 points. Thus, all things being equal, traders should buy the most expensive index and sell the least expensive contract if they are bullish and vice versa. The usual spread will be the Value Line versus the S & P 500. More aggressive traders could do Value Line versus NYSE Index or S & P 500 versus NYSE Index as there is a bias of almost two to one in favor of the Value Line or S & P 500 against the NYSE Index.

The second important consideration is how many contracts one should trade in inter-index spreads. The most common is to do one Value Line contract versus one S & P 500 contract, two contracts versus one contract in the Value Line versus NYSE Index or S & P 500 versus NYSE Index spreads, and five contracts of S & P 100 versus two S & P 500. In general, this is a good rule of thumb. However, the spread will be weighted by the contract with the largest value. This adds another factor to consider. It may be helpful or unhelpful to the particular spread. For example, if one is bullish on the Value Line and bearish on the S & P 500, then doing one Value Line versus one S & P 500 will help the spread if it works but will be an additional negative factor if it goes against traders. If traders believe that the wrong sizes between contracts will be helpful, then traders can leave the weighting nonequal. If it is unhelpful then traders should neutralize the weighting by making the value of the two sides of the spread as equal as possible. To do this simply divide the value of one side of the spread by the price or value of the other side. For example, if the Value Line is trading at 177.50 and the S & P 500 is at 151.60, then the division yields a 1.17 ratio of the Value Line prices versus the S & P 500 price. This means that the value of almost 12 S & P 500 contracts is worth the same as 10 Value Line contracts. To give another example, let us say that the Value LIne at 177.40 versus the NYSE at 87.45 equals a 2.03 ratio of Value Line price to NYSE Index price. Traders should then initiate almost exactly two contracts of the NYSE Index for every one contract of the Value Line. Technically one would want to do 203 Value Line versus 100 NYSE indexes, but the lack of precision will not be a major factor when we get a difference of two decimal places.

Conclusion

The valuation of stock index futures in relation to the cash index is an important yet subtle problem. We have focused on the various factors that should go into the valuation of stock index futures. We have focused particularly on the basis, the relationship between the cash and futures indexes. In the following chapter, we will examine how some of the theoretical concepts outlined in this chapter can be applied in a practical manner by investors and hedgers.

Investment and Hedging Strategies

There are many investment and hedging strategies available to users of stock index futures. Many of the strategies are derived from the concepts of the preceding chapter as well as from basic hedging theories. The hedging concepts have been around for years and have been thoroughly discussed in many books. We will apply these concepts to specific situations in this chapter and outline strategies that can be used by the hedger.

Investment strategies are virtually infinite. We will therefore focus on individual circumstances that are common and peculiar to stock index futures. In other words, we will not be looking at situations where the business cycle has turned up and traders wish to be long the stock market. This style of analysis is applicable to both stock index futures and the stock market and has been thoroughly discussed in many other books. We will instead focus on strategies that are peculiar to stock index futures. For example, if traders are more bullish on secondary stocks than on the big industrial issues, then they can buy the Value Line and sell the S & P 500. This strategy is only practical with stock index futures. It is possible to do it in the cash market, but commission and other transaction costs would be extreme.

In our discussion of investment strategies we will address a single issue as if the rest of the world were static. In other words, we will treat the situation that we are describing as if it exists in a vacuum, and we will consider no other influences on that situation in relation to that particular strategy. The real world, of course, is far more complicated. It may be that the situation described in this chapter and the strategies are applicable but that the particular circumstance is overwhelmed by a contrary influence. For example, we may believe that the intra-commodity spreads will widen in the New York Stock Exchange Index because we believe the carrying charges will widen out due to higher prices. This may be true and the analysis may be highly accurate and applicable. Unfortunately, there may be other pieces of information that are not taken into account that will turn this correct analysis into a losing trade. Perhaps dividend flows change dramatically and move the spread in a direction opposite to the effect given by the higher prices. Therefore, it is necessary for the investor to examine each of the situations outlined in the chapter to ensure that there are no other factors that will eliminate the profitability of the trade.

In effect, we are using what is called a static model of the universe. We are assuming that there are no changes other than those we have set up in our laboratory. Reality is not so simple, and caution is advised.

Hedgers or investors are urged to examine those parts of this chapter that are most applicable to their situations. There is no need for broker dealers to read the section devoted to small investors and holders of call options.

Investment strategies should be examined carefully by investors so that there is a full understanding of the variety of ways to handle possible situations. This will help traders stay out of unprofitable situations, as they will have the means to discover possible conflicts. It is conceivable and even likely that a given stock index future at a given time may fit into several of the situations outlined below.

We will spend some time discussing the basic concepts of hedging before getting into the specific situations and strategies. This will allow commodity futures novices to get a background in the important concepts necessary to understand the strategies given to hedge price risk. Experienced traders and hedgers are encouraged to read the following section. Many traditional concepts of hedging have to be changed because we are hedging an index, not a given product. There are also many concepts of hedging that are peculiar to stock index futures.

Hedging Concepts

Time is one of the critical components of business. Manufacturing is the transformation of materials into goods over time. Investors seek returns on their investments over time. The ability to address the time aspect of an investment is one of the critical values of futures markets.

Prices are another critical element in the manufacturing and investing businesses. Indeed, investing is the art and science of being able to evaluate the price of various investments over time. The ability to reduce price risk is a major goal of all investors.

In addition, investors are constrained by their inventories of investments, their desires to change their inventories, and contractual demands on their investment decisions. All of these constraints create risk due to fluctuating prices. Hedging with futures can help reduce these risks.

In the past, a money manager has been able to rank in the top performance decile by having a track record with a return only a few percentage points higher than the return from holding the market as a whole. If the S & P 500 index dropped 15 percent in 1 year, money managers who lost 13 percent were considered good managers. The commodities industry has a different criterion for excellence in money management. Commodity futures money managers who lose money are considered failures no matter what the market does. This is largely a function of the different psychologies of the two markets. Stock traders are less likely to profit in bear markets. Some institutions may have legal restrictions on their ability to go short. Commodity traders usually have no psychological restrictions. It is as easy to go short as it is to go long. Thus, commodity futures money managers are expected to perform as well in bear markets as in bull markets.

Stock index futures give traders an easy, inexpensive way to sharply reduce price risk in their trades. Bear markets may not be profitable for the traders, but there no longer exists any excuse for not splitting even. Stock money managers will be judged now more on absolute gain or loss of customers' equity than on their ability to beat a random portfolio.

Nonetheless, futures contracts and specific stocks or portfolios are not completely interchangeable. We showed the theory behind the valuation of the futures contract versus the cash index. We will consider this issue further in this chapter. Using futures contracts for hedging will not eliminate risk, but it will reduce it. This point cannot be overemphasized. Many stock traders believe that stock index futures will put an end to stock price risk. Risk can be sharply reduced, but it can never be eliminated.

Hedging is offsetting a cash position by taking an opposite position in the futures market. The purpose of hedging is to reduce exposure to risk due to price movements. Hedgers can be long hedgers or short

221

hedgers. The most common type of hedger is the short hedger. Short hedgers own or are carrying an inventory of the commodity they wish to hedge. Their concern is that prices may go down while they carry the commodity and decrease the value of the inventory. For example, there are millions of owners of stocks. When the price of their inventory of stocks goes down, they lose money. Thus, owners wishing to reduce their price risk will short-hedge by selling short futures contracts against their long stock position. Long hedgers are those who are short the cash market and must deliver stocks or stock substitutes in the future. These hedgers will buy futures to offset their short cash positions. These two small examples highlight the idea that hedging is the offsetting of an existing position to reduce risk. Hedging only takes place in goods that have significant unpredictable price movements. Without significant price movements there is little risk and therefore little reason to hedge. If hedgers could predict the future price direction of the inventory of stocks they hold, they could adjust their portfolio according to their price expectations instead of hedging. If potential hedgers believe they can predict the market they are probably better off speculating than doing their usual business!

The problem with hedging is that it is rarely perfect. Futures contracts call for the delivery of specified commodities in a specified manner. In the case of stock index futures, cash must be delivered based on the closing price of the cash stock index. No one can exactly duplicate this portfolio, and therefore no one will have a portfolio with exactly a one-to-one relationship with the underlying index. Another problem with hedging is that commissions must be paid to execute the futures contracts. This makes the return on the futures contract less than expected based solely on the price movement. The final problem that can make a hedge less than perfect is that the futures contract can be liquidated usually very easily while the cash side of the hedge is often very hard to liquidate with ease. For example, a portfolio of $100 million can be hedged with about 1300 futures contracts. It may take a full day to liquidate 1300 contracts at a reasonable price, but selling $100 million worth of stock would be a major sell program. It would be difficult to get a reasonable price for the stock, particularly if smaller issues are held.

In spite of the problems, hedging represents a method of reducing risk due to adverse price movements. If the problems just outlined did not exist, the hedge would be perfect and price risk could be eliminated. However, the hedge is not perfect because of the outlined problems. The hedge sharply reduces risk but does not eliminate it. It substitutes the risk of change in the relationship between the futures and the cash for the price risk. We outlined the ways of evaluating the relationship between the cash and futures in the previous chapter.

As was mentioned, the most common type of hedger is a short hedger. A short hedger is one who shorts the futures contract in order to reduce the risk of holding inventory, or commitments to hold inventory. Examples of a long hedger would be a portfolio manager, mutual fund, and pension fund. The portfolio will typically be constructed of long positions in stocks but may also contain commitments to purchase stocks such as call options or convertible bonds. The short hedger will ascertain his or her net exposure in the marketplace and essentially sell an equivalent number of futures contracts.

A long hedger is the opposite. Long hedgers are much rarer in stock index futures, but they do exist. A long hedger is one who is short the cash stocks and needs to buy an equivalent number of stock index futures. An example of a long hedger is one who is carrying a portfolio of short stocks, has written a call, or has made a contractual commitment to deliver stocks.

Basis Profits

In fact, the problems outlined above are the foundation for potential profits. Hedging exchanges price risk for basis risk. Wherever there is risk, there is the potential for reward. Sophisticated hedgers look at the basis inefficiencies as opportunities for profit. The fluctuations of the futures versus the cash can often be predicted and traded.

The relationship between the cash and the futures can be split into an analogous part and a nonanalogous part. The analogous part represents the similarities between the cash and the futures. The nonanalogous part represents the differences. The Value Line cash and futures indexes are similar in that they have a similar base and method of computation. They differ in the ways outlined in the last chapter, such as carrying charges and market expectations. Basis traders will focus their analyses on the differences in order to understand and, it is hoped, profit by the changes in the differences between the two indexes.

Hedging is often rightly thought of as giving up the chance of price profit to avoid price risk. Hedgers instead substitute price risk and the potential for basis profit.

Hedgers will find the differentials between the cash and the future to be the most important factor, while speculators will view the price swings as the most significant factor. Speculators must need to forecast absolute price changes, while hedgers focus on the factors affecting the basis. Thus, hedgers wishing to profit through basis movements must have a deep familiarity with the valuation techniques outlined in the previous chapter.

Many hedgers will not fully hedge their inventories or commitments. These hedgers will be looking at both absolute price changes and basis movements. An incomplete or partial hedge is probably the most difficult position to be in as it requires the hedgers to be cognizant of more factors affecting their profits or losses. In addition, many hedgers will find that they have more differences between their particular cash stocks or commitments than the market as a whole.

For example, a portfolio consisting only of machine tool manufacturers will not track the broad stock indexes as well as the cash index on which the futures contract is based. This means that the differences that make up the basis are going to be significantly larger than they would be when hedging a widely diversified portfolio. As a result, there is additional basis risk but also additional basis profit potential.

It should now be clear that hedging is a method of changing risk—changing the character of the risk the hedgers acquire by being in business. In addition, the risk and potential reward vary all the way from virtual speculation to a very conservative hedge program.

The futures hedge therefore serves two roles: (1) It transfers to others the price risk associated with the holding of stocks or commitments in the stock market; and (2) it isolates those factors that form the basis between the cash and futures from which hedgers expect to profit. This means that hedgers should look upon hedging not as a neutral strategy to nullify all risk but as a strategy for attaining profits, albeit at a lower level than might be earned by outright speculation in the cash stocks.

Alternate Marketing Strategy

Futures contracts can be used by hedgers to provide an alternate marketing strategy to their usual procedures. Marketing in this case simply means the sale of stock that has previously been purchased or the covering of a short position already established. An extremely large portfolio would have a difficult time eliminating price risk due to the large transaction costs incurred when trying to move huge blocks of stock at a given time. For example, let's assume that hedgers have decided that the market has peaked and they wish to unload large quantities of stocks from diversified portfolios. The futures contracts can be sold that best correspond to a particular portfolio at that time. For example, if the hedger makes the decision to sell a September contract on June 1, he or she then has 3 months in which to wind down the portfolio. By giving additional time, the hedger should be able to reduce commission and other transaction costs. In addition, flexibility is retained to change opinions and reinstate the net long position. It is this flexibility to timing that can provide one of the greatest values to a hedger.

Management Problems

Without changing prices, there would be no need for hedging. Corporations would not need to use the futures market to hedge price risk. However, there are few people in the stock investment field who are not at risk through price changes. Indeed, the magnitude of average price changes has been increasing as wild market swings rock the market. We now see daily price changes in the Dow Jones Industrials that would have been equivalent to a month's range only a decade ago.

Management has problems greater than just the price changes. They have basically three problems. The first problem is inventory requirements. This can be the holdings of securities or it can be the commitments to buy or to sell that have been prearranged. For example, a pension fund has the problem of trying to maintain the proper inventory of stocks given its mandate. In addition, it will know to the exact date and to within a few pennies how much it will be receiving because of pension payments into its fund. This means that a pension fund has a commitment to purchase securities at a certain dollar level on a certain day.

The second management problem is the financial requirements of holding and hedging the inventory. This includes such things as the fiduciary responsibility for making sure that the money is not poorly invested. Financing becomes a major problem as well. The inventory of stocks may be financed or margined, and certainly the hedge itself must be financed. We will be discussing further in this chapter the cash flow considerations of hedgers, so let's sidestep that issue here.

Let us simply point out that if the futures side of the hedge is not the profitable side, then additional capital must be committed to the hedge even though the net position is flat; that is, there is no profit or loss. This additional margin money will likely be financed through bank loans. An additional financial requirement is the insurance and safekeeping of both the cash stocks and the futures contracts. Due to regulatory requirements and the firm action of the clearinghouses, there is little need to worry about insurance and safekeeping on the futures side. The cash side, however, presents a far more serious problem, and hedgers must be cognizant of it to ensure that an intelligent hedge is not placed on stolen securities.

A more abstract requirement on management is that of time. The most significant problem concerning time is the performance of the portfolio. A poorly performing portfolio will reflect poorly on management and place pressures that may result in personnel changes. In addition, future commitments to buy or sell mean that hedgers must attain some kind of ability to move purchases and sales through time. This time flexibility is an issue that has been difficult for hedgers to deal with but has become significantly easier with the advent of stock index futures.

Net Position

It is essential for hedgers to evaluate their net exposure to price change. First, an inventory should be taken to establish the exact position in the marketplace. The most obvious starting point is to examine the long or short position of the outright securities. Thus, a portfolio holding 100,000 shares of IBM can be simply tabulated as such.

The trickier part is to examine those other commitments, or securities, that may be translated into inventory. This can be such investments as options or convertible bonds, which commit hedgers to price risk in an indirect fashion. For example, hedgers owning options may be in the position of acquiring the stocks represented by the options. It is therefore necessary that hedgers count in the position of convertible securities as part of their portfolios.

Commitments to buy due to contractual arrangements should also be counted in the listing of the portfolio. We have already given the example of the pension fund that knows that it must commit certain funds on a certain date due to payments into that fund.

The anticipated, or implied, exposure is the hardest part for hedgers to get a handle on, but it must be considered to appreciate fully the price risk of the portfolio. It is often easy for individuals to forget money that they may have tied up in a pension fund or in an IRA while establishing their exposure to the market.

It may be that hedgers are able to offset the risk from the implied positions through such means as offsetting contracts, changes in contract terms, or escape clauses. In addition, these additional implied security commitments must be examined to determine their impact on the basis. Securities committed in an implied form may have different characteristics than the securities that are known and shown outright.

It would be easy to establish the price risk if each of the units in the portfolio had identical price characteristics and an identical degree of parallelism to the futures contract. This would be quite possible if all of the securities were essentially identical or moved in a parallel fashion. It might also be possible if accounting procedures were available so that all price changes would be accounted for immediately. An additional problem is that it may be difficult to evaluate and to establish prices for implied commitments.

Because these problems exist, it is necessary to shift our attention from the quantity of the portfolio to the absolute price risk. This is not necessarily a simple or precise operation, because of the problems surrounding the implied commitments. A portfolio of simply outright long or short positions becomes a significantly easier problem to deal with. It may be that the hedging manager is only able to estimate the value of some of the components of the portfolio. In spite of the difficulty, it is imperative that this be done. Without this effort, it becomes extremely difficult for a proper hedge to be constructed.

The identification of the value of the portfolio allows the manager to ascertain which portion of the risk can be offset through futures contracts and how much will remain as basis risk. It is for this reason that the management of hedges must include a description of those components that are different between the cash and the futures. These components of the basis should be made explicit so that they can be managed and profitable.

Cash Flow Considerations

We discussed in an earlier chapter the fact that margin money must be kept at a specified level each day. If there is a surplus of funds in the account, the owner can receive a check for the surplus amount. The owner must deposit sufficient funds if the margin in the account is deficient. This ebb and flow of cash occurs due to changes in the price of the futures contract. The net value of the hedge, combining the value of the futures and cash positions, may not fluctuate an iota, but the cash position of the hedger may have great fluctuations. Hedgers should be aware of this problem and be prepared to deal with it. They will often make arrangements for banks to provide the maintenance margin for the futures account. Most hedgers do not consider it a problem to be generating surplus funds in their futures account and are usually able to find ways to use the funds. Nonetheless, a negative cash flow is an additional cost in hedging that is often overlooked.

In sum, there are basically three types of transactions that hedgers will consider: (1) ownership of the stocks; (2) commitments to purchase stocks; and (3) futures contracts.

Each of these has a different effect as far as a holder of a portfolio is concerned. The cash stocks may be financed 50 percent. Additional margin must be placed if the positions go against them. Alternately a fully margined position will have no cash flow consequences unless the hedger decides to use it as collateral for a loan. Commitments to purchase stocks, whether exchange-traded, options, convertible bonds, or contractual agreements, will have no cash flow consequences as no cash has been posted or need be posted. The futures contracts will generate or consume cash depending on their value. If the futures contract goes up in value, then a positive cash flow results. A negative cash flow will result when the futures contract goes against the portfolio manager.

The futures market provides for time flexibility. The time factor of the price risk can be allocated wherever hedgers desire within the limitations of the contract months. We will discuss risk more later.

Every stock has two types of risk: systematic and nonsystematic. These were examined in great detail in the previous chapter. Let's quickly review the high points. Systematic risk is the risk of a stock associated with the market as a whole. It has been shown that a large percentage of most stocks' price movements are related to the movement of the whole market. In other words, when the stock market goes up, most individual stocks go up. It should be noted that the percentage gain of the individual stocks may be more or less than that of the market.

The second risk associated with stock ownership is the risk associated with the particular stock, or unsystematic risk. This risk would include such changes as market competition, hirings and firings, and the introduction of a new product.

When we speak of risk we speak as the academics do. Risk is the same as reward. For each degree of risk there is some degree of possible reward. The point is that when we use the word "risk" we are also referring to reward. This perspective allows us to have a positive or potentially profitable risk. An example of potentially profitable risk would be the introduction of a new product that is extremely successful. This would be a profitable situation for the person who is long the stock but an unprofitable situation for one who is short the stock. It can easily be seen that the risk and reward are identical but depend on the position of investors or their attitude toward the market.

The two types of risk combined give the total risk for a given stock. Investors can theoretically eliminate systematic risk from their investments in a specific stock. Theoretically a sale of a stock index futures contract will eliminate the market risk from the trade. When investors buy an individual stock they are "long" both the systematic and nonsystematic risk in the market. They are now liable to both the risk and the reward that come from the individual stock as well as the total market. To eliminate the systematic risk they can "short" the market by selling stock index futures. Thus, they are long the market for some proportion of their investment and short the market through the futures contract for a net flat position in the market. They are still liable to the risk and reward associated with the individual stock, but, if the hedge is properly constructed, they will have eliminated the systematic risk through the selling of the stock index futures. The tricky part is deciding how many futures contracts to sell against the stock position. We will cover this issue later in this section. First we need to discuss the basis.

The Basis

The basis is the difference between the cash and futures prices. Simply subtract the futures price from the cash price. This is the most important and powerful of the tools necessary to understand for hedging.

In general, the basis refers to the cash price minus the price of the nearest futures contract. Usually, hedgers stop using the nearest contract and start using the next furthest contract after the first notice day. On February 15, the hedger would compute the basis using the cash price and the March futures contract. The hedger would shift to the June contract after March 1. This has been a rule of thumb in the traditional commodities for years. It is done this way because a contract about to expire tends to have few contracts outstanding. There is also less time value to the contract. In other words, there are fewer people who are worried about price risk in the next few days than in the next few months. This pushes the interest of the market and liquidity into the later months. This rule of thumb is less valid for stock index futures than for traditional commodities. Liquidity dries up in the traditional commodities in the last month of trading largely because the speculators are afraid of having to take or make delivery. Stock index futures have a cash delivery system, and delivery is marked to the market as if it were any other trading day. This greatly reduces the speculators' fears of delivery. There still is a greater time value for the next contract month over the current contract month. Speculators going through the delivery process in stock index futures may pay an extra commission if they want to stay in the market and roll into the next contract month. It can be argued that speculators must pay the extra commission anyway if they want to roll over the position. The rollover forced by the delivery process necessitates a commission. Speculators not forced by delivery to roll over may be stopped out or change their minds on their positions and liquidate them, thus saving the extra commissions. The net effect is that hedgers are not changing the futures contract in the basis computations until later in the delivery month.

The basis is a simple concept when hedgers are dealing with homogeneous commodities. The corn futures contract calls for the delivery of 5000 bushels of number 2 grade corn. The cash price of corn at a point of delivery minus the futures contract price is the corn basis. The corn contract has a few complicating factors, such as the ability to deliver other grades of corn. These other factors are taken into consideration when determining the basis as they have a very solid relationship with the main deliverable grade of corn. For example, there is a penalty for delivering corn of a lesser grade against the contract. This penalty is known in advance and is easy to factor into basis relationships.

There are two ways to compute the basis. One is simple and the other is much harder. The simple basis is the cash index minus the futures contract. The basis between a particular portfolio and a particular stock index futures contract is more difficult to compute.

The basis between the cash index and the futures index was discussed in Chapter 6. The reader should be able to understand basic basis movements and their application by studying the previous chapter. This chapter will focus on the more practical aspects of the basis. Most portfolios are not large or diversified enough to be considered as a proxy for the market. The basis composed of the cash index minus the futures index is useful in analyzing the relationship between the cash and futures markets. Except perhaps for the largest of the pension and mutual funds, there will be few individuals or institutions who have portfolios that duplicate the market. Most hedgers will have portfolios that behave differently from the market as a whole. For example, a portfolio composed only of shares of Homestake Mining will behave in a significantly different manner from the market. Stock index futures would have very little correlation with the price of the stock. The use of stock index futures to hedge would be very unwise because of the lack of correlation between the futures and the cash. The vast majority of hedgers must instead consider the basis between their portfolios and the stock index futures contract.

To determine the basis relationship between a particular portfolio and a particular futures contract, the hedger must first determine the number of contracts that are going to be necessary for the hedge. This will cause us to detour into a discussion of risk and the hedge ratio before we come back to the basis.

The investor or hedger must determine how many contracts of futures are necessary to hedge the risk being held in the cash market. This is called the hedge ratio. It is the ratio of the number of dollars of stock index futures necessary to hedge a certain dollar amount of cash holdings.

The best approach to determining the hedge ratio is to examine the beta of the portfolio. We examined in close detail the concept of beta in Chapter 6. If you are unsure of the meaning of beta and of r^2, then it is recommended that you reread those sections of Chapter 6. A firm understanding of those concepts is very helpful in determining the proper heading strategy. The hedger can ignore the deep understanding of beta and just follow the instructions outlined in this chapter, but it will be difficult for him or her to progress beyond this chapter without a firm understanding.

The portfolio owned by the hedger must be adjusted by the beta to determine the correct number of stock index futures necessary for the hedge. The hedger in effect weights his or her portfolio by the value of the shares times the beta of the stock. This process adjusts the portfolio as a whole to its relationship to the market.

The market is represented by the stock index futures contract that is being used for the hedge.

Let us look at the situation in Exhibit 7-1 as an example. The investor (whether the investor is an individual or institution is immaterial) holds a portfolio composed of three stocks. The investor wishes to know how many stock index futures contracts are necessary to hedge this portfolio. Note that the investor is also asking what the relationship is between the portfolio and the market. The investor needs to

EXHIBIT 7-1 Sample portfolio.

Stock	Price	No. of shares	$ Value
ABC	50	1000	50,000
BCD	20	2500	50,000
CDS	100	2000	200,000

discover two relationships between the portfolio and the market. The first relationship is in terms of relative volatility. In other words, what happens to the portfolio if the market changes price by 1 percent? The second question is how firm the relationship is between the portfolio and the market. In other words, how closely will the portfolio track the relationship between the portfolio and the market? If the investor has determined the average move the portfolio makes when the market moves 1 percent, how close will the portfolio come to hitting the average?

These two considerations have been studied. Two basic measurements can provide insights into the problem. The measurement to determine the relationship between the volatility of the portfolio and the market is called the beta. The measurement to estimate the tracking error is the r^2.

The concept of beta was explained in some detail in the previous chapter, but let us review some of the high points. The beta measures relative volatility of the individual stock or portfolio. If the market advances and the stock advances .80 percent, then the beta of that stock is .80. A beta of 1.40 would mean that the stock will go up or down 1.40 percent every 1.00 percent the market moves. In other words, a beta of 1.40 means that the stock is 40 percent more volatile than the market in both advancing and declining markets. A beta of .80 means the stock is 20 percent less volatile than the market.

Note that the beta is a measurement that represents an average relationship over a set period of time. This presents two problems. First, the average relationship may have a wide variance and may change over time. A stock may have a long-run beta of 1.10 but may vary between .50 and 1.75 during a given time. This may be because of changes in factors affecting the specific company. For example, the stock may rise on the same day the government brings a lawsuit against the company. The company's stock may dip 1 percent while the stock market is rallying 1 percent. What is the beta? For this one day the beta is actually negative.

The beta of a stock can change over time. A stock will tend to be more volatile, on a percentage basis, at lower price levels than at higher price levels. It takes much more buying power to move a $100 stock a dollar than to move a $10 stock. This means that a given dollar purchase will move a $10 stock a greater percentage than an equivalent purchase of a $100 stock. The volatility on the lower-priced stock is therefore greater. This means that the beta for a stock can be substantially different at a lower price than at a higher price. This change can occur over a very short time.

Portfolio Dividend Flows

We discussed in great detail in Chapter 6 the effect of dividend flows on the basis. The same type of analysis must be applied to construct the basis between a futures contract and a specific portfolio. This information can be of use when timing hedges as it will provide greater insight into the over- or undervaluation of the futures contract versus the cash portfolio.

This particular factor will work best in a highly diversified portfolio, whose actions mimic the futures contract. The difficulty will be in the tracking of the ex–dividend dates and the calculation of the resulting dividend yield. Serious hedgers managing large portfolios will find the time to be worthwhile, but most hedgers will typically substitute the valuation of the cash index dividend flows for the specific dividend flows of their portfolio.

The net effect of this is that hedgers will have a basis that is particular to their needs and situation. It will be composed of market expectations as well as carrying charges.

Net Present Value

All carrying charge calculations that we have talked about have been predicated on the assumption that hedgers are carrying portfolios until the final trading day of the futures contract. Instead, it may be that traders and hedgers expect to be carrying portfolios and investments for time periods different from the final expiry day of the futures contract. The basis will respond as if this assumption were true. Nonetheless, individual hedgers may wish to calculate their own personal basis on the assumption of their actual intended holding period.

In addition, one of the major assumptions built into most valuations of stock index futures is that the dividend flows and T-bill yields are equivalent. In fact, this is not true. The T-bill yield will not accrue to the owner until the T-bill is cashed in or rolled over, while the dividend flows are occurring through time.

Certainly hedgers will prefer to receive dividends in this case because they are able to reinvest the money, whereas the T-bill yield comes at the very end and cannot be utilized in other forms. Thus, the dividend and T-bill yields should be looked at on a discounted basis rather than on an outright basis. This requires using calculators or more sophisticated math than is suitable in this presentation. Traders should be discounting the net present value of the dividends and T-bills based on the expected dividend and T-bill yields.

Hedge Ratio

It is important for the hedger to be able to identify the number of contracts needed to hedge his or her portfolio. This is extremely easy for specific hedgers because they can merely use the beta-adjusted value of the portfolio and divide it by the current price of the stock index futures contract to determine the number of contracts needed.

The general rule for determining hedge ratios of storable commodities (stock index futures are considered storable commodities) is simply to find the number of contracts that are equivalent in dollar value to the underlying cash instrument, in this case stock index. For example, if the value of the cash index is 100.00 and the stock index futures contract is priced at 110.00, then 10 contracts of futures will be used to hedge the equivalent of 11 cash indexes. This 11:10 ratio will equalize the total dollar value of the cash and futures.

Management of Hedging

The first function that a corporation should consider when entering into a hedging program is the appointment of a hedge manager. This person can come from within the firm, but he or she should be thoroughly trained in both the futures and the cash sides of the business. Alternatives to the internal hedge manager are the paid consultant and the brokerage firm. Paid consultants will typically have the advantage of being objective in their work for the hedger. In addition, their consultation fee may be less than the cost of hiring an in-house manager. Brokerage houses will often provide excellent advice as part of their service if you use their brokerage firm for the hedging transactions. There are often highly qualified individuals within brokerage firms who are experienced at placing hedges. All three choices should be considered in detail as a hedging program can have a major impact on the bottom line of the portfolio.

It is also important that there be a management information system that keeps track of the hedging program. This is to provide some quantification of the success or failure of the program and also to provide the feedback necessary for changing policies and actions.

Each management information system should have a written statement of policy and purpose about the hedging program. It should provide exclusive instructions for the hedge manager, consultant, and/or broker for them to carry out their duties.

The hedge manager should be keeping track of the net position of the hedges. This could be completed on whatever basis is necessary for tracking of the portfolio. Smaller portfolios may consider a weekly review sufficient, while major pension funds may prefer a minute-by-minute accounting. This statement should be available to both the hedging manager and the top management of the entity doing the hedging. The net position statement should include all outright positions as well as implied commitments such as options, contracts, and convertible bonds.

It is also suggested that a plan be devised similar to that outlined in the next chapter before hedges are initiated or liquidated. The plan should outline the method of decision making that will go into the placing and liquidation of hedges. Without this explicit plan it becomes extremely difficult to adjust one's actions if they are not successful. The hedging plan should contain a list of those differences that make for changes in the basis. In stock index futures, this will include such factors as dividend flows, T-bill rates, and financing rates. Indicators of market expectations might also be included.

The management plan should address such issues as the amount of risk the investor wishes to consider and how aggressively it wishes to use the futures market.

Timing of Hedges

The timing of initiating and liquidating hedges is vitally important to hedgers. The timing of hedges is the essential task of hedging. Only by timing hedges well can hedgers expect to make any basis profits. The maximum impact of hedging comes when the initiation and liquidation of the hedges are timed properly.

There are two major factors that go into the valuation of the basis: carrying charges and market expectations. Chapter 6 discussed this in detail. These two factors combine to give the present price of the futures contract and, hence, the basis. Unfortunately, we never know exactly the market expectations except by subtracting the carrying charges from the basis and attributing the remainder to market expectations. This means that we can never know the exact relationship between the cash and the futures except by looking at the last price. Certainly, hedgers should be striving to develop techniques of predicting market expectations. This could greatly increase the return from the hedging program. The hedger would initiate the hedge whenever basis profits were expected based on the analysis of the carrying charges and market expectations.

There is another way of timing hedges that is somewhat easier. It can also be used in conjunction with analysis of the components of the basis. The basic technique is to study the historical price relationship between the cash portfolio and the futures contract. When the relationship is out of line, hedgers can initiate hedges with a reasonable idea of eventual basis profits. The method of examining the historical relationship between the portfolio and the futures contract is the scatter diagram.

The Scatter Diagram

The scatter diagram is a graphical representation of the relationship between two things. In our example, the two things being examined are the value of the cash portfolio and the value of the futures contract.

The scatter diagram is drawn on graph paper with the value of the cash portfolio on the left side of the page and the value of the futures contract on the bottom. For example, let us suppose that the value of the portfolio on Day 1 was $1.00 and the value of the equivalent futures contract was $1.05. A dot would then be drawn on the graph at the intersection of the lines formed by the two values. In other words, an imaginary line would be drawn from the left side of the graph paper at the point labeled $1.00, representing the value of the cash portfolio. Another line would be drawn from the bottom at the $1.05 point, representing the value of the futures contract. A point would be drawn at the intersection of the two lines, which represents the relationship of the two instruments. This process is repeated for, say, 50 days so that a large enough sample is used.

The result of the graphing should be a series of dots on the graph paper lying in a ragged line. We discussed in the previous chapter the interpretation of the scatter diagram. The closer the dots come to forming a straight line, the closer the relationship of the two instruments.

The closer the relationship between the portfolio and the futures contract, the less basis risk there is. A perfectly straight line would mean that the portfolio and the futures contract were perfectly correlated, the basis would never change, and hedging with the futures contract would totally eliminate the price risk of holding the portfolio. There would be no basis risk or opportunity for basis profit.

The wider the distribution of points around the center of the line, the greater the basis risk and potential reward. Let's take a look at Exhibit 7-2 to get a good idea of this in action.

Exhibit 7-2 shows a random portfolio selected from the first stocks listed in *Barron's Financial Weekly*. We are assuming a position of 5000 shares in each stock. The beta figures come from the table given in the previous chapter. The prices are those given as the last for the week in *Barron's*. The value is the price of the stock times the 5000 shares owned. The beta-adjusted value is the value of the stock times the beta. This gives a weighted value that is necessary for the computation of the hedge. At the bottom of each table is the total value of the portfolio, in the first case $1,225,125 and the beta-adjusted value of the portfolio, $1,327,302. The beta of the portfolio is derived by dividing the beta-adjusted value of the portfolio by the value of the portfolio. Thus, the beta of the portfolio is 1.08, which means it has slightly greater volatility than the market. The closing price for the S & P 500 is then listed. The number of contracts needed to equal the beta-adjusted portfolio value is found by dividing the total beta-adjusted portfolio value by the dollar value of the S & P 500. This result, 24.28, is rounded off to 24 to give the number of contracts needed to hedge the portfolio. The value of the contracts is found by multiplying the value of the S & P 500 by the rounded-off number of contracts. The result is plotted from the bottom of the scatter diagram, while the beta-adjusted value of the portfolio is plotted from the left side of the diagram.

This graph will show the closeness in the relationship between the S & P 500 and the particular portfolio. Exhibit 7-3 shows the results of graphing all the points specified in Exhibit 7-1. Notice how the points lie within a fairly narrow band. This shows that there is a

EXHIBIT 7-2 Random portfolio selected from the first stocks listed in Barron's *Financial Weekly* (Paine Webber) (*Continued*).

STOCK	PRICE	5000 SHRS	BETA	BETA ADJ.VALUE
AMF	17.375	86,875	1.10	95,563
Abt Lab	28.25	141,250	0.87	122,888
AlisCh	12.75	63,750	1.20	76,500
Alcoa	24	120,000	1.01	121,200
Amax	25.375	126,875	1.89	239,794
AHes	16.375	81,875	1.97	161,294
ABrand	40.625	203,125	0.71	144,219
ABdcst	27.625	138,125	0.86	118,788
AmCan	26.825	134,125	0.86	115,348
ACyan	25.825	129,125	1.02	131,708
TOTAL		1225125		1327302

S&P= 109.34
(TOTAL 5000 SHRS/S&P 500)= 22
PORTFOLIO BETA= 1.08

S&P 500= 54670
TOTAL CONTRACT VALUE=1,202,740
DATE=3/8/1982

STOCK	PRICE	5000 SHRS	BETA	BETA ADJ.VALUE
AMF	18.5	92,500	1.10	101,750
Abt Lab	29.375	146,875	0.87	127,781
AlisCh	12.625	63,125	1.20	75,750
Alcoa	25.125	125,625	1.01	126,881
Amax	26	130,000	1.89	245,700
AHes	18	90,000	1.97	177,300
ABrand	40.75	203,750	0.71	144,663
ABdcst	34.25	171,250	0.86	147,275
AmCan	27.825	139,125	0.86	119,648
ACyan	27.375	136,875	1.02	139,613
TOTAL		1299125		1406361

S&P= 115.12
(TOTAL 5000 SHRS/S&P 500)= 23
PORTFOLIO BETA= 1.08

S&P 500= 57560
TOTAL CONTRACT VALUE=1,323,880
DATE=4/5/1982

STOCK	PRICE	5000 SHRS	BETA	BETA ADJ.VALUE
AMF	18	90,000	1.10	99,000
Abt Lab	30.5	152,500	0.87	132,675
AlisCh	14.5	72,500	1.20	87,000
Alcoa	25	125,000	1.01	126,250
Amax	27.25	136,250	1.89	257,513
AHes	19.625	98,125	1.97	193,306
ABrand	42.825	214,125	0.71	152,029
ABdcst	37.125	185,625	0.86	159,638
AmCan	27.5	137,500	0.86	118,250
ACyan	29.125	145,625	1.02	148,538
TOTAL		1357250		1474199

S&P= 116.44
(TOTAL 5000 SHRS/S&P 500)= 23
PORTFOLIO BETA= 1.09

S&P 500= 58220
TOTAL CONTRACT VALUE=1,339,060
DATE=5/3/1982

STOCK	PRICE	5000 SHRS	BETA	BETA ADJ.VALUE
AMF	15.375	76,875	1.10	84,563
Abt Lab	29.125	145,625	0.87	126,694
AlisCh	12.75	63,750	1.20	76,500
Alcoa	23.125	115,625	1.01	116,781
Amax	21.25	106,250	1.89	200,813
AHes	20.625	103,125	1.97	203,156
ABrand	39.125	195,625	0.71	138,894
ABdcst	35.375	176,875	0.86	152,113
AmCan	27.5	137,500	0.86	118,250
ACyan	27.375	136,875	1.02	139,613
TOTAL		1258125		1357377

S&P= 110.09
(TOTAL 5000 SHRS/S&P 500)= 23
PORTFOLIO BETA= 1.08

S&P 500= 55045
TOTAL CONTRACT VALUE=1,266,035
DATE=6/7/1982

STOCK	PRICE	5000 SHRS	BETA	BETA ADJ.VALUE
AMF	15.25	76,250	1.10	83,875
Abt Lab	28.375	141,875	0.87	123,431
AlisCh	12.625	63,125	1.20	75,750
Alcoa	22.25	111,250	1.01	112,363
Amax	20.25	101,250	1.89	191,363
AHes	18.125	90,625	1.97	178,531
ABrand	39.625	198,125	0.71	140,669
ABdcst	37.375	186,875	0.86	160,713
AmCan	28.25	141,250	0.86	121,475
ACyan	28.5	142,500	1.02	145,350
TOTAL		1253125		1333520

S&P= 107.65
(TOTAL 5000 SHRS/S&P 500)= 23
PORTFOLIO BETA= 1.06

S&P 500= 53825
TOTAL CONTRACT VALUE=1,237,975
DATE=7/5/1982

STOCK	PRICE	5000 SHRS	BETA	BETA ADJ.VALUE
AMF	14.75	73,750	1.10	81,125
Abt Lab	30.125	150,625	0.87	131,044
AlisCh	8.625	43,125	1.20	51,750
Alcoa	23.5	117,500	1.01	118,675
Amax	19	95,000	1.89	179,550
AHes	16.75	83,750	1.97	164,988
ABrand	38.875	194,375	0.71	138,006
ABdcst	39	195,000	0.86	167,700
AmCan	27.875	139,375	0.86	119,863
ACyan	28.75	143,750	1.02	146,625
TOTAL		1236250		1299326

S&P= 107.09
(TOTAL 5000 SHRS/S&P 500)= 23
PORTFOLIO BETA= 1.05

S&P 500= 53545
TOTAL CONTRACT VALUE=1,231,535
DATE=8/2/1982

EXHIBIT 7-2 Random portfolio selected from the first stocks listed in Barron's *Financial Weekly* (Paine Webber) (*Continued*).

STOCK	PRICE	5000 SHRS	BETA	BETA ADJ.VALUE
AMF	15.125	75,625	1.10	83,188
Abt Lab	36.25	181,250	0.87	157,688
AlisCh	10.125	50,625	1.20	60,750
Alcoa	27.375	136,875	1.01	138,244
Amax	21.5	107,500	1.89	203,175
AHes	23.375	116,875	1.97	230,244
ABrand	44.25	221,250	0.71	157,088
ABdcst	47.5	237,500	0.86	204,250
AmCan	31.125	155,625	0.86	133,838
ACyan	29.5	147,500	1.02	150,450
TOTAL		1430625		1518915

S&P= 122.68
(TOTAL 5000 SHRS/S&P 500)= 23
PORTFOLIO BETA= 1.06

S&P 500= 61340
TOTAL CONTRACT VALUE=1,410,820
DATE=9/6/1982

STOCK	PRICE	5000 SHRS	BETA	BETA ADJ.VALUE
AMF	15.125	75,625	1.10	83,188
Abt Lab	35.125	175,625	0.87	152,794
AlisCh	8.625	43,125	1.20	51,750
Alcoa	26.625	133,125	1.01	134,456
Amax	21.5	107,500	1.89	203,175
AHes	25.25	126,250	1.97	248,713
ABrand	44.25	221,250	0.71	157,088
ABdcst	46.25	231,250	0.86	198,875
AmCan	30.5	152,500	0.86	131,150
ACyan	31	155,000	1.02	158,100
TOTAL		1421250		1519289

S&P= 121.97
(TOTAL 5000 SHRS/S&P 500)= 23
PORTFOLIO BETA= 1.07

S&P 500= 60985
TOTAL CONTRACT VALUE=1,402,655
DATE=10/4/1982

STOCK	PRICE	5000 SHRS	BETA	BETA ADJ.VALUE
AMF	17.125	85,625	1.10	94,188
Abt Lab	37.625	188,125	0.87	163,669
AlisCh	23.375	116,875	1.20	140,250
Alcoa	28.375	141,875	1.01	143,294
Amax	20.5	102,500	1.89	193,725
AHes	26.75	133,750	1.97	263,488
ABrand	47.5	237,500	0.71	168,625
ABdcst	57.75	288,750	0.86	248,325
AmCan	31.5	157,500	0.86	135,450
ACyan	38.375	191,875	1.02	195,713
TOTAL		1644375		1746727

S&P= 138.69
(TOTAL 5000 SHRS/S&P 500)= 24
PORTFOLIO BETA= 1.06

S&P 500= 69345
TOTAL CONTRACT VALUE=1,664,280
DATE=12/6/1982

STOCK	PRICE	5000 SHRS	BETA	BETA ADJ.VALUE
AMF	17.875	89,375	1.10	98,313
Abt Lab	39	195,000	0.87	169,650
AlisCh	12.5	62,500	1.20	75,000
Alcoa	33.125	165,625	1.01	167,281
Amax	24.625	123,125	1.89	232,706
AHes	28.5	142,500	1.97	280,725
ABrand	47.375	236,875	0.71	168,181
ABdcst	51.5	257,500	0.86	221,450
AmCan	32.875	164,375	0.86	141,363
ACyan	35.5	177,500	1.02	181,050
TOTAL		1614375		1735719

S&P= 145.18
(TOTAL 5000 SHRS/S&P 500)= 22
PORTFOLIO BETA= 1.08

S&P 500= 72590
TOTAL CONTRACT VALUE=1,596,980
DATE=1/10/1983

STOCK	PRICE	5000 SHRS	BETA	BETA ADJ.VALUE
AMF	18	90,000	1.10	99,000
Abt Lab	39.75	198,750	0.87	172,913
AlisCh	11.75	58,750	1.20	70,500
Alcoa	32.75	163,750	1.01	165,388
Amax	24.5	122,500	1.89	231,525
AHes	24.5	122,500	1.97	241,325
ABrand	45.375	226,875	0.71	161,081
ABdcst	52.125	260,625	0.86	224,138
AmCan	31.5	157,500	0.86	135,450
ACyan	36	180,000	1.02	183,600
TOTAL		1581250		1684920

S&P= 146.14
(TOTAL 5000 SHRS/S&P 500)= 22
PORTFOLIO BETA= 1.07

S&P 500= 73070
TOTAL CONTRACT VALUE=1,607,540
DATE=2/7/1983

STOCK	PRICE	5000 SHRS	BETA	BETA ADJ.VALUE
AMF	17.875	89,375	1.10	98,313
Abt Lab	44	220,000	0.87	191,400
AlisCh	12	60,000	1.20	72,000
Alcoa	34.625	173,125	1.01	174,856
Amax	23.875	119,375	1.89	225,619
AHes	23.625	118,125	1.97	232,706
ABrand	45.875	229,375	0.71	162,856
ABdcst	60.5	302,500	0.86	260,150
AmCan	32	160,000	0.86	137,600
ACyan	40.5	202,500	1.02	206,550
TOTAL		1674375		1762050

S&P= 153
(TOTAL 5000 SHRS/S&P 500)= 22
PORTFOLIO BETA= 1.05

S&P 500= 76500
TOTAL CONTRACT VALUE=1,683,000
DATE=3/7/1983

EXHIBIT 7-2 Random portfolio selected from the first stocks listed in Barron's *Financial Weekly* (Paine Webber) (*Continued*).

STOCK	PRICE	5000 SHRS	BETA	BETA ADJ.VALUE
AMF	16.25	81,250	1.10	89,375
Abt Lab	43	215,000	0.87	187,050
AlisCh	13.75	68,750	1.20	82,500
Alcoa	32.125	160,625	1.01	162,231
Amax	22.875	114,375	1.89	216,169
AHes	24	120,000	1.97	236,400
ABrand	48.75	243,750	0.71	173,063
ABdcst	63.25	316,250	0.86	271,975
AmCan	33.75	168,750	0.86	145,125
ACyan	42.5	212,500	1.02	216,750
TOTAL		1701250		1780638

```
S&P= 152.96                         S&P 500= 76480
(TOTAL 5000 SHRS/S&P 500)= 22       TOTAL CONTRACT VALUE=1,682,560
PORTFOLIO BETA= 1.05                DATE=4/4/1983
```

STOCK	PRICE	5000 SHRS	BETA	BETA ADJ.VALUE
AMF	16	80,000	1.10	88,000
Abt Lab	46.5	232,500	0.87	202,275
AlisCh	14.375	71,875	1.20	86,250
Alcoa	32	160,000	1.01	161,600
Amax	27.5	137,500	1.89	259,875
AHes	27.125	135,625	1.97	267,181
ABrand	54.625	273,125	0.71	193,919
ABdcst	66	330,000	0.86	283,800
AmCan	38.25	191,250	0.86	164,475
ACyan	45.5	227,500	1.02	232,050
TOTAL		1839375		1939425

```
S&P= 164.42                         S&P 500= 82210
(TOTAL 5000 SHRS/S&P 500)= 22       TOTAL CONTRACT VALUE=1,808,620
PORTFOLIO BETA= 1.05                DATE=5/2/1983
```

STOCK	PRICE	5000 SHRS	BETA	BETA ADJ.VALUE
AMF	16.75	83,750	1.10	92,125
Abt Lab	42.75	213,750	0.87	185,963
AlisCh	16.625	83,125	1.20	99,750
Alcoa	38.375	191,875	1.01	193,794
Amax	27.75	138,750	1.89	262,238
AHes	26.125	130,625	1.97	257,331
ABrand	49.75	248,750	0.71	176,613
ABdcst	61.5	307,500	0.86	264,450
AmCan	42.75	213,750	0.86	183,825
ACyan	46.25	231,250	1.02	235,875
TOTAL		1843125		1951964

```
S&P= 162.68                         S&P 500= 81340
(TOTAL 5000 SHRS/S&P 500)= 23       TOTAL CONTRACT VALUE=1,870,820
PORTFOLIO BETA= 1.06                DATE=6/13/1983
```

EXHIBIT 7-3 Results of graphing all the points specified in Exhibit 7-1 (Paine Webber).

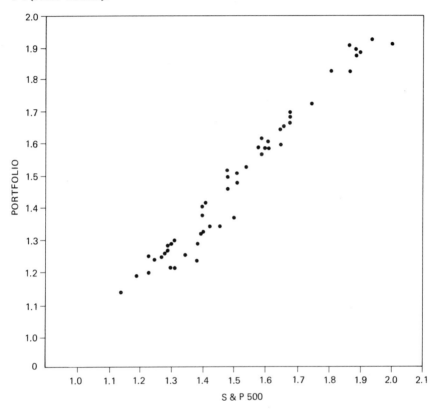

strong relationship between the index and this particular portfolio. A band can be drawn around the points that show the relationship. Exhibit 7-4 shows the band.

But also notice how the points are scattered within the band. When the point lies near the top of the band, it means that the portfolio is overvalued versus the index. When the point is near the lower edge of the band the portfolio is undervalued versus the index. Notice that the width of the band represents a value of around $180,000. This means that the relationship of the value of the portfolio and the index can vary by up to $180,000 without going outside the band. In other words, we would expect the value of the portfolio and the index to fall within a range worth about $180,000 in normal circumstances.

This $180,000 also defines the basis risk and potential reward. If the

EXHIBIT 7-4   The band (Paine Webber).

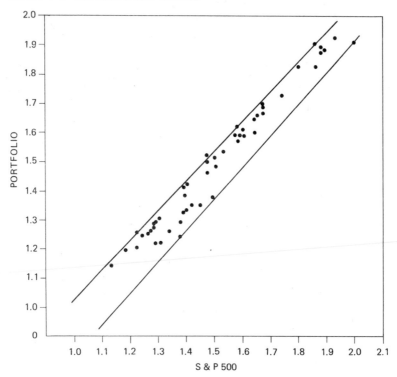

hedge was initiated on the worst side of the band and liquidated on the opposite side, the hedge would lose $180,000. Notice that the reverse would have been highly profitable. If the hedge was initiated and liquidated at the optimal times within the band during normal circumstances, the hedge would have created a profit of $180,000!

The value of the scatter diagram should now be clear. It tells hedgers when their particular portfolios are under- or overvalued versus any given index. Hedgers should construct scatter diagrams of their portfolio versus each of the stock index futures contracts. It may be that the basis between their portfolios may be overvalued versus one futures contract but undervalued versus another contract. Thus, a hedger can select the futures contract that is the furthest away from its expected value and use that one for the hedge.

Hedgers should not assume that they will be able to make the amount of profit represented by the width of the band every time they put on a hedge. It should be assumed that it will be rare when the point moves to one extreme of the band. One suggestion is to initiate hedges when the point approaches the midpoint of the band. More aggressive basis traders may want to wait until the point has reached two-thirds of the way to the other side of the band before liquidating the hedge. Either way, basis traders are cautioned against greed. The points may stay on one side of the band for months at a time, thus creating an uncomfortable situation. Common sense should be a reasonable guide.

One of the best aspects of this technique is that it is applicable to virtually every reasonably large portfolio. In addition, it is relatively easy to implement and apply every day.

Technical Analysis

Some basis traders and hedgers will shy away from the scatter diagram and valuation models and simply use technical analysis on the graph of their particular basis. They may not initiate hedges until, say, a trendline is broken on the basis chart, which may imply a change in trend in the basis. Some technically oriented basis traders will wait until the basis has moved to an extreme position on the chart or on momentum before initiating hedges.

Dividend Flows

Another technique for initiating hedges is to use the dramatic changes in dividend flows that change the basis. We showed in the previous chapter that the dividend flows in the last 2 months of the life of a futures contract could have a significant impact on the basis. Hedgers could use the changes in the basis caused by the dividend flows to initiate and liquidate hedges. For example, we know that dividend flows will tend to increase the value of the cash index relative to the futures index about 6 weeks before the expiry of the futures contract. This would therefore be the best time to place long hedges. This is the time when the futures contract is least valued relative to the cash. The next major swing in dividend flows is in favor of the futures contract. Short hedges should be initiated about 10 weeks before expiration of the futures contract because this is just prior to the most significant increase in the value of the cash relative to the futures.

Remember that we are discussing a general rule and that other

245

short-term factors may override the effects of dividend flows. Thus, hedgers are cautioned to examine the current situation carefully instead of blindly trusting dividend flows to cause significant changes in the basis.

The Importance of Basis Timing

A well-designed hedge program can go awry if hedges are placed poorly. Timing is probably the most important skill hedge managers can acquire. The basics of evaluating the hedge are extremely important and provide the base for hedging and basis trading. It is the timing that is the frosting on the cake, allowing the trader to move from an adequate hedge program to a highly profitable one.

ACLI did a study that highlights exactly this situation. It analyzed the consequences of arbitraging a small portfolio of stocks versus the stock index futures. ACLI constructed two portfolios of the same stocks but with differing numbers of shares. Exhibit 7-5 shows the two portfolios. Portfolio A was constructed because it had a beta extremely close to that of the market and an r^2 that was also high and suggested reduced tracking errors. Portfolio B was constructed of the same eight companies but with equal weightings to provide a contrast to the weighted Portfolio A.

Exhibit 7-6 shows the price behavior of the two portfolios and the S & P 500 stock index over the test time period. It can be seen that all three portfolios moved roughtly with each other, though Portfolio B

EXHIBIT 7-5 Stock components in sample portfolios.

Company	Portfolio A	Portfolio B
Dupont	35	100
GE	35	100
GF	95	100
IBM	20	100
AT&T	100	100
U.S. Steel	140	100
Exxon	360	100
U. Technologists	65	100
Total shares	850	800
Value on 6/1/82	$28,719	$33,163
Historical beta	.95	.80
r^2	.97	.83

EXHIBIT 7-6 S & P 500 Stock Index (line). Price index for Portfolio A (dot) and price index for Portfolio B. Indexes = 133 on May 1, 1981 (ACLI International).

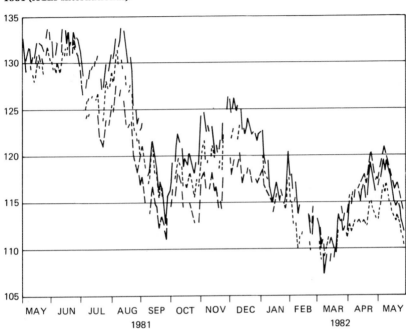

underperformed the market through most of 1981 but outperformed it in the first 5 months of 1982. This suggests that the basis risk of holding Portfolio B was higher than that for Portfolio A, which tracked the market more closely.

ACLI used much the same evaluation technique outlined in Chapter 6 for its study. It was therefore able to identify periods when the futures were over- or undervalued versus its portfolios. Transaction costs were estimated at about $300 per contract and each trade was held to the maturity of the stock index futures contract. This basically means that there were no timing considerations when initiating or exiting the hedge—only the over- or undervaluation of the futures versus the portfolio. There were 75 trading days during the test period, and the holding period of each particular arbitrage trade could be as long as 107 days and as short as 1 day.

Portfolio A was undervalued for 33 days and overvalued for 42 days during the 75 trading days of the test. On 27 of the 33 days that the futures prices were undervalued, long futures/short stock positions were implemented. All of these 27 positions made money. There were

247

29 short futures/long stock trades implemented on the 42 days that futures prices were overvalued. Only 8 of these 29 trades were profitable. Exhibit 7-7 outlines the results of the profit and loss for hedge positions for both Portfolio A and B.

Notice that the trading results of Portfolio B were almost a complete flip-flop of those for Portfolio A. The short futures/long stocks trades were 96.3 percent profitable, while the long futures/short stocks trades were only 32 percent profitable.

Nonetheless, the net result would have been profits for arbitrageurs using this strategy. All profits and losses shown take into account dividend and interest flows as well as commissions. It was assumed that futures traders were holding cash T-bills and holders of long stocks were receiving dividends. Exhibit 7-8 shows the arbitrage profits and losses for Portfolios A and B.

We discussed before the importance of basis risk in selecting the hedge and how the basis risk could also provide a profit opportunity. Exhibit 7-9 shows the basis of Portfolios A and B during the test. It shows that even Portfolio A, with its high beta and r^2, has significant basis risk. This highlights the fact that a constant monitoring of the basis is of critical importance to hedgers or arbitrageurs. For example, Portfolio A underperformed the index futures value by 7.3 percent from August 18 to the expiry date of the futures contract of September 16. In fact, for the whole test period, Portfolio A underperformed the index futures prices.

It must be noted, though, that the results are taken by assuming that the position is liquidated on the last trading day of the futures con-

---

EXHIBIT 7-7 Profit/loss for hedged positions.

	Long futures/ short stocks	Short futures/ long stocks	Total
Portfolio A			
no. of trades	27	29	56
profitable trades	27	8	35
winning percentage	100%	27.6%	62.5%
avg. profit per trade ($/$1000)	$41.87	$−10.17	$14.92
Portfolio B			
no of trades	25	27	52
profitable trades	8	26	34
winning percentage	32.0%	96.3%	65.4%
avg. profit per trade ($/$1000)	$−25.66	$30.60	$ 3.55

EXHIBIT 7-8 Arbitrage profits/losses for Portfolio A (line) and Portfolio B (dot). All hedged positions mature on September 16, 1982 (ACLI International).

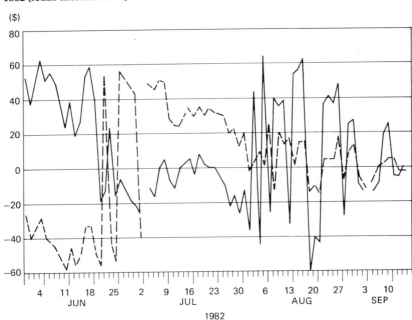

tract. In fact, on every day after initiating the arbitrage, or hedge, the position could have been liquidated. In other words, as the basis moved up or down, additional profits or losses might occur. For example, Exhibit 7-10 shows the tracking of a single trade of a long futures/ short stocks position implemented on June 18 and liquidated on the last trading day of the futures contract. Notice that Portfolio A showed a final profit of $58.50 per $1000 but was at an unprofitable position during two time periods in August. It also showed an almost $60.00 profit in July.

Portfolio B could have been profitable if liquidated during the first month of holding but became unprofitable in late July and never did regain an even position. This should highlight the fact that the monitoring and analysis of the basis are critical to the performance of any hedge program. Even a well-constructed hedge will have significant basis movements during its life. Intelligent hedgers will keep an eye on these levels, stopping profitable hedges from turning into unprofitable hedges and monitoring unprofitable hedges for signs of coming profitability.

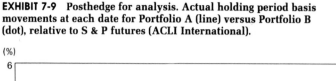

EXHIBIT 7-9   Posthedge for analysis. Actual holding period basis movements at each date for Portfolio A (line) versus Portfolio B (dot), relative to S & P futures (ACLI International).

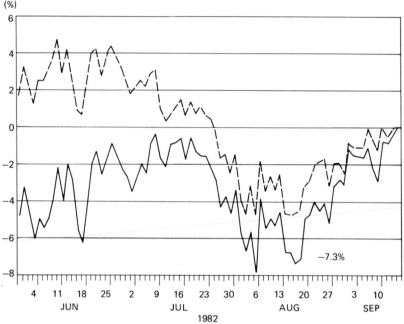

(%)

Eliminating Systematic Risk

Most traders believe that their stock picks will outperform the stock market as a whole. This is a common situation though most people will not recognize it. Most individuals analyze stocks with the idea that they will go up in price. An underlying assumption is that their particular stock picks will appreciate more rapidly than the average of all stocks. If they did not believe this, they would use a dart board to select their portfolios. The key to the situation is that holders are confident of the ability of their stocks to do better than the market whether the market moves up or down.

Most traders usually think little of the general direction of the stock market when they select their stocks. These traders are concentrating on the nonsystematic portion of their portfolio at the expense of the systematic.

Most traders, even excellent selectors of individual securities, lose

250

money in bear markets. This is because a high percentage of the value of a stock is related to the value of the market as a whole. Some studies have estimated around 50 percent of the value of the average stock on the New York Stock Exchange is related to the value of the general market. This means that traders may select extremely strong stocks and still lose money. Stock index futures give traders a way of eliminating this problem by eliminating the systematic risk in the market.

Chapter 6 showed how the value of an individual security contains both systematic and nonsystematic risk. We can apply that concept to this situation by selling futures contracts to eliminate the systematic risk in holding a stock portfolio.

This means that even traders who are unsure of the market direction but feel confident of their ability to pick stocks can make money. The sale of futures contracts against a stock portfolio can sharply reduce the need to worry about the future direction of the market. This futures hedge means that the value of the investor's portfolio will rise and fall with his or her ability to select stocks—not with the direction of the market.

The critical part is to determine the number of contracts that must

EXHIBIT 7-10 Tracking a single trade. Arbitrage profit/loss for long futures/short stocks position implemented on June 18 and matured on September 16, Portfolio A (line) versus Portfolio B (dot) (ACLI International).

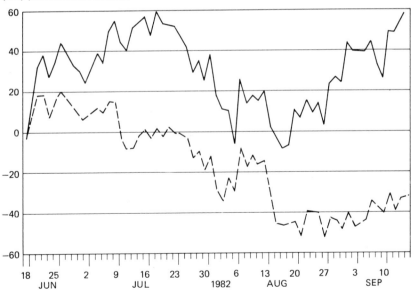

be sold to eliminate the systematic risk. This is where r^2 comes in. It was introduced in Chapter 6 and represents that portion of the individual's total risk that is attributable to the stock market. Thus, a stock with an r^2 of .68 has 68 percent of the total risk of that stock coming from the stock market as a whole and 32 percent coming from that particular stock.

The process for determining the r^2 of a portfolio is identical to that for finding the r^2 for a stock. The total returns of the portfolio, both dividends and price appreciation or depreciation, are correlated with the returns of the market as a whole. Chapter 6 outlines this process in detail, and readers are referred to that chapter for a more thorough discussion. This process should be updated periodically to ensure that the r^2 of the portfolio is up to date. A change in the r^2 would have an impact in the value of the hedge. An increase in r^2 would mean that more futures contracts must be sold, while a decline in r^2 would mean that fewer futures contracts would be sold.

Let's presume that hedgers have discovered r^2 for their portfolios. This r^2 represents the portion of the total risk of the portfolio that is attributable to the stock market as a whole. The r^2 represents that portion of the portfolio value that should be eliminated to isolate the non-systematic risk. In other words, if the portion of the value of the portfolio represented by r^2 could be eliminated, the portfolio would rise and fall solely on the merits of the individual stocks and be neutral to the movements of the stock market.

Hedgers then take the r^2 for the portfolio and mutliply that times the total value of the portfolio. Thus, for a portfolio of $1 million with an r^2 of .80, $800,000 of the value of the portfolio is related to the stock market as a whole and $200,000 is related to the individual stocks.

The systematic portion of the portfolio is then hedged by selling an equivalent dollar amount of stock index futures. For example, if the systematic portion of the $1 million portfolio was $800,000, then $800,000 worth of stock index futures would be sold to offset the systematic risk in holding that portfolio. Obviously it will be extremely difficult to sell an exact number of equivalent contracts. The portfolio will thus become slightly overhedged or underhedged depending on the decision of the hedger. In addition, as the r^2, portfolio value, and stock index futures values change, the hedging will also change. Hedgers should monitor these three variables to make sure that the proper number of stock index futures contracts are being utilized in the hedge.

The discussion earlier in this chapter on timing hedges should be applied to this kind of a procedure. Scatter diagrams may be a useful tool in timing the hedge, entry, and exit points. Nonetheless, stock index futures and this hedge method provide an excellent technique for allowing stock pickers to trade those stocks that they feel will out-perform the market but still be immune to general market trends. Obviously, this may be a positive or negative influence on any individual's portfolio. Stock pickers may find that their selections lag the market averages and that they will be reducing their performance by selling stock index futures.

The ability to eliminate systematic risk will also put pressure on fund or pension managers to improve their performance. They are currently able to claim that they are doing an excellent job if they simply lose less than the market averages. If the S & P 500 average is down 12 percent in a year and they are only down 11 percent, they claim to be doing an excellent job. With the new option of using stock index futures to hedge, they will have to do better. Now fund managers will be graded on their ability to make money regardless of the level or direction of the market. This will have a profound effect on the management of equity portfolios.

Call Options

Holders of call options can also use stock index futures to eliminate the systematic risk involved in their portfolios. Holders of call options assume that their particular portfolios will do better than a random selection of call options. This is therefore a very similar situation to the one just outlined. Stock index futures can be sold against the options to reduce the total risk of the portfolio by eliminating that portion of the portfolio attributable to the underlying market.

The process is more complicated, however. The one difference is the amount of leverage that has been added through the use of the call option instead of the underlying stock. Traders must therefore determine the sensitivity of each call to the underlying stock and the sensitivity of the portfolio to the underlying stock market.

The sensitivity of price movements between the individual stock and its option is called the delta, or neutral hedge ratio. For example, a delta of .40 means that the option will change 40 cents for every $1.00 that the stock moves. This is a simplistic description of delta and readers are advised to refer to the last section of the book for additional sources of detailed information on stock options. Nonetheless, this description will suit our purposes. Traders should examine the delta of the portfolio by adding together the net deltas of the individual stock options. In addtion, traders will have to adjust this value by the r^2s of the underlying stocks to find that portion of the price volatility that is associated with the systematic risk.

One critical feature to monitor is the delta, as deltas do oscillate with price movement at all times. This information can be obtained from private services or possibly from your broker.

Warrants

Warrants are similar to options in that they give the holder the ability to purchase shares of an underlying common stock at a set price within a certain time limit. However, they are not standardized and their conditions rarely change, unlike puts and calls, which have a very short-term delivery cycle and changing strike prices. Warrants can also be hedged using stock index futures.

Warrants have a concept similar to delta in that their value will change according to the change in the price of the underlying stock. This relationship changes as the price moves higher or lower. The price relationship between the warrant and the underlying stock tends to be more than that between a call option and the stock. Warrants can almost be thought of as deeply in-the-money calls.

The first goal of the warrant hedger is to determine the relationship between the warrant and the stock. Then, by adjusting the value of the warrant by the r^2 of the underlying stock, a value of the warrant that must be hedged to eliminate systematic risk is discovered.

It is important to remember that warrants often call or give the right to purchase an odd number of stocks. For example, a particular warrant may require 14.32 shares to be delivered for each warrant exercised. In addition, these exercise conditions may change due to stock splits and other factors.

Convertible Bonds

Holders of convertible bonds can also hedge somewhat with stock index futures. In addition, they may want to use T-bond futures in their hedge.

A convertible bond is composed of two factors: the bond and the

convertible-into-stock features. The bond feature will be the dominant feature when stock prices are low against the value specified in
the convertible bond. The stock feature, or the convertible feature of
the bond, will be the dominant factor when the underlying stock is
selling for a price above the call price in the convertible option. There
are thus two kinds of risk in holding a convertible bond: that associated with the underlying stock and that associated with the bond market. It is for these two reasons that stock index futures and T-bond
futures are necessary to hedge against a possible decline in value for
a convertible bond portfolio.

The tricky part is to determine how much of the current value of
the bond is reflecting the interest-bearing aspect, or the equity investment aspect. After this has been decided, then traders can adjust their
portfolios to account for the weighting.

Short Positions

Stock index futures can also be used to eliminate the systematic portion of the portfolio of short securities, or short security substitutes.
Thus, individuals who are short stocks and believe that their stocks
will underperform the marketplace could buy stock index futures to
offset the systematic risk in holding the portfolio of short stocks. The
same procedure can be done with convertible securities. Thus, holders of puts, short warrants, and short convertible bonds could also be
buyers of stock index futures to offset systematic risk.

Temporary Setback

Holders of large portfolios of stocks or convertible securities sometimes believe that there is a major bull market but that a temporary
dip may reduce their equity. Many traders and portfolio managers are
unwilling to eliminate their positions in such a circumstance. It is
often difficult to reduce holdings without incurring extremely large
transaction costs and depressing market prices. It would be very difficult for a major pension fund managing hundreds of millions of dollars to dump all of its holdings of many stocks over a short period of
time merely because it believes the market is about to go into a 1- or
2-month correction.

In any given portfolio there are several methods available to reduce risk temporarily. One is to liquidate the entire portfolio, but, as we have seen, this is a very expensive and difficult process. Another method is to write a portfolio of options. This is only possible if the portfolio is constructed of stocks that are optionable and if market conditions are correct. In addition, transaction costs can be very high for this procedure.

Probably the best alternative is to sell stock index futures against the long portfolio. There are other strategies than these simple ones outlined, but these are the most common and widely used.

Traders and portfolio managers may wish to liquidate their portfolios if there is a belief that the dip will be fairly lengthy and/or severe. Once again, though, the problem with this approach is that it has very high transaction costs for both commissions and poor fills on the stock liquidation.

The second strategy will be to write a portfolio of calls against the underlying stocks. This can be a very attractive proposition if the calls are overvalued and increased revenues can be picked up by investors. The disadvantage with the option-writing scheme is that it can also include heavy transaction costs that may not be covered unless the downturn is lengthy and/or severe. The best approach to take when the downturn is expected to be short or not too severe is to use shorting stock index futures.

The advantages of shorting stock index futures against the portfolio are that transaction costs are virtually negligible and positions are highly liquid. In addition, the leverage is very great as each stock index futures contract can eliminate tens of thousands of dollars' worth of risk in the portfolio. Investors will use the hedge timing devices outlined earlier in this chapter and sell contracts at essentially the full value of the portfolio. In particular, hedgers should be examining the example we used of the randomly selected portfolio of 10 stocks that was outlined in some detail earlier in this chapter. Stock index futures have a value that could be used to offset trading setbacks that are expected to be as short as several days. The market is extremely large and liquid and therefore poor fills are sharply reduced.

There are a number of institutions that find themselves lacking flexibility in market timing decisions. These include employee benefit plans, insurance companies, institutional endowments, foundations, trust companies, banks, mutual funds, and other managed accounts. The cumulative value of these institutions is measured in the tens of billions of dollars. Some of these investors may be constrained by federal regulations on using stock index futures.

Convertible Securities

Much the same procedure can be used to hedge a portfolio of convertible securities such as calls, convertible bonds, or warrants. Once again, the alternatives would be to eliminate the portfolio or possibly to write options against the existing convertible security. It is likely that the best alternative is to sell stock index futures against the portfolio as a means of hedging against a price decline. This has the advantage of being liquid, inexpensive, and significantly easier to actualize.

Short Positions

Traders who are short a portfolio of securities or convertible securities and believe the market is due for a temporary rally can use the same strategy just outlined, except that they will go long stock index futures instead of short. The advantages remain the same. Stock index futures will be a constant and valuable aid to the portfolio manager.

Near-Term Expected Purchases

Some individuals or institutions know that they will be buying stock in the near future. Pension funds may know exactly how much money they will be receiving at a particular time in the future for investing in stocks. Individuals may be ready to cash in a certificate of deposit or receive an insurance settlement that will be invested in securities. These same individuals and institutions may be worried that the price of the stock or of the portfolio of stocks may rally between the time of their decision to buy and the actual purchase date.

Stock index futures can be a valuable aid, allowing the institution to buy a stock index futures contract now and liquidate it when the actual stocks are purchased. This has the effect of getting the purchaser long at current levels. This may be an advantage or disadvantage depending on the subsequent price action.

Thus, a significant advantage of flexibility comes to individuals and firms who use stock index futures to aid in their buying programs. Typically, large institutions have problems rapidly implementing a buying program. Stock index futures allow them to purchase the level of the market they wish and then proceed in an orderly and controlled fashion to purchase the individual securities. This enables them to profit by any interim market rally while helping to achieve better pricing of the individual securities.

Institutions who will use stock index futures should be alert to the underlying value of the futures contract. A contract that is overvalued will reduce the attractiveness of using the stock index futures. The purchase of stock index futures contracts that are undervalued will enhance the portfolio return.

Index Funds

Stock index futures represent a perfect alternative to index funds. Index funds are those funds that were constructed to perform as close to general market indexes as possible. Their object was neither to beat nor to be beaten by the market in performance. Thus, if the market as measured by the S & P 500 was up 12 percent a year, index funds would also strive to be up 12 percent in a year. Index funds do this by investing in a very broad range of stocks in weighting similar to those in the major market indexes.

Stock index futures, being based directly on the indexes them-selves, will have a price appreciation or depreciation essentially the same as the indexes. In addition, they have the significant advantages of lower transaction costs and no tracking errors. The major differ-ence, as pointed out in Chapter 6, is that an investment in an index fund derives a yield from dividends, while a stock index fund is going to have a yield in the form of T-bills. This means that if there were, for argument's sake, $100 million in an index fund, the index fund could be constructed by buying stock index futures and investing the rest of the principal in treasury securities.

It has been shown that there are opportunities for a stock index fund to outperform the underlying index, largely due to inefficiencies in the market. It may be that innovative market managers in the future will use a combination of cash stocks and stock index futures. In other words, when opportunities exist to outperform the market through investing in stock index futures and T-bills, money managers will take that course of action instead of investing in new securities. Thus, in the future we may see stock market funds ranging from being totally invested in cash stocks to being totally invested in stock index futures.

Issuing Corporate Stock

Corporations that are issuing stock may be worried that the value of the stock market will drop as they ready the stock for issuing. These companies could sell stock index futures equivalent to the value of the stock to be issued as a hedge against possibly declining stock market values in the interim.

In theory, a corporate treasurer could hedge a potential drop in stock values before issuing the stock through a stock index futures contract. The procedure would be simply to determine the r^2 of the company's stock and use the futures market accordingly.

Specialists

Specialists are members of the stock exchange who often carry an inventory of stock that they are responsible for. Stock index futures may be a viable means to offset some of the risk of their inventory. The main problem with stock index futures for a specialist is that the specialist may not be carrying an inventory broadly based enough for the very broadly based stock index futures to be a suitable hedge. On the other hand, many specialists do carry a fairly wide inventory, and for them stock index futures would be suitable. Typical specialists carry 15 to 20 issues in their portfolios, and this is unlikely to be broadly diversified enough to benefit from stock index futures. However, the specialist may be part of a larger firm that is much more broadly based, covering around 100 different stocks. These large specialist firms will find stock index futures to be very useful.

The value of the portfolio should be adjusted by the r^2 to determine the number of stock index futures contracts necessary. Once again, the problems inherent in hedging a small portfolio should be addressed. In particular, the amount of systematic risk is highly variable.

In spite of these problems, we have seen specialists become major users of the NYSE Index futures contract. They have found it to be a useful tool to lay off at least some of the risk that they carry at all times. In addition, they have found it to be a useful speculative tool, as they are able to look at their books to determine what buy or sell orders are going to enter the market and are able to step into the futures markets to profit by it.

Equity Dealers

Equity dealers, or securities dealers, often hold large portfolios of stock in which they make a market. Equity dealers find themselves in the same position as many wholesalers of more traditional commodities. Their situation is analogous to that of a corn wholesaler who can suffer losses in profit should the value of the inventory decline. Wholesalers of any commodity, including equities, are typically trying to profit through marking up the inventory they hold rather than speculating in the value of the inventory. The use of stock index futures can eliminate much of the price risk from holding the inventory and allow merchandisers of securities to make their profit through merchandising rather than speculating. The obvious drawback to this is that equity dealers must be carrying diversified portfolios or the basis risks outlined above will also apply in this case.

Block Traders

Block traders carry portfolios that are generally long and typically large and well-diversified. Block trading is often done as a profitable enterprise or as a loss leader for other investment banking or underwriting business. Block traders often lose as they position their blocks and the market drops while the distribution is taking place. This loss sometimes overrides the fees received for the service. Thus, stock index futures can appropriately hedge a major portfolio of stock blocks. Losses on block positioning would be decreased and profitability increased for block traders. Block traders could increase their operations significantly over current levels and still merely be losing the same as they might be losing now.

Market Leads

One of the intriguing features of stock index futures is that they appear to lead the cash stock market. Studies that have been completed, particularly by ACLI, suggest that S & P 500 futures lead the cash index by about 5 to 20 minutes. Exhibit 7-11 shows this relationship very clearly on April 4, 1982.

It is hypothesized that this may be due to the fact that money can more directly affect stock index futures than it can the stock market.

EXHIBIT 7-11   Minute-by-minute TIC chart, April 4, 1983. June 1983
futures = upper, S & P Index = lower (ADP/Comtrend).

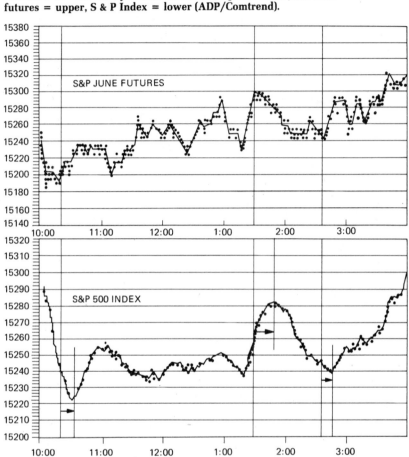

That is to say, investors who turn bullish on the market can buy the
whole market by buying a stock index futures contract, whereas it
will take a much more significant amount of money and time to affect
the underlying cash index. Thus, changes in market sentiment will
show up sooner in the index futures than they do in the cash market.

Outperforming the Market

It appears that stock index futures can be used to outperform the market. We have pointed out their uses as an index fund and the ways to

evaluate stock index futures, and we have suggested that buying futures when they are undervalued versus the cash index can become a way to outperform the market. Value Line, in its August 26, 1983, issue of *Selection and Opinion*, discussed a study that it had completed showing the use of stock index futures to outperform the marketplace. Exhibit 7-12 gives the results of purchasing stock index futures and posting T-bills as margin as a substitute for an index fund. The net result was, indeed, that stock index futures would have produced a return several percentage points above the market in both bull and bear markets. In fact, Value Line points out that the additional performance does not take into account the higher transaction costs of cash securities.

Value Line also examined the use of stock index futures to eliminate systematic risk from holding a portfolio of its top-rated stock selections. Value Line ranks stocks according to its criteria in five categories ranging from the best, Rank 1, to the worst, Rank 5. It has shown that Rank 1 stocks consistently outperformed Rank 5 stocks. Value Line monitors its ranks according to two methods, frozen and unfrozen.

The frozen method assumes that Rank 1 stocks are purchased on the first of each year and held for the entire year regardless of any changes in rank. The unfrozen method assumes that if stocks drop out of Rank 1, they are replaced by new stocks that have become Rank 1.

EXHIBIT 7-12 Futures contracts as an index fund. (Reprinted by permission of the publisher, © 1983, Value Line, Inc.)

	1982 First Half	1982 Second Half	1982 Full Year	1983 First Half	18 Months 1/1/82-6/30/83
Interest Income	6.1%	6.2%	12.2%	4.0%	16.2%
(Minus) Premium	(1.0)	(1.0)	(2.0)	(1.0)	(3.0)
Plus (Minus) Change In VL Composite	(12.2)	31.4	15.2	28.7	48.6
Total Return of Futures Contract	−7.1%	+36.6%	+25.4%	+31.7%	+61.8%
Dividend Income	2.5%	2.7%	5.0%	2.0%	7.2%
Plus (Minus) Change In VL Composite	(12.2)	31.4	15.2	28.7	48.6
Total Return of Average Stock	−9.7%	+34.1%	+20.2%	+30.7%	+55.8%
Advantage of Futures Contract (Percentage points)	2.6	2.5	5.2	1.0	6.0

EXHIBIT 7-13   Hedging strategy—frozen basis. (Reprinted by permission of the publisher, © 1983, Value Line, Inc.)

	1982 First Half	1982 Second Half	1982 Full Year	1983 First Half	18 Months 1/1/82-6/30/83
Gain (Loss) On					
1-Ranked Stocks	(1.5%)	35.7%	33.6%	49.5%	99.7%
Plus Premium Received	1.0	1.0	2.0	1.0	3.0
Plus Dividend Income	2.5	2.7	5.0	2.0	7.2
Gain (Loss) On					
Futures Contract.	12.2	(31.4)	(15.2)	(28.7)	(48.5)
Total Return					
From Hedging	+14.2%	+ 8.0%	+25.4%	+23.8%	+61.4%
Total Return					
From Average Stock*	−9.7%	+34.1%	+20.2%	+30.7%	+55.8%
Return From					
Treasury-Bill**	+6.1%	+6.2%	+12.2%	+4.0%	+16.2%

*From Table 2
**Assuming rate is locked in at beginning of period.

However, Value Line points out that high transaction costs may make it difficult to duplicate the unfrozen strategy and that the true results probably fall somewhere in between, such as quarterly revisions of the portfolio.

Investors who follow Value Line's ranking system are likely to outperform the market, but, as we pointed out earlier in this chapter,

EXHIBIT 7-14   Hedging strategy—unfrozen basis. (Reprinted by permission of the publisher, © 1983, Value Line, Inc.)

	1982 First Half	1982 Second Half	1982 Full Year	1983 First Half	18 Months 1/1/82-6/30/83
Gain (Loss) On					
1-Ranked Stocks	1.3%	48.7%	50.6%	50.2%	126.2%
Plus Premium Received	1.0	1.0	2.0	1.0	3.0
Plus Dividend Income	2.5	2.7	5.0	2.0	7.2
Gain (Loss) On					
Futures Contract	12.2	(31.4)	(15.2)	(28.7)	(48.5)
Total Return					
From Hedging	+17.0%	+21.0%	+42.4%	+24.5%	+87.9%
Total Return					
From Average Stock*	−9.7%	+34.1%	+20.2%	+30.7%	+55.8%
Return From					
Treasury-Bill**	+6.1%	+6.2%	+12.2%	+4.0%	+16.2%

*From Table 2
**Assuming rate is locked in at beginning of period.

they may proceed to lose tremendous quantities of equity if there is a prolonged bear market. However, the use of stock index futures to hedge against this systematic risk can leave the outperformance of Rank 1 stocks while eliminating the negative aspects of a bear market. In other words, an index fund could be constructed with only Rank 1 stocks with short sales of futures contracts to hedge out the systematic risk. Exhibit 7-13 and Exhibit 7-14 show the results of this strategy from the beginning of 1982 to the middle of 1983 for both the frozen and unfrozen method. It can be seen that this strategy was a consistently profitable strategy for conservative traders. One of the most interesting aspects is that the investor would have outperformed the market yet would actually have had less risk than an investor in a true index fund.

chapter 8

Trading plan and money management

We have spent a tremendous amount of time examining the techniques that go into the analysis and use of stock index futures. There are two more aspects of our subject that are extremely important for investors: the trading plan and money management.

The most important part of a trade is the trading plan, though most traders are not familiar with the concept of a trading plan and will find this statement somewhat hard to accept. Without proper monitoring of information, traders drown in an overwhelming flood of data. With a trading plan, all of the relevant fundamental and technical indicators can be stored in one spot. It allows traders to outline a scenario of the expectations for the future. In addition, it provides a place for the exact entry and exit points to be delineated and necessary money management principles to be applied.

Money management is also incredibly important, though it is often overlooked. Money management is the proper utilization of the capital that is the lifeblood of the investor.

Let us first examine the trading plan. A classic study was done in the 1960s by the Commodity Exchange Authority, the predecessor of the Commodity Futures Trading Commission. It showed that approximately 85 percent of commodity speculators were losers, 10 percent split even, and 5 percent made money. This has been erroneously given as an example of how the 5 percent of winners will take the money from the 85 percent of losers. This is not true at all. Other studies have indicated that the 85 percent who were losers were actually winners on their trading but became losers when commissions were deducted. It has been shown that over the long run speculators will lose money at about the same rate that they pay commissions. This chapter will address itself to the basic problem of profitability.

There are numerous trading systems on the market that are profitable. There are numerous trading advisers that have had long, profitable track records. Yet the average speculator is a loser. The average speculator, when handed sound advice, will still lose money. There are several reasons for this.

The first reason is perhaps the most controversial, or perhaps the most basic. Several writers have theorized that commodity speculators lose money because they want to lose money. They are driven by a sense of guilt over their successes in other areas of their lives and want an area in which they can lose and thus assuage that guilt. They do this by speculating in commodity futures without using the intelligence that made them successful in the other areas their lives. Commodity futures trading provides an excellent way to eliminate the guilt because of the quick pace. Traders are forced into a position of having to take their losses by the fact that a commodity futures contract is an expiring product. Finally, they can easily blame their losses on the broker or the markets when they succeed in failing.

There is a common perception among successful traders that a loser will find a way to lose even if given a profitable trading system. The main factor that is cited is that the difference between successful and unsuccessful speculators is discipline. It takes discipline to examine objectively and fully all the factors affecting the trade before the trade is entered. It takes discipline to eliminate the emotional responses of the speculator, which create the largest number of losses in the market. It is not a lack of information or wisdom but a lack of ability to control one's own mind that is the creator of most losses in the marketplace. Too often speculators will see a market moving strongly to the upside, get excited, and buy. The classic situation is that the market then turns and collapses. This scenario occurs frequently for a reason. Most speculators buy at the highs and sell at the lows because they have an inability to eliminate their emotional desires from the marketplace. When the market rallies, their greed becomes overriding. When the market moves against them, their fear becomes so great that they are paralyzed and unwilling to admit the failure of the trade. Average speculators are thus savagely whipsawed not by the market but by their own minds.

This chapter will present techniques and methods that will help traders acquire the discipline to trade markets profitably. These techniques will not replace the discipline of traders but will help them establish a frame of mind so that they can have no more excuses for lacking discipline.

A prime example of the emotional nature of traders is their inability to cut losses and let profits run. The first rule of every trader is to buy low and sell high, but surely the second rule must be to cut losses and let profits run. Speculators show their inability to accept failure as they allow an unprofitable position to continue to go against them. They hope that something will change and will relieve them of the psychological and financial burden they have acquired. They begin to justify and rationalize their initial position and explain why the market will turn and go in their direction. This is obviously no time to be justifying and rationalizing a position. That process should be completed before the trade is initiated. Conversely, as prices move in their direction, they are eager to grab a quick profit. They rationalize this by claiming, "You can't go broke taking a profit." On the contrary, over the long run, traders will go broke taking quick profits. Less than 50 percent of all trades are profitable in most technical trading systems. This means that traders can only become profitable if the gains on the winning trades are greater than the losses on the losing trades. The gross profit must be greater than the commission. By taking the quick profit, they have limited their profits and reduced their lifeblood.

One of the important features of the trading plan is that it is devised before money is risked. Traders are typically far less emotional about a trade before the money is committed. Typically, traders lose their objectivity when they are on the firing line and money is committed.

The trading plan also helps to educate traders. After a trade, investors can go over their trading plans and what actually happened. They have an opportunity to examine how accurate the pretrade analysis was and discover areas of weakness in their own education or insights. Often, investors will realize that certain facets of their trading technique have been over- or underestimated. Traders can refer back to the trading plan while in the trade to determine whether things are going as planned and whether there have been significant changes that will affect the analysis that led to initiating the position. The trading plan thus becomes a rudder for the average speculator, who tends to trade like a rudderless ship. When investors are forced to commit thoughts to paper before initiating the trade, their thoughts must be more logical and coherent. The record of the thoughts before the trade is initiated provides a useful insight for future growth.

It should be clear to the reader that I believe that investing in stock index futures is a serious endeavor. Many traders trade futures for the action and excitement. They view the market as a legalized gambling casino that saves them the airfare to Las Vegas. Nothing could be further from the truth. There are significant economic values to having speculators in a market. The amount of money that can be gained or lost in a single day can be awesome. Investors should take speculating on a serious level if there is to be success. Speculators should not expect to consider the market as a plaything and still make money. If traders are honest with themselves and acknowledge that action and excitement are the primary goals that they derive from trading commodity futures, then I have no objection to their frivolous attitude. On the other hand, if investors desire profits, then a structured, disciplined approach must be taken.

Many commodity speculators will say that they have a hard time sleeping at night. The most common reason for this is that they are overtrading and that their psychology will not allow them to risk the level of money that they are currently risking. The easiest way to eliminate this problem is to liquidate the trade or to reduce the number of contracts outstanding. The use of a trading plan is also a viable way of reducing mental fatigue and anxiety. The trading plan is a record of the thoughts of the trader before the trade is initiated. It represents a more calm, detached state than will exist when money is on the line. Traders who have committed money based on a rational trading plan will be able to refer back to that trading plan and use it as a touchstone of calm.

Trading Plan

Many investors believe a trading plan is a waste of time. Filling out a trading plan takes time but is probably a major time saver in the final analysis. Most average speculators will spend a tremendous amount of time and valuable energy watching the market on almost a tick-by-tick basis. This seems to be based on the psychological idea that if they do not watch the market it will go against them. This constant staring at a screen is an incredibly time-consuming activity. There is a major loss of energy when the trader's mind is unfocused. The trading plan enforces a certain discipline, requiring that traders specify the entry and exit points and the method of stop placement before the trade is initiated. This means that traders can enter entry and exit points once a day rather than staring at a screen all day long looking for clues to the future direction of the market. The trading plan will reduce impulsive behavior by traders when prices get close to entry or exit points. There are often nagging second thoughts about a trade when prices begin to get close to the entry point. This doubt about the trade is really a form of self-doubt, and it occurs often when traders are not using a trading plan. The use of a trading plan releases traders from having to watch the market on a micro level. The time saved can be spent analyzing the markets and acquiring more knowledge.

Remember, the main point of a trading plan is to help increase discipline. A written plan is far superior to a mental plan. It is extremely difficult for the human mind to take into account all possible factors in a rational manner when they are not written down. A mental trading plan tends to become a plan composed of wishful thinking rather than hard critical analysis. Furthermore, the written plan provides the opportunity for traders to conduct a postmortem analysis on the trade. It is probably easier for traders to acquire the discipline to fill out the trading plan than it is to acquire the psychological discipline necessary to function without a trading plan.

A trading plan should address the two major styles of analysis, technical and fundamental. It is suggested that traders analyze each trade from both perspectives. The elimination of one technique will leave the trader trading with one eye. The use of both techniques combined provides a synergy. It also allows traders to eliminate absurd trades. For example, it may be that a trader wants to put on an intra-index spread for technical reasons. It may also be that the spread is already at full carrying charges and has virtually no chance of moving any further. This is an example in which a knowledge of the fundamentals enables traders to eliminate unprofitable errors.

The first section of the trading plan should be composed of general information such as the name of the index, the contract month, date, margin, and commission. A second section should be devoted to some of the technical considerations necessary for the analysis, and a third section should be devoted to fundamental indicators. A final section is the punch line of the report. This is the action section, detailing specific plans to actualize.

Let us examine a specific trading plan. Exhibit 8-1 shows an example of a two-page plan. The plan that we are presenting is not necessarily the best plan for all traders but should provide a general framework that readers can adjust to suit their own particular needs and desires.

General Area

The first area of the trading plan is the general area. It contains some general information about the specific trading plan. The date entered

EXHIBIT 8-1 Example of a two-page trading plan.

```
GENERAL
  DATE _____ STOCK INDEX _____ CONTRACT MONTH(S) _____
  MARGIN _____ EACH      COMMISSION _____ EACH

TECHNICAL - FUTURES
  TREND _____
  CHART SUPPORT: _____
  CHART RESISTANCE: _____
  FORMATIONS: _____
  VOLUME AND OPEN INTEREST CONSIDERATIONS: _____
  CYCLES: _____
  TRADING SYSTEM(S): _____
  OVERBOUGHT/OVERSOLD: _____

  COMMENTS: _____
  _____
  _____
  _____
  _____


TECHNICAL - CASH
  DOW SUPPORT _____
  DOW RESISTANCE _____
  DOW FORMATIONS _____
  DOW TREND _____

  INDEX SUPPORT _____
  INDEX RESISTANCE _____
  INDEX FORMATIONS _____
  INDEX TREND _____

  UP VOLUME _____
  DOWN VOLUME _____
  ACCUMULATING VOLUME _____
  VOLUME CONSIDERATIONS _____
  _____

  TRIN _____
  TRIA _____
  TICK _____
  TIKI _____
  TIKA _____

  ADVANCES _____
  DECLINES _____
  A/D LINE _____
```

NEW HIGHS _____

NEW LOWS _____

HIGHS - LOWS _____

MOST ACTIVE STOCKS _____

FUNDAMENTAL

ROTATION CONSIDERATIONS _____
_____

INFLATION CONSIDERATIONS _____
_____

INTEREST RATE CONSIDERATIONS _____
_____

MONEY SUPPLY CONSIDERATIONS _____
_____

ECONOMIC OUTLOOK _____
_____

FOREIGN STOCK MARKETS _____
_____

OTHER

BASIS _____

BASIS CONSIDERATIONS _____
_____

INTER-INDEX SPREAD CONSIDERATIONS _____
_____

OTHER _____
_____

SCENARIO AND MILESTONES _____
_____
_____
_____
_____
_____
_____
_____
_____
_____

ACTION

POSITION: BUY _____   SELL _____

INITIATE POSITION AT _____

INITIAL STOP LOSS _____

PARTIAL PROFITS _____

271

should be the date that the trading plan is filled out. The next section gives the name of the stock index. This is S & P 500, S & P 100, NYSE Index, or Value Line. The section beside it is the contract month, or months in the case of a spread. Traders enter "Sep" if the September contract is to be traded or "Sep/Dec" if the September/December spread is to be done. The margin requirements are placed in the next section and commissions are placed in the final section.

Technical Analysis

The next major area is for technical analysis of the futures. The first section is for the trend. There can be many definitions of the trend, and traders should use whatever indicator they prefer. For example, the trend could be a 10-day or 20-day moving average of the closing price. An alternative would be to examine price charts. There are obviously a number of different ways to determine the trend, and whichever has been found to have the greatest success should be used by traders. Some traders may wish to expand this area and have both short- and long-term trends.

The next section is for chart support, and following that is chart resistance. Traders should examine their price charts to determine where the support and resistance lie. This is useful in determining the price levels that will be difficult to break. In addition, it can be very useful in obtaining entry and exit points.

The formation section is devoted to listing price chart patterns such as pennants and trendlines. An example might be to list a recently broken uptrend line as a bearish factor.

The next section is for volume and open interest considerations. Traders should not be listing the volume and open interest here but should instead be outlining what they believe the volume and open interest are implying. In other words, traders should be discussing the relative bullishness or bearishness of the volume and open interest in relation to recent price action.

The cycles section is similar to the volume and open interest section in that a discussion of recent price action in relation to the cycles should be included. More important, though, traders should be outlining the coming cyclical situation, both short- and long-term.

The next section, the trading systems section, is another that traders have a lot of freedom to change. In this section traders should be monitoring mechanical trading systems as further confirmations of trends. Such trading systems as the moving average crossover system could be examined. If, for example, the moving average crossover system is long, then traders would place "bullish" in this section. Traders may want to monitor more than one trading system to acquire even more input into the decision-making process. I would not recommend putting a countertrend system in this section, though that might be an interesting possibility for another section of the trading plan. The problem with a countertrend system is that most trades will not be going with the trend, and using a countertrend system might confuse the decision-making process. A possible reason to include it would be to try to get some idea of whether the market has gone too far in a particular direction and might be susceptible to a setback.

The countertrend system would most likely be based on an overbought or oversold model. In most cases it would not be necessary to include a countertrend system as we have already placed "overbought/oversold" on the form. The overbought/oversold indicator is an excellent means for keeping traders out of trouble. Typical losing traders will buy highs and sell lows. Traders can provide a double check against buying an overbought market or selling an oversold market by monitoring overbought/oversold indicators.

The final section of the technical analysis of futures area is the comments section. This is where traders should outline their conclusions, based strictly on technical indicators. They should clear their minds of all other considerations and focus only on technicals. An expected price scenario could be outlined as well as possible entry and exit points.

Technical Analysis of Cash Indexes

The next area deals with the technical analysis of the cash indexes. It follows much the same format as the area for technical analysis of the futures. The major difference is that there are far more ways to analyze the cash index than the futures.

The first four sections are devoted to the support, resistance, formations, and trend of the Dow Jones Industrials. This is done because the Dow Jones Industrial Index has a major psychological impact on the marketplace, not because it is used for direct trading purposes.

The next four sections give the support, resistance, chart formations, and trend of the cash index that underlies the futures contract being traded. For example, traders would discuss the S & P 500 cash index if the S & P 500 futures were being traded.

The next three sections deal with volume. This up volume and down volume are obviously placed in the first two sections. These refer to the volume of advancing and declining issues. The third section is used for the accumulating volume as outlined by Stan Weinstein or for the onbalance volume technique of Joe Granville. The section for volume considerations is provided to allow investors to draw conclusions about future price directions solely on the basis of volume. For instance, suppose that two of the three volume sections are bullish. The investor filling out this section may sum up by saying that volume is bullish but flashing a warning signal.

The next two indicators, TRIN and TRIA, are technical indicators that can be obtained from brokers. Issued over the Quotron quote system, they are based on volume and are indicators of the underlying breadth of the market. TICK, TIKI, and TIKA are based on the up ticks and down ticks of the market. They can be obtained from quote services and look like excellent indicators. These indicators give short- and intermediate-term insights into the technical strength of the market.

One of the classics of technical analysis of cash stocks is the advance/decline line. The next three sections on the trading form give spaces for writing down the advances, declines, and the advance/decline line.

A similar indicator is given by highs-minus-lows. This is outlined in the next three sections on the trading plan. The highs-minus-lows can be used like the advance/decline line. The most active stocks can also be used as an adjunct to the highs-minus-lows.

That completes the technical considerations on the cash index. Additional lines could be added or subtracted depending on the trader's trading style. Some investors may want to eliminate entire sections or add a multitude of additional indicators. Traders are referred to the last section of the book for references on the various indicators.

Fundamentals

The next section is a bit harder to outline on the trading plan as it requires more subtle and analytical skills. The fundamental area is the next major area. The questions are not as specific as they are in the technical sections, as each day brings a new set of factors that move to the forefront of the market's consideration. Nonetheless, several major areas of concern can be outlined that affect the stock market's performance. They are listed on the form and are:

- Rotation
- Inflation
- Interest rates

- Money supply
- Economic outlook
- Foreign stock markets

The only one that may be somewhat confusing to the reader is rotation considerations. It is sometimes, though not always, useful to know which stock groups are leading the market. This is a very important factor when trying to analyze the inter-index spreads.

Miscellaneous Sections

The area on the plan for "other" is devoted to miscellaneous indicators and considerations. The first consideration is the basis. Two sections have been placed on the form concerning the basis. The first section is for recording the basis or recent basis action. The second section is for considerations based on the basis and is devoted to the more analytical side of the basis.

The next section is for inter-index spread considerations. This section allows traders to write down any additional factors that are necessary for analyzing the inter-index spreads. Traders may also wish to write down the recent action of the inter-index spreads as a means of analyzing an outright position.

The "other" section should be considered a catchall for any rare occurrences. Bad weather, war, price controls, and so on are examples of exogenous shocks to the system that can be placed in this particular section.

The scenario and milestones sections are vital parts of the trading plan. Traders should be examining every trade from the point of view of projecting a scenario of the future. The scenario should address itself to both near-term and long-term horizons. Specific prices and times should be mentioned. For example, one sentence in a scenario could be: "Prices should rally to 152.50 due to an oversold condition and dropping interest rates some time in the next week." The milestones section is a useful adjunct to the scenario section. This becomes a checklist of both bullish and bearish occurrences. Investors should list expectations of future fundamental and technical occurrences and when they are likely to occur. One suggestion is to put the bullish factors on the left and the bearish factors on the right. This is better than mixing them together as it allows traders to examine the relative bullishness or bearishness of events as they unfold. The usefulness of the milestones section is that it gives the investors a quick idea of expected events and whether they are unfolding as

275

expected. If events are unfolding as expected, then the trade will be profitable. If they do not unfold as expected, then we would expect to see the trade go sour. This may encourage the investors either to take profits or to cut losses quicker.

Action Section

The action section is the most important area of the trading plan. This is the culmination of all the analysis that has gone into the trading plan. This is where the rubber meets the road. This is where traders must move out of fantasyland and put down cold cash.

The first section simply allows futures investors to write down which contract is being bought; for example, "Buy two June NYSE Index." The suggested initiation price is listed in the next section. In addition, traders could write the style or method that was used to determine the initiation point. This is similar to the next section, where the initial stop loss is listed and the method of determination could also be noted. The final section lists the point at which to take partial profits. Partial profits will be discussed in more detail later in this chapter, when we take up money management. For now, let us just say that we can place the point at which we wish to take partial profits as well as the reason for doing so at that point.

This concludes our discussion of the trading plan. The most important thing to remember is that it is a tool to help the trader build the self-discipline necessary to profit in commodity futures trading. The suggested trading plan should be modified to fit the needs and desires of the individual trader. It is a guideline that is not set in stone. Play with it. Make it your own.

Money Management

Perhaps the most important skill that a commodity trader can acquire is that of money management. The selection of trades should take a back seat to the proper management of trading funds. Without proper money management, any trading system can become a loser, but with proper money management some unprofitable trading systems can become profitable.

The main thrust of this book has been offensive; that is, it has been directed toward conveying the skills necessary to make money. Money management is a defensive tactic; it strives to protect traders and their capital. The first goal of any trader is survival. If survival is ensured, profits will likely follow.

There are two major techniques I recommend to help decrease risk in trading. The first is the multiunit tactic and the second is a capital management plan. Neither of these techniques is complicated. Better techniques exist, but these two have the major advantages of being simple and usable.

Multiunit Tactic

"Multiunit tactic" means having more than 1 unit of a given trade. A unit can mean as few as 1 contract or as many as the trader can handle. We use the term "units" because we do not wish to imply that large traders should be limited to only 1 or 2 contracts. To a large trader, one unit may be 10, 20, or even 100 contracts. The same concepts apply with little modification to positions of any size. In fact, we call this the multiunit tactic because traders can be utilizing as many units as desired. We will use 2 units as our example though the principles apply to 2 units or 20.

Positions should be initiated in units of 2 or more. This requires additional margin and initial risk but the eventual trading will be less risky if combined with the cash management principles outlined below. The basic tactic is to eliminate the 2 units if the trade becomes unprofitable and breaks below the stop loss point. However, if the trade is profitable the trader liquidates 1 of the 2 units very early and takes partial profits. The stop loss on the remaining unit is moved up to the entry point and the trade now becomes a "no lose" proposition. (It could still be a loser if the price opens beyond the stop loss point, but this is an unlikely situation.)

The first unit thus becomes a trading unit and the second unit is used to hang on for the big move. The first unit is entered and exited on short-term technical movements whereas the long-term unit is carried in an effort to gain very large profits and is only liquidated when the fundamentals say that the market is no longer underpriced or overpriced or when the major technical trend changes.

An additional way would be to stagger the stop losses as well as the objectives. This allows traders more flexibility in exiting the positions. The stop loss point can be placed close to the entry point of the trading unit to reduce dollar risk. This might be appropriate because the return on the investment is expected to be low. This would leave the stop loss relatively wide for the second unit. This is reasonable as much larger profits are expected on the second unit. The staggered

277

stop loss also provides more flexibility if money management is kept in mind.

Cash Management

Cash management is another critical issue that can be used by the trader to reduce risk and potentially increase profit. Studies have shown that approximately 85 percent of commodity traders lose money. Approximately 10 percent of traders split even, and 5 percent make money after commissions are deducted. The first goal of every commodity trader should be survival. If survival is ensured or the probabilities increased to a high level, then profits will likely occur. There is a 98 percent chance of survival if the money risked on any given trade is no more than 5 percent of the total equity in the account. This rule assumes that dollar losses are equal to gains and occur with equal frequency. For example, a $10,000 account should have a stop no more that $500 away from the entry point. Obviously, an excellent trading system or technique can accentuate the positive aspects of this rule. In addition, a very poor ratio of gains to losses will make this a less attractive proposition.

The use of a 5 percent cash management stop means that there is only a 2 percent chance of a trader's being wiped out. This simple technique of cash management moves the trader from the category of loser to that of very probable survivor. It is my contention that one who survives in the commodity market long enough will be a net winner over the long run. To help move from survivor to winner, stops can be placed even tighter. A stop that represents only 2 to 3 percent of total equity will reduce the chances of being wiped out to only 1 percent. It shuld be noted that when using the multiunit tactic the total risk of all units combined must be within the cash management limits given here. For example, a trader has decided to trade two units of the NYSE Index. The trader wishes to risk 100 points on each unit for a total of $500 per contract or $1000 as the total risk for the two units. This means that the trader must have $20,000 or more in the account to come under the 5 percent cash management stop rule.

Traders should first determine the trade and then the stop that they wish to use that present the optimal chance of success. The technique used may be fundamental, technical, or a combination of the two. But through whatever means, the trade, the initiation point, and the stop loss point must be selected first. Only then should the decision be made as to whether or not the trade should be placed in the trader's account. In other words, only after the risk has been determined

278

should that be translated into a dollar risk and the 5 percent of equity rule be applied.

There is no way that we can overemphasize the importance of money management. Improper money management is, I believe, the major reason that most traders fail in trading commodities.

A combination of the trading plan and money management will help provide the discipline necessary for trading profits. This self-discipline is vitally important for investors looking to make money trading in stock index futures.

Sources of Information

There are very few sources of information specifically about stock index futures. The best source is your broker. Brokerage firms maintain stocks of brochures issued by the exchanges. The brochures that have been issued by the Chicago Mercantile Exchange, the New York Futures Exchange, and the Kansas City Board of Trade are excellent, and all stock index futures traders and hedgers should obtain copies.

In addition, I have compiled information about stock index futures that may be interesting to readers. You may receive this packet simply by writing me at 675 West Hastings, Suite 1614, Vancouver, British Columbia, Canada V6R 4W3.

Books

The Commodity Futures Game, by R. J. Teweles, H. L. Stone, and C. Harlow, McGraw-Hill Book Company, New York, 1974.

This is the best introduction to commodity futures. Both novice and experienced traders will appreciate it. *The Commodity Futures Game* covers the basics as well as providing an overview of major trading techniques. The major drawbacks are that it was published 10 years ago, does not cover the financial futures, and is therefore very agriculturally oriented. Highly recommended.

Commodity Spreads, by Courtney Smith, John Wiley & Sons, New York, 1982.

This book provides the only significant coverage of the spread market. The book is mainly concerned with the concepts and techniques for analyzing and trading spreads. Traders interested in pursuing stock index spreads will find the more in-depth coverage useful.

Security Analysis, by B. Graham, D. L. Dodd, S. Cottle, and C. Tatham, McGraw-Hill Book Company, New York, 1962.

This is the standard text on the fundamental analysis of stocks. The techniques outlined here can be used not only for specific stocks but often for the market as a whole.

The Stock Market, by R. J. Teweles and E. S. Bradley, John Wiley & Sons, New York, 1983.

This is the best introduction to the stock market. Recommended for novices.

Investments—Analysis and Management, by Jack Clark Francis, McGraw-Hill Book Company, New York, 1972.

This textbook goes into detail about the capital asset pricing model. The basics of risk and return are covered in an easy-to-understand manner. The only drawback is that some readers may be uncomfortable with the math used in the explanations.

Newsletters

There are no private newsletters that are exclusively for stock index futures. Some stock brokerage firms have started newsletters for stock index futures though most of them are really on the stock market and do not address the issues specific to the futures. This poor situation is likely to change, so we recommend keeping in contact with your broker and watching for ads in investment journals for new publications.

Software

The only software specifically available for personal computers is the Stock Index Futures Valuation Model. This is an overlay for a popular spreadsheet program. The model gives the theoretical value of each futures contract, the basis, and the major intra-index spreads. It is available from the Delta Group. Highly recommended for hedgers and serious investors.

There are several time-sharing companies that have evaluation routines for stock index futures. The Options Group and Tradecenter both have interesting products. The cost is fairly high, but hedgers should have little problem justifying the cost. The main advantage of the time-sharing companies is that they have the actual dividend yield. This is the hardest number to find when evaluating the futures contracts.

Purchases

Delta Group, 520 Ridgecrest Drive, Abingdon, Virginia 24210, (703) 628-9678. The best place to buy many of the reference materials mentioned is through Delta Investment Systems Group, Inc. They have a catalog of investment products that contains software, chart services, newsletters, and books. Highly recommended.

Index

About the Author

Courtney D. Smith is vice president and director of the Commercial Support Group for PaineWebber, Inc., a major New York Stock Exchange brokerage house. He was formerly president of Gruschow & Smith, Inc., an investment advisory firm. Mr. Smith is the author of two books about commodity futures, *Commodity Spreads* and *Profits Through Seasonal Trading*.